THE NEW GLORIOUS AMERICAN FOOD

A COLLECTION OF CLASSIC AND
QUINTESSENTIALLY AMERICAN FARE

CHRISTOPHER IDONE

PHOTOGRAPHER TOM ECKERLE
FOOD EDITOR DIANA VAN BUREN

welcome
BOOKS

NEW YORK ○ SAN FRANCISCO

FOR THE FARMERS, THE FISHERMEN,
THE RANCHERS, AND THE VINTNERS
WHO LOVE THIS LAND.
—Christopher Idone,
New York City, December 2004

CONTENTS

NORTHWEST 304

BASICS 330

OLD STANDBYS 338

INTRODUCTION

Twenty years ago I took a journey across the United States to compile a book of our culinary history, record the lives of fishermen, farmers, and ranchers, and select dishes which represented and differentiated one region from another. It was a time when America could still be divided into parts, when the cooking in these regions relied on local produce and recipes passed from generation to generation. It was a time when Cajun gumbos could only be found in the Bayou, grits and spoon breads in the Carolinas, quilcine oysters and wild mushrooms were limited to the northwest, and barbeque from Texas to Kansas had to be eaten there.

Twenty years ago I went out to meet the men and women who worked the land, and was captivated by their devotion to their crops and livestock, their care and desire to offer the best, and the freshness and quality of their products. I was impressed by their struggle and determination to survive as they were buffeted by financial burdens, government sanctions, and the enormous subsidies offered to the agro-farmers.

Twenty years ago much of the country I visited, the kitchens I cooked in, and the places we photographed were still rural. Small cities were small, and country towns were exactly that—enclaves tucked away off the blue highways of America.

Twenty years ago I introduced the book as follows.

○　○　○

Every other Sunday, when I was a kid, my siblings and I were packed into the car and driven off to my maternal grandmother's house. It smelled of yeast and butter and roasting meats. My grandmother would drink a bit of sherry before dinner, and we children would drink milk warm from the cow when we sat down to the roast accompanied by mashed potatoes swimming in gravy and butter. On alternate Sundays, we visited my paternal grandfather. His house smelled richly of olive oil, garlic, and tomatoes bubbling on a wood burning cast-iron cook stove, and a line stretched across the kitchen was hung with noodles like ribbons drying in the air until they were ready to be tossed into a cauldron of boiling water. While I sat on my grandfather's knee, I would chew a golden slice of bread with a crust so hard it hurt my teeth, and he would nibble slices of sausage spiced with fennel seeds or flecked with red hot pepper.

At home we drank milk from our pet goats (long before I knew what a chevre was). The goats lived among the menagerie of rabbits, chickens, and dogs that always were around. Sometimes we ate cream cheese with jelly and sometimes we had fresh mozzarella melted on fragrant oily bread. We brought vegetables from a local farm stand and every Friday a truck pulled up with fish, clams, and mussels from the harbor fishing boats. The fisherman, for that's what we called him, would draw back the canvas to reveal all kinds of terrors pulled from the local waters, spread out on heaps of snow-white crystals of ice. He weighed my mother's choice, collected her money, and wrapped our dinner in newspaper.

We pulled up rhubarb stalks out behind the shed, and my mother served them stewed, with puddles of thick cream. Rhubarb was followed by a season of asparagus and strawberries picked from a local patch. We cranked out ice cream tinted with luscious berries and peaches of a hot summer. But it was apple picking I remember most about my childhood. The baskets of apples that weren't to be stored or turned into applesauce, pies, and crisps were packed along with empty bottles and

corks into the back of my mother's Ford wagon. My father took us to the local cider mill, part of a huge orchard that belonged to a friend who allowed my father to make his own cider. Inside the barn was what looked like a jerry-rigged wooden machine—a huge tub with a wheel spiked with dowels attached to a jib. A crank turned by hand crushed the apples and from the spout autumn's brown juices would flow into a bucket. The barn's pine walls were damp with apple moisture and the floorboards slippery. A hill of fermenting skins, stems, and seeds were piled in a corner giving off gasses so sharp the smell made the little kids reel. The pile was destined for the farmer's pigs to get them drunk, no doubt, but also to sweeten them up. We bought pork and hams from that farmer, and oh, were those dinners a delicious memory. Apples were a part of almost every fall and winter meal in my family's house. We ate applesauce with cream for breakfast and had it again with warm gingerbread when we got home from school, and sometimes sandwiched between anise-scented Zweiback that my mother called Icebox Cake. Stewed apples were served with pork chops at supper time and baked apples were turned into pies, cobblers and turnovers, or

put on sticks and dipped into hot sugar syrup colored with Red Dye Number 2. A crisp, rosy apple always found its way into our lunch box.

Such childhood memories as these are the roots of my love for honest food, and the beginning of a curiosity that would flourish throughout my life. It was a long time before I realized that food served in one house differed from that served in another—that food tastes different in different places, that what flourishes in one area withers somewhere else. But now, I know. Surely food will always vary from home to home, and dishes will vary from cook to cook. American cooking developed with a sense of thrift—simple, basic, rooted to the land, and it didn't lack inspiration. When I set out to do this book, I had an idea of what I might find in America. Certainly I thought I knew a great deal about this country's food. I'd read and traveled and tasted so many dishes I couldn't begin to count them. What I had suspected, but was not sure of, was the truth about the source of our food: that it springs from great pride, and from tremendous bounty.

I divided the United States into regions, not so much geographically as historically, following the trail of food. The experience was a history lesson for me, one I wanted to record. I decided to start with our entry into the magnificent ports and harbors of the continent and trace the paths of pioneers who crossed what was an unimaginable expanse of land. I wanted to see firsthand how people cook at home, in what ways their cookery depends on local produce, and if local cookery is still based on regional dishes of the past or if it has become homogenized. So I went to find the farmers and fishermen and ranchers, people of the country. I went to the source and found cooks, wonderful cooks, young and old, who shared their company, their charm and generosity, their experience, their memories, and their secrets.

I followed the water everywhere I went. Many of the fishermen I met were doing the work their families have done for thirteen generations, but I found time had taken its toll. The haulseiners of Long Island depend on a depleting population of bass and are further hampered by state laws and by the sports fisherman who claims this fish as his trophy. The old-time Baymen of the East Coast, whose hand-shuck scallops are the best in the land, are slowly losing their livelihood as the scallop beds become over-fished or polluted. Shrimp boats rot in the channels along the intercoastal water route from Charleston to the Bayou, because the independent shrimper has lost his mortgage to the banks and his catch to the trawlers that sift our waters and send back to us "fresh frozen" seafood. I've seen the versatile rice grower of the South turn his off-season fields into flooded crawfish farms or catfish ponds. I've watched the delicate shad travel up a cleaned-up Hudson River to the point where sweet water meets the salty current—so docile in their abundance that they are netted like pets, deposited in aerated water tanks, and trucked to the Susquehanna to replenish the stock there. And I have stood in the wood shavings of the first skipjack to be built on the Chesapeake in more than seventy years.

I learned about the land from those whose livelihood depended on it. I spoke with the children who had been to college and pursued a career, and had then experienced a change of heart, returning to the farm that was their birthright. I talked to the professor who gave up his tenure to cultivate his own small parcel of land, growing tender lettuces, herbs, and vegetables. I chatted with the farmer who left his farm at 4 A.M. to drive 140 miles to the Decatur Street Market in New Orleans, his pickup filled with the most beautiful ivory turnips I have ever seen—he just beamed when they were photographed. I bought an overripe melon for a dime from a dejected farmer who stood by his truck sipping coffee from a tin cup, knowing his day was over before it barely started. I found that the "western cowboy" works from Texas to Montana, from Bakersfield, California to the Santa Lucia Range on the Pacific. I tasted the beef the ranchers keep for themselves—from cattle that aren't sent off to the corn feedlots for a final fattening—much gamier to my city palate, but delicious and pleasing. Whole communities eat this way, consuming beef as they prefer it; who, outside of these areas, would ever know of it?

I was looking for the flavor of America, and I found that no single flavor exists. The menus and recipes in this book are made from regionally available foods, the ingredients and techniques adjusted to reflect local influences. I followed tradition and custom to the point where it made sense to me. In essence, I took the liberty of adapting these dishes to please contemporary palates. I realized, too, that if indeed there exists a homogenized "American flavor," it belongs only to fast food. But around the corner there is always a reminder: overstuffed sandwiches of pastrami and corned beef, pickled, cured, peppered and smoked on the premises; a toasted roll filled with half a lobster, boiled up on a one-burner stove and moistened with mayonnaise and a hint of celery; a burrito stuffed with meats and beans, and salsa lovingly simmered for hours; a trio of steamed dumplings selected on the street, served up from a bamboo steamer. At times, I wondered whether what I was seeing and recording would ever be seen by a future generation. But ways of life are ever *changing; the side of American life that fascinates me so has been in the process of fading since long before I was around, or my grandmother and grandfather, for that matter. Every generation talks of hope and despair as though experiencing it for the first time.*

○　○　○

That was written twenty years ago. In the intervening years, much has changed.

Back then people were beginning to become aware that there were better and healthier ways to eat. Young chefs, mainly in California and on the East Coast, were earning their stripes by offering the public the best possible ingredients the country had to offer. They encouraged farmers to suppress herbicides and pesticides, to grow organic fruits and vegetables, and heirloom varieties. The farmers obliged and these new ways of eating filtered down to supermarkets and the consumer. Chefs were joining cooperatives, working with local farmers, dairies, cheese makers, fishermen, and cattle producers. Some even bought land to grow their own produce. Food writers and critics bestowed well-earned praise on these innovators and created the celebrity chef, who in turn fueled the public's insatiable appetite for all things culinary.

By the mid-seventies, California had the lead on organic produce, but small farmers' markets were being established throughout the east, particularly in New York City. Today there are thirty markets among the five boroughs. The largest and most appealing is the Greenmarket at Union Square. Four days a week farmers and the public mingle and exchange cooking tips with some of the city's most talented and celebrated chefs who come to buy and be inspired. Home cooks flock to the market too, delighted with the opportunity to buy fresh fish, organic meats, wild ramps or a bag of apples when the harvest is abundant.

Even fast food has changed over the past twenty years. Today, push carts and holes-in-the-wall

specialize in baked potatoes stuffed with Ementhal, Cheddar, and Brie; Middle Eastern inspired skewers of beef and chicken are offered curbside from a fired grill; an Indian or Pakistani serves up curries, sates, chickpeas, and hot papadam and nan bread; empanadas and rotis based on recipes from Jamaica to Bolivia are sold on city streets; and quality sushi and sashimi can often be had from the Asian-run deli on the corner. The choices come from all over the world—as culturally diverse as those who prepare the food. Eclectic, yes; foreign, no—they're all now part of America's culinary lexicon.

During the past two decades I have seen dozens of diet fads come and go. At the same time I've watched Americans become fatter and fatter as they cook fewer meals at home and rely more on fast and packaged foods. As a cook, I look for taste first, and I want my bread and cake and eat it too! I have always cooked with butter and eggs and sometimes lard when I know a crust will be flakier with it. Yes, I remove as much fat as possible without losing the integrity of the meals I put forth, but the recipes here are dishes that have been part of the American dining experience for generations—they are classics just as they are. We will always hanker for a good meat loaf and a steaming casserole of baked macaroni and cheese.

I have revisited many of the regions that were on my journey twenty years ago, and all is not the same. What was once farm acreage abutting the dunes of the East Coast is now covered with houses that compete with Versailles. Potato fields have been sub-divided or in some instances replaced by rows upon rows of ornamental shrubbery to landscape those mansions. I have witnessed the end of fishing for the Baymen at the east end of Long Island, who lost their livelihood to over-fishing. I have seen the reduction of shellfish in the Chesapeake because of pollution, and watched the schooners that dredged these waters for oysters and crabs all but disappear. And I have observed the

mountains and hills from the Columbia River in Oregon to the heights of Washington State denuded of their forests, their crowns as bald as an old man's head.

There is still hope. Fish farms, which protect and breed certain species (although these will never taste like true wild fish or shellfish), are growing in numbers. There are the farmers who replenish the earth with what is good, and grow the best produce we've had available to us in our lifetimes. There are cattlemen who graze their beef on grass-fed ranges and never use hormones. There are still dairy cows left out to pasture rather than pent up in closed barns and fed harmful nutrients and hormones to increase their milk production. On the other hand, most small dairy farms cannot make a living—as the economics of scale make clear, a farm of fifty cows cannot compete with farms of four or five hundred (but the smaller dairy provides better milk)—and therefore much of what was once farm acreage has been lost to development. Today, to make ends meet, these farmers have formed cooperatives to make cheese, and, happily, cheese has captured the public

imagination and is much in demand—especially when it is local.

What inspires the farmer's devotion, this willingness to marry your life to the land, knowing it will be a struggle, knowing you may make a decent living, but will never get rich? What keeps him going when after days in the field, his evenings are spent trying to protect the land, working in community groups, lobbying government agencies, passing on new and vital information, and encouraging his competitors? And how does he continue to believe—and I mean *happily* believe—that there is a future in good and honest crops? I think it's a deeply ingrained passion for the land, a passion which harks back to the American Indians and the country's earliest settlers.

○   ○   ○

Today, one of the largest industries to contribute to preserving our land is the wine business. From the splendid vineyards of the North and South Forks of Long Island to the burgeoning wineries of Connecticut and on down to Virginia, wineries are tucked amongst the hills as far west as Texas and Arizona. All fifty states—including Alaska and Hawaii—are producing wines. But the mother lode is found in California—particularly in the Napa Valley.

My love affair with California wines began in the early 1970s. Early one sunny spring morning I crossed the Golden Gate Bridge and drove up into burnished grass hills tunneled by soaring eucalyptus trees, passing lumbering tractors and pick-up trucks to Saint Helena. I had no particular plan and I wandered the back roads until I came upon a sign announcing Stag's Leap Winery. I braked, backed up, and drove up a gravel drive to what I remember as a small white house perched on a green lawn overlooking rows of neatly pruned vines months away from bearing grapes. A screen door opened and out walked a well groomed, gray haired man who offered his hand as I approached. Warren Winiarski is the proprietor of a vineyard that was already then synonymous with great California wines. There was no tasting room or shop selling wines, but after introductions he brought out a bottle with a couple of glasses and led me to a worn oak bench and barrel, which served as a table. He uncorked the bottle and someone brought a plate with little bits of semi-hard tangy cheese and crackers. And we tasted the wine.

It was a Cabernet—the likes of which I had never tasted, from this country anyway—and while we sipped, he talked about his wines and his work. Winiarski was slightly shy, unabashedly but charmingly proud of his vineyard, thoughtful, and devoted to his grapes. It was straight wine talk, and the proof and thrill were in the bottle. Today Stag's Leap is among the most respected and well-known winery's of the region. Winiarski was one of the trailblazers who went to the Valley, earned his stripes, and revolutionized the industry. The rest is history.

New to this edition are both updated wine recommendations and suggestions of regionally brewed beers. The history of beer-making in America began as early as 1587 when Virginia colonists brewed ale made from corn. The first brewery established in the New World was at the southern tip of New Amsterdam (Manhattan) in 1612 and other colonies quickly followed. During the Revolutionary War, Congress rationed every soldier one quart of beer or cider per man per day. And by 1789 George Washington declared he would only drink beer made in America—an early version of the "buy American" policy. By the mid-19th century, 431 breweries throughout the country produced 750,000 barrels of beer (31 gallons per barrel) for a population of 23 million people.

When researching this book in 1983, beer was something I rarely thought of suggesting with menus, and only when it seemed appropriate. Back then, brewing was at its lowest point with only 51 brewing companies operating a total of 80 breweries throughout the country, and the word 'microbrewery' was virtually nonexistent, but it soon entered the vocabulary. By 1984 the Manhattan Brewing Co. opened in New York City's Soho, becoming the first 'brew pub' on the East Coast. By 1995 approximately 500 microbreweries were operating throughout the U.S. with another three or four opening each week. Microbreweries are a regional phenomenon—most of them are craft beers, distributed in a fairly limited region—as opposed to the national reach of the big breweries. These crafted beers include ales, lagers, porters, meads and even ciders and Perry—an early colonial beverage made from fruit, vegetables, or herbs, and coffee. There are yeasty beers and hoppy beers and, yes, even dessert beers which suggest chocolate and wine.

○   ○   ○

The glory of American food derives not only from the natural bounty our country provides (and which we must protect) but also from the people inspired by that bounty—the farmer and the fisherman who nurture and harvest it, and the cook who shapes it. It is to them I am most indebted.

NEW ENGLAND

NEW ENGLAND

In the beginning, the crow flew from the great fields of the Southwest, carrying a kernel of corn in one ear and an Indian bean in the other. So goes the myth of how farming was brought to the American Indians of the New England coast.

Where are the sources of American cookery more invitingly encountered than in New England's familiar and fertile tradition? After all, it was Colonial America's first chapter. Any schoolchild knows that those early colonists surely would have perished without the single greatest gift from the American Indians: corn. In 1605 the explorer Champlain records that planting should begin no sooner than "when a white-oak leaf approximated a red squirrel's foot-print," or when it was "the size of a mouse's ear." Captain John Smith (whose expedition of 1614 landed the first Englishmen on these shores) records that squaws roasted corn at the side of the very fields they were tending. For the 102 Pilgrim settlers who followed in Smith's wake, corn became the mainstay. They ate it roasted, grilled, or pounded to a paste and formed into little hot cakes called "bannocks." The early settlers would pull back the corn husks to remove the silk, wrap the ear with thin slices of bacon, pull up the husks, and roast the corn to succulence. They popped corn in hot kettles as the American Indians taught them, adding a little of their treasured lard. They ate succotash fresh in the summer, and in the winter they would make the same dish from dried beans and corn, boiled in potash and water and dried, called samp. They planted corn rows that then served as nature's beanpoles.

To this day, descendants of some of those first families celebrate Forefather's Day (December 21), dining on succotash at the Old Colony Club in Plymouth, Massachusetts. Corn was a part of early New England clambakes, which remain the region's quintessential summer feast; settlers learned from the American Indians of Cape Cod and Nantucket how to build a fire in a rock-lined pit on the beach to steam oysters, clams, and corn by sandwiching them between two layers of wet seaweed. In time the settlers learned to grind and sift corn by mill and left their mortars and pestles behind. As the coast became more diversely and widely settled, different regions came to be known for their own corn specialties (pones, hush puppies, corn sticks, corn bread, johnnycakes, Indian mush, and so on). Far into the nineteenth century corn was indispensable to the diet of not only New Englanders but colonists of the South, the Deep South, and the Midwest.

In early spring the New Englanders caught herring with their bare hands, selecting the swollen roe-filled females as the prize and discarding their partners on the rocks. They feasted on the bass, shad, salmon, trout, and sturgeon that spawned upriver from the ocean. They ate sweet scallops harvested from shallow bays, oysters and clams the size of hazelnuts, mussels picked from rocks, and periwinkles plucked from stony beaches. They fished for lamprey, flounder, whiting, cod, and its smaller cousin, haddock. The colonists found a market for cod dried on wooden frames and sent shiploads to England and to Catholic Spain and Portugal, thus building a thriving commerce. John Smith called this land Massachusetts.

Surely there was much to marvel at in unfamiliar foods. Smith describes dining on stewed squashes and varieties of pumpkins, watermelons, and what we know today as Jerusalem artichokes. They snacked on pemmican, a paste made of dried venison strips pounded together with berries and bear or deer grease. They gorged on wild berries and smoked tobacco. Game was plentiful and consisted of swans, geese, ducks, woodcocks, pheasants, partridges, deer, rabbits, squirrels, turkeys and more. Still, the Pilgrim newcomers, familiar as they were with the country of rolling

green meadows which reminded them of their own southern England, were probably as unaccustomed to handling a gun as they were to plowing or clearing a field. In their homeland, hunting remained the privilege of the landed gentry, and few of the virtuous Pilgrims were accomplished hunters, let alone crack shots.

Farming was a communal effort for the American Indians and the colonists followed suit. Planting and cultivation were commonly the work of the women, children, and older men of the villages. They worked with crude hoes, sometimes fashioned out of long poles with large clamshells affixed to the ends. Most English farms of that time were villages adjoining the great estates, with houses, stables, and gardens clustered near the village church. The early settlers adhered to this feudal arrangement in the colonies, and the close-knit community provided mutual protection and governing authority. Barns and sheds were often connected to their dwellings, and the family garden and fruit trees flourished close by. Crops were planted on individual plots apportioned according to the size of the family, in one common field. The town provided an ox or two to cultivate them and a single herdsman collected the few cows, sheep, or goats each farmer owned and took them to pasture as one herd.

Everyday life encompassed a hundred small economies, but was softened by some few luxuries that the colonists had brought from their homeland, such as seeds and saplings. Craving more luscious fruits than the tart beach plums, cranberries, and other wild berries they found here, they soon sent for apple, pear, plum, and even apricot trees and seeds from Europe. Longing to recreate dishes from home and missing beer fiercely, they rushed to import wheat, rye, barley, and hops. The first licensed brewery was established as early as 1640. Sadly, wheat and barley grew poorly in the rocky Eastern soil, and if it ever chanced to mature it was beset by blackbirds and the imported rat.

And so the beer they loved was replaced by hard cider from the flourishing apple trees, and when the cider turned they used it for vinegar. In those colonial cellars another alcoholic drink called perry was made from pears, and there were many wines made with cherries, mulberries, and dandelion blossoms. By the late seventeenth century, rum had won tremendous popularity among the colonists, a new rival to hard cider. A profitable exchange of cows, beef, hogs, sheep, dry biscuits, butter, salt cod, and tobacco were being shipped to New York ports and the West Indies in return for molasses (the thick, black, syrupy by-product of the sugar plantations). To some extent molasses was used for sweetening, although maple syrup and maple sugar were used regionally in New York, Massachusetts, Vermont, and New Hampshire by the close of the eighteenth century. For the most part, molasses was used to make rum, and many of the existing cider mills of the day were converted to that purpose. This rum was shipped to Africa in exchange for slaves, who then were sent to the cane fields of the West Indies and later to Virginia plantations and the prosperous estate farms of Massachusetts,

Rhode Island, Connecticut, the Hudson Valley, and Long Island, New York.

The hearth was the heart of early American homes, the one unfailingly warm corner. A large iron pot invariably hung over glowing coals all day, stewing and bubbling with boiled chickens, corned beef, codfish, hams, and the vegetable greens that would become known as pot liquor. The result was a plain style of cooking, but a style just the same. The cooking pot was brought directly to the table, where each family member ladled out a portion into shallow wooden bowls or trenchers: carved hollows in the tabletop itself. Preparation for winter was a year-long occupation, and included the growing and putting up of fruits and vegetables and the fattening of the hog.

The network of one-farmer households spread as towns grew and generations settled further into the woodlands. The old New England villages remain, a reminder of those first dependent, frightened flocks. At the outset of the nineteenth century, most of New England looked as Iowa does today. Hills and valleys were denuded of their timber to be used for building homes, barns, and ships, and for desperately needed warmth. In turn those soft, fertile, but rocky rolling hills were cultivated and the rocks themselves were used to fence open fields and separate neighbor from neighbor. Today one finds those walls on walks through groves of birch, pine, and maple. Those farmers, like the American Indians before them, moved on to more fertile fields when the land was exhausted. Eventually they would move west.

Breakfast

OATMEAL ○ CODFISH BALLS ○ BACON ○ CURRIED STEWED TOMATOES ○ RYE AND CHEDDAR BISCUITS ○ TEA ○ Casco Bay Riptide Red Ale, ME

Historically, codfish balls were a standard Sunday breakfast—especially from Boston up through Maine—often served with Saturday night's baked bean dish. Salt pork from the pork barrel supplied flavor and seasoned vegetables, meats, poultry, and fish. It was often a foundation for main dishes when nothing else was available. The lard was used for frying, as well as in the making of sweets and pastries—it was their butter. Coupling fish and pork renderings may seem odd, but it satisfied the New Englander's craving for the flavor of meat, and "Cape Cod turkey" wasn't turkey at all, but rather cod larded with salt pork or bacon. The China trade and whaling expeditions brought in a profusion of spices and exotic fruits that swiftly found their way into the kitchens of the colonies. Rye flourished in the rocky New England soil, and provided a pleasant change from corn breads.

CODFISH BALLS

INGREDIENTS

1/2 pound salt cod, (approximately
    1 cup shredded)
1/4 cup milk plus additional milk for soaking the
    salt cod
1 cup hand-mashed boiled potatoes
3 eggs, lightly beaten
Freshly milled black pepper
Dried unseasoned bread crumbs
Vegetable oil

METHOD

Soak the cod in cold water and cover for 12 hours,
    changing the water 2 or 3 times.
Replace water with milk and soak cod for an
    additional 6 hours. Drain and discard the milk.
In a bowl, shred the fish and mash together with
    the potatoes.

Combine with 1 egg and season with pepper.
Shape the mixture into walnut-sized balls.
In a shallow bowl, whisk the remaining 2 eggs with
    1/4 cup milk. Place the bread crumbs in another
    shallow bowl.
Dip each ball in the egg-and-milk mixture and
    then roll in the bread crumbs. Refrigerate for
    20 minutes.
In a large-deep skillet, add enough oil to fill the pan
    to 1 1/2 inches. Set over moderately high heat.
When the oil is hot but not smoking, add one fish
    ball to test. Working batches, add the fish balls
    without crowding the pan.
Fry quickly, turning regularly, until golden brown.
Drain on paper towels and keep warm.
Fry the remaining fish balls and serve.

Makes 12 codfish balls

Add the buttermilk and cheese and mix thoroughly.
Place the dough on a lightly floured surface and
knead for 2 minutes.
Roll out the dough to $3/4$-inch thickness. Cut the
dough with a 3-inch round cookie cutter and
place the biscuits on an ungreased baking sheet.
Bake for 12 to 15 minutes, or until golden brown.
Serve warm.

Makes 8 to 10 biscuits

CURRIED STEWED TOMATOES

INGREDIENTS
4 large ripe tomatoes, peeled and seeded, with
the juice reserved (approximately 4 cups)
Salt and freshly milled black pepper
1 teaspoon curry powder
1 tablespoon snipped fresh chives

METHOD
Coarsely chop the tomatoes and place them in a
heavy saucepan. Add the reserved juice and set
over moderate heat.
Bring the tomatoes to a slight boil and reduce the
heat to low.
Add salt and pepper to taste and the
curry powder.
Simmer 15 to 20 minutes or until the tomato pulp
is soft.
Place in a serving bowl and sprinkle with chives.

Makes 4 cups

RYE AND CHEDDAR BISCUITS

INGREDIENTS
1 cup rye flour
1 cup all-purpose flour
1 tablespoon baking powder
1 teaspoon baking soda
$1/2$ teaspoon salt
6 tablespoons unsalted butter, slightly chilled and
cut into bits
$3/4$ cup buttermilk
4 ounces cheddar cheese, grated (approximately
1 cup)

METHOD
Preheat the oven to 450° F.
In a mixing bowl, combine all of the dry ingredients.
Using your fingers or an electric mixer, blend the
butter into the dry ingredients.

Succotash Dinner

GREEN TOMATO TART ○ SUCCOTASH WITH STEAMED FISH ○ STEWED TOMATOES WITH ROSEMARY ○ FRIED BAKED GRITS (see page 116) ○ JASON'S BLUEBERRY PIE WITH ROSE PETAL ICE CREAM ○ Palmer Vineyards Chardonnay, NY or Peconic Bay Riesling, NY

At harvest's end, green tomatoes were pickled, fried, or seasoned with sugar and spices and baked into pies. This tart fruit on a flaky crust coated with sweet honey mustard is a savory introduction to an end-of-summer menu. It was not uncommon to add bits of meat, fowl, or fish to succotash, which was frequently enjoyed as a meal in itself. The wild beach rose, Rosa rugosa, *grows in the crests and valleys of the dunes on the Atlantic coast. This Arabian strain was introduced purely by accident when English wrecks washed up on our Eastern shore. The fragrant petals found their way into potpourris and recipes, and the rose hips made delicious jelly. Those who live far from the sea can substitute a few drops of rose water to make this whimsy.*

GREEN TOMATO TART

INGREDIENTS

$^1/_2$ recipe pie dough, made with lard
   (see Basics, page 353)
2 teaspoons vegetable oil
1 large onion, thinly sliced
$^1/_3$ cup honey mustard
2 medium-sized green tomatoes, cut in
   $^1/_4$-inch slices
Salt and freshly milled pepper
2 tablespoons unsalted butter, melted
2 tablespoons fresh Italian parsley, lightly chopped

METHOD

Preheat the oven to 350° F.

Prepare the pie dough and while the pastry is chilling, heat the oil in a skillet and add the onions.

Slowly cook the onions over low heat, stirring occasionally, until wilted and lightly browned, about 20 minutes.

Set aside and cool.

On a floured surface, roll out the dough into a 10-inch circle.

Carefully lift the pie dough and place it on a baking sheet lined with parchment paper or foil.

Evenly spread the mustard over the surface of the pie dough, leaving a 1-inch band around the circumference of the dough.

Evenly spread the onions over the mustard.

Arrange the tomatoes in a spiral, covering the caramelized onions.

Lightly season the tomatoes with salt and pepper.

Bake the tart for 25 minutes, or until the edges of the crust are crisp.

Remove the tart from the oven, brush with melted butter, and sprinkle with the parsley.

Serve warm.

Serves 4 to 6

SUCCOTASH WITH STEAMED FISH

INGREDIENTS

10 ears fresh sweet corn

2 cups small, shelled fresh lima beans

1/2 cup water

2 cups fresh string beans, cut into 1-inch pieces

1/4 pound unsalted butter

3 pounds white fish fillets, such as scrod, halibut, bass, or weakfish

1 bunch small scallions, including some of the green, trimmed

2 to 3 tablespoons heavy cream

1/3 pound salt pork, cut into 1/4-inch cubes

METHOD

Cut the kernels of corn from the cobs into a bowl.

With a large spoon, scrape the milk from the cob into the bowl with the corn and set aside.

Blanch the lima beans in boiling water until almost tender.

Cool under cold water, drain and set aside.

Blanch the string beans, cool, drain, and set aside.

In a large, heavy saucepan, melt the butter and add the corn, lima beans and their juices, and 1/2 cup water.

Place fish fillets on top of the corn mixture. Place scallions on top of fish and cover. Cook over moderate heat for 10 minutes or until the fish is flaky and opaque. Add cream and blanched string beans to mixture.

Meanwhile, in a skillet, render the salt pork until golden brown. Set aside on paper towels to drain.

Pour the succotash onto a heated platter. Arrange the fish, scallions, and rendered salt pork over the succotash and serve.

Serves 6

STEWED TOMATOES WITH ROSEMARY

INGREDIENTS

4 to 5 large, very ripe tomatoes (approximately 3 pounds)

1 sprig fresh rosemary

Salt and freshly milled pepper

METHOD

Blanch, peel, and seed the tomatoes, reserving the juice.

Chop the tomatoes.

Place the tomatoes and their juice in a heavy saucepan.

Crush the rosemary by bruising it between your fingers.

Add the rosemary and salt and pepper to taste.

Simmer over moderate heat, stirring occasionally, until the liquid reduces and tomatoes are cooked through.

Serve hot.

Note: Fresh, ripe tomatoes are one of summer's joys. They need little seasoning and the fresh taste is incomparable. After stewing, the tomatoes may be cooled and frozen in plastic containers or put up in jars for a wintertime treat.

Makes 1 1/2 to 2 quarts

JASON'S BLUEBERRY PIE

INGREDIENTS

$^1/_2$ recipe pie dough, made with lard
  (see Basics, page 335)
2 pints blueberries, washed and drained
$^1/_4$ cup sugar
1 $^1/_2$ tablespoons quick cooking tapioca
1 lemon, seeded and sliced paper-thin

METHOD

Preheat the oven to 400° F.
Prepare the pie dough and chill it.
In a mixing bowl, mix the blueberries with the sugar
  and tapioca.
Line a 9-inch glass pie pan with enough lemon
  slices to cover the bottom.

Fill the pan with the blueberry mixture.
On a floured surface, roll out the pie dough
  $^1/_4$-inch thick.
Cover the berries with the dough. Trim and crimp
  the edges.
Bake in the center of the oven 35 minutes, or
  until golden.
Serve warm with vanilla ice cream or the rose
  petal variation.

Serves 6

ROSE PETAL ICE CREAM

INGREDIENTS

1 quart English Cream (see Basics, page 336),
  made without the vanilla
2 cups rose petals from *Rosa rugosa* (see Note)

SPECIAL TOOLS

Ice cream maker

METHOD

Prepare the English Cream, omitting the vanilla.
Freeze the mixture in an ice cream maker,
  following the manufacturer's directions.
    When the cream begins to thicken, fold in the
    rose petals.
Spoon the ice cream into a container and freeze
  until ready to serve.
The ice cream will take on the perfume flavor of
  the petals.

Note: *Rosa rugosa* flourishes in the dunes along the Easter shoreline. The fruit is rich in vitamin C and is considered medicinal as well as wonderful for making jellies. It is one of nature's most fragrant wild roses. The petals are five to a blossom, ranging in color from white or pale pink to a deep rich pink. You may substitute a few drops of rosewater in place of the petals.

Makes 1 quart

Baked Bean Dinner

BAKED BEANS WITH BLACK DUCK BREASTS AND LINGUIÇA SAUSAGES ○ BROWN BREAD ○ SUSAN WILBUR'S CORN RELISH ○ PICKLES ○ APPLE CHARLOTTE ○ Lenz Estate Merlot, NY or Bar Harbor Cadillac Mountain Stout, ME

Though they take hours of slow cooking, baked beans require little tending. To a New Englander the dish is not just a pot of beans, but a casserole that might be cooked with a partridge, accompanied by a fresh goose breast, or finished with the addition of Portuguese Linguiça sausage. Rich, dark molasses flavored the dish but was used sparingly so as not to oversweeten. With these embellishments the simple pot of beans becomes a New England cassoulet. Steamed brown bread always accompanied the dish, along with pickles and relishes to satisfy the Yankee passion for sweet and sour. The apple was the one fruit that thrived, and the colonial housewife's countless variations on the apple dessert are a credit to her imagination.

BAKED BEANS WITH BLACK DUCK BREASTS AND LINGUIÇA SAUSAGES

INGREDIENTS

Beans:

2 pounds dried navy, cranberry, or yellow eye (favored in Maine) beans

1 pound salt pork with skin attached (see Note)

2 tablespoons dry mustard

1 teaspoon cider vinegar

1/4 dark rum

1/2 cup molasses

1 teaspoon salt (optional)

1 medium-large onion, studded with 12 cloves

Meat:

3 Linguiça sausages

3/4 pound lean pork fat, cut into 1/4-inch cubes

6 boneless, skinless Black Duck breasts (also called Canadian Redleg), or substitute Mallard or Muscovy duck breasts

Salt and freshly milled pepper

1/2 pound unsalted butter, clarified (see Basics, page 333)

Small bunch fresh sage leaves

METHOD

The beans:

Thoroughly wash and pick over the beans. Place in a soup kettle with water to cover and set aside to soak overnight.

Drain the beans, place them in a large kettle and add cold water to cover.

Bring to a boil over high heat. Reduce the heat to low and simmer for 30 minutes.

Drain the beans and reserve the cooking liquid.

Preheat the oven to 200° F.

Cut away the salt pork skin in one sheet.

Line a bean pot or deep oven-proof casserole with the skin, skin-side up.

In a small bowl, combine the dry mustard, vinegar, rum, molasses, and salt. Mix into the beans and fill the pot one-third full with the bean mixture.

Add the clove-studded onion and cover with half the remaining bean mixture. Then add the salt pork and cover with the beans that are left. Fill with enough liquid to cover the beans.

Cover the bean pot and bake for 10 to 11 hours, checking the liquid from time to time. If the beans begin to dry out, add some of the reserved bean liquid to moisten them. Uncover the beans for the last hour of cooking and bury the Linguiça sausages in the beans. About 30 minutes before serving, render the cubed pork fat over moderately low heat until golden, draining off the fat as it cooks.

Drain the cubes on paper towels and set aside in a warm place.

The duck breasts:

Lightly season the duck breasts with salt and pepper.

Warm the butter in a large ovenproof skillet over moderately high heat.

Add some of the sage leaves and sauté the breasts for 2 minutes on each side, until rare.

Raise the oven temperature to 275° F.

Place the skillet in the oven while you assemble the dish. For a rare breast bake for 6 to 7 minutes, for a well-done breast bake for a total of 11 minutes.

To assemble:

Remove the onion from the beans and discard.

Remove the sausage from the beans. Peel off the skin and slice 1/4-inch thick.

Arrange the sliced sausages in the center of a warm platter. Surround the sausages with the duck breasts and place one or two whole sage leaves over each breast.

Sprinkle with the reserved rendered pork fat.

Serve with the beans.

Note: If the salt pork is very salty, boil it first. Otherwise it will burn and brown before the fat is rendered.

Serves 6 to 8

BROWN BREAD

INGREDIENTS

2 tablespoons butter, for the mold
1 cup whole wheat flour
1 cup all-purpose flour
1 cup yellow cornmeal
2 teaspoons baking soda
1 teaspoon salt
2 cups buttermilk
3/4 cup molasses
1 cup seedless raisins

SPECIAL TOOLS

Two 1-quart steamed pudding molds or one
    2-quart steamed pudding mold

METHOD

Butter the pudding mold, including the cover.
In a large bowl, combine the flours, cornmeal,
    baking soda, and salt.
Add the buttermilk and molasses and stir thoroughly.
Fold in the raisins.
Pour the mixture into the mold and cover lightly.
Place the mold in a large pot and fill with hot
    water to reach halfway up the sides of the mold.
Cover the pot and steam over moderate heat for

3 hours, replenishing the water as necessary
    every 30 to 40 minutes.
When the bread is cooked, unmold and serve
    warm, slicing the loaf with strong kitchen string.

Makes 1 large or 2 small loaves

SUSAN WILBUR'S CORN RELISH

INGREDIENTS

2 dozen large ears sweet corn, husked
1 large green cabbage (approximately
    3 pounds)—outer leaves removed, cut in half,
    and cored
4 green bell peppers—halved, cored, seeded,
    and deveined
1 sweet red bell pepper—halved, cored, seeded,
    and deveined
4 large onions
2 quarts cider vinegar
1 cup all-purpose flour
4 1/2 cups sugar
1/4 cup salt
3 1/2 tablespoons dry mustard
1 teaspoon turmeric

METHOD

Using a sharp knife, cut the corn kernels from the
    cobs and set them aside in a large bowl.
Using a spoon, scrape the milk from the cob into
    the bowl of kernels.
Thinly slice the cabbage and chop.
Cut the green and red peppers into thin strips
    and dice.
Chop the onions.
In the kettle, bring 1 quart of the vinegar to a
    simmer over moderate heat.
Whisk in the flour, sugar, salt, dry mustard,
    and turmeric.
Add the remaining 1 quart vinegar and fold in the
    vegetables. Simmer for 30 minutes.
Ladle the relish into sterilized canning jars and
    refrigerate for up to 3 months or seal according
    to manufacturer's directions.

Makes 5 1/2 quarts

APPLE CHARLOTTE

INGREDIENTS

8 to 10 thin slices white bread, crusts removed and
    cut in half (see Note)
$^1/_2$ pound unsalted butter, melted
6 pounds semi-tart cooking apples, peeled, cored,
    and thinly sliced
2 cups dark brown sugar
$^3/_4$ teaspoon ground cinnamon
$^1/_2$ teaspoon ground mace
$^1/_2$ teaspoon ground allspice
Heavy cream or whipped cream for serving

METHOD

Preheat the oven to 350° F.
Working in batches, brush the bread with
    $^1/_4$ pound of the melted butter and brown lightly
    in a heavy skillet set over moderate heat. Allow
    to cool slightly.
Line the bottom and sides of the soufflé dish with
    bread, cutting as necessary to fit the dish. Set
    aside the remaining slices of bread.
Add the remaining $^1/_4$ pound butter to the skillet
    and return it to moderate heat.
In a bowl, toss the apples with sugar and spices
    and add the mixture to the skillet.
Cook, stirring until the apples wilt and the sugar
    melts. The filling will resemble a chunky sauce.
Pour the filling into the lined dish and top with the
    reserved slices of bread.
Place the mold in a hot water bath and bake for
    30 to 50 minutes, until crisp and golden.
Remove from the oven and cool on a rack for
    15 minutes.
Place a serving dish over the mold and invert
    to unmold.
Serve warm with heavy cream or whipped cream.

Note: Slice some of the bread crosswise to line the
sides of the dish. Diagonal slices are easier to fit on
the top and bottom.

Serves 6 to 8

Lobster Lunch

WHITE FISH CHOWDER ○ BOILED LOBSTERS ○ BLACKBERRY COBBLER WITH CREAM OR VANILLA ICE CREAM ○ Bedell Cellars Viognier, NY or Southampton Publick House Grand Cru Pale Ale, NY

At one time, coastal New England's chowder was a simple combination of fish or clams with water, pork, and onions, thickened with flour. The Portuguese prepared a richer version using olive oil, tomatoes, peppers, and garlic. By the middle of the nineteenth century, a true New England chowder was a milky stew, served with water biscuits or hardtack of a rocklike texture that was meant to be crumbled and soaked in the chowder as filler. Salt cod substituted when fresh fish was unavailable. Lobster, once considered a food of the poor, has become a luxury and is served here at its simplest— boiled. A true down-easter prefers his lobster boiled or steamed, flavored with nothing more than the sea water in which it cooks.

WHITE FISH CHOWDER

INGREDIENTS

1 pound salt cod (as prepared on page 23)
1 pound fresh cod fillet, skin removed
1 pound halibut fillet, skin removed
4 tablespoons unsalted butter
1 medium yellow onion, chopped
4 cups heavy cream
2 cups milk
1 teaspoon fresh thyme leaves
1/4 pound fresh pork fatback
2 cups peeled, diced, waxy potatoes such as
   Yukon Gold
Freshly milled black pepper
3 tablespoons chopped fresh parsley

METHOD

Cut all of the fish into 1 1/2-inch cubes.
Cover and refrigerate.
In a soup kettle, melt the butter over
   moderate heat.
Add the onions and sauté until translucent,
   3 to 5 minutes.
Add the heavy cream, milk, and thyme and
   reduce the heat to low. Simmer for 20 minutes.

Meanwhile, dice the fatback and cook over
   moderate heat until rendered golden brown.
   Drain on paper towels and set aside on a warm
   part of the stove.
Add the potatoes to the chowder and simmer until
   the potatoes are almost fork-tender.
Add the fish and simmer for about 10 minutes, until
   just cooked through. Season to taste with
   pepper. Serve the rendered pork on the side and
   let each guest sprinkle some over the chowder.

Serves 6

COOKING LOBSTER

METHOD

The sweetest and tenderest lobsters are under 1 1/2 pounds, and the easiest way to cook live lobsters is by boiling or steaming.

To boil lobsters, fill a lobster kettle with enough water to cover the lobsters and add 1 teaspoon of salt for every quart of water, if you are not using sea water. Cover the kettle and bring to a rolling boil.

Plunge the lobsters head first into the pot and cover. When the water begins to boil, cook a 1-pound lobster for 10 minutes, and 1 1/2-pound lobsters for 14 minutes. Cold live lobster will cool down the water and it will take from 3 to 5 minutes for the water to return to a boil.

To steam lobsters, layer the bottom of the kettle with about 1/2 pound of seaweed, if possible. Add several quarts of water, and bring to a boil, covered. Add the lobsters, cover, and cook according to the individual size. Most lobster kettles will hold 4 to 5 lobsters at a time, but it is best to cook them a few at a time rather than overcrowding the pot. If steaming, the lobsters on the bottom will cook faster. Lobsters should cool slightly before handling.

For easy serving, use a sharp sturdy knife to cut the lobster from the point where the tail and body meet down to the end of the tail. Turn the lobster around and cut through the head. Remove and discard the sand sac from the head of the halved lobster. Crack each claw at its widest point and serve with lobster crackers.

Boiled or steamed lobster may be served plain or with warm drawn butter.

BLACKBERRY COBBLER

INGREDIENTS

2 quarts blackberries
About 1/2 cup sugar, depending on the sweetness of the berries
Biscuit dough:
4 cups all-purpose flour
2 teaspoons salt
2 tablespoons baking powder
2 teaspoons sugar
2 cups heavy cream
Heavy cream, for serving

METHOD

Preheat the oven to 400° F.

Toss together the berries and sugar in a large oven-proof casserole.

Place in the oven for 20 minutes, or until the sugar melts and the berries soften.

Meanwhile, prepare the biscuit dough.

In a large bowl, combine the dry ingredients.

Gradually pour in the cream and mix into a sticky dough.

Remove the casserole from the oven and spoon the biscuit dough over the berries.

Reduce the heat to 350° F and bake for 20 to 25 minutes, or until the cobbler is golden brown.

Serve warm with heavy cream.

Serves 6

Boiled Dinner

STEAMED MUSSELS WITH FENNEL AND HERBS ○ GLAZED CORNED BEEF WITH ROOT VEGETABLES ○ PIQUANT RELISH (see Basics, page 332) ○ JOHNNYCAKE ○ APPLE PIE WITH CHEDDAR CHEESE ○ Paumanok Estate Cabernet Sauvignon, NY

In addition to the pork and apple barrels, most homes had a pickling barrel. The process of salting and brining beef resulted in corned beef, so called because the pellets of salt resembled grains in size, and at that time all grains were called corn. Until the invention of the icebox, homemakers depended on snow and pickling to preserve their meat. The corned beef is dressed up with a sweet glaze and an assortment of winter vegetables. It was often something of an "extender" meal that made a weekly appearance. The leftover beef was served up cold, which was the preference, with hot vegetables and then yet a third time, hashed. The cornmeal johnnycake, sweetened with molasses, was one of the first faintly elaborate breads. The name "johnny" came from "journey" and the cakes, tucked into saddlebags, traveled to the four corners of the country. Long before pie à la mode became popular, cheddar was the common accompaniment to homemade apple pies. Americans had not yet developed their legendary "sweet tooth" and preferred to end the meal with a savory. The cheese is served as a final course, to be enjoyed with the last of the wine.

STEAMED MUSSELS WITH FENNEL AND HERBS

INGREDIENTS
1/4 cup olive oil
2 cups dry white wine
1 small fennel bulb—halved, cored, and cut into
   2-inch julienne, reserving fennel fronds
4 quarts mussels, scrubbed and debearded
1 bunch scallions, including some of the green,
   thinly sliced lengthwise
1 tablespoon finely chopped parsley
1/2 cup fennel fronds
Freshly milled black pepper

METHOD
In a large soup kettle, combine the oil and wine
   over high heat.
Bring to a boil, add the fennel julienne, and reduce
   the heat to low. Simmer until tender, about
   8 minutes. Increase the heat to moderately high
   and add the mussels and remaining ingredients.
   Cover tightly and steam until the mussels open.
   Discard any that do not open.

Serve the mussels in heated bowls with some of
   the liquid ladled on top.

Note: Place the mussels in the freezer for 10 minutes before cooking so they will open faster.

Serves 6 to 8

GLAZED CORNED BEEF WITH ROOT VEGETABLES

INGREDIENTS

Brisket:

1 corned brisket of beef (4 to 5 pounds)

2 bay leaves

8 peppercorns

2 allspice berries

1 small cinnamon stick

1 teaspoon mustard seed

Glaze:

1 dark brown sugar

1 tablespoon dry mustard

$^1/_4$ cup molasses

$^1/_3$ cup bourbon

Vegetables:

8 small golden beets

12 small new potatoes, with a strip of peel removed around the center

12 white radishes, including $^1/_2$ inch of the green tops, peeled

12 large scallions, trimmed

12 small carrots, including $^1/_2$ inch of the green tops, peeled

2 parsnips—peeled, cut lengthwise in half, and quartered lengthwise

24 brussels sprouts, cleaned and trimmed

1 small head Savoy cabbage or white cabbage, cored and cut into 1-inch-thick slices

METHOD

Wash the brisket thoroughly to remove any brine.

Place the brisket in a large kettle with the spices and add enough water to cover.

Bring to a boil and simmer over moderately low heat for approximately 1 hour per pound, or until the center of the meat can be pierced easily with a 2-prong kitchen fork.

Meanwhile, make the glaze.

In a bowl, mix the sugar with the dry mustard. Add the molasses and fold in the bourbon. Set aside.

Wash the beets thoroughly. Trim, leaving the roots and 2 or more inches of stem attached to prevent bleeding while cooking.

Cook the beets in a pot of lightly salted boiling water until tender, about 12 minutes. Blanch in cold running water and slip off the skins.

Return the beets to the pot and keep warm.

When the corned beef is cooked, preheat the
   oven to 375° F.
Remove the beef brisket and 2 cups of the
   cooking liquid to a large baking pan. Set aside.
Bring the remaining cooking liquid to a rolling
   simmer and cook the vegetables, starting with
   the potatoes for 10 minutes. Add the radishes
   and scallions and simmer for 10 minutes. Add the
   remaining vegetables and cook for 10 minutes.
While the vegetables cook, spoon over enough
   thickened glaze to coat the corned beef and
   bake in the oven, basting with an additional
   glaze, for 10 to 15 minutes.
Serve the corned beef on a large platter,
   surrounded by the vegetables.

Serves 6 to 8

JOHNNYCAKE

INGREDIENTS
Butter for greasing baking pan
1 cup yellow cornmeal
$1/4$ cup sugar
$1/2$ teaspoon baking soda
1 teaspoon cream of tartar
$1/4$ teaspoon salt
1 cup buttermilk
1 egg, well beaten
1 tablespoon molasses
1 tablespoon unsalted butter, melted

METHOD
Preheat the oven to 425° F.
Lightly butter an 8-inch square baking pan.
Sift together the dry ingredients in a large
   mixing bowl.
Add the buttermilk, beaten egg, molasses, and
   melted butter and mix until smooth.
Pour the mixture into the prepared baking pan
   and bake for 30 minutes.
Unmold the johnnycake and let cool slightly
   before cutting.
Serve warm.

Serves 6 to 8

APPLE PIE WITH CHEDDAR CHEESE

INGREDIENTS
2 recipes pie dough, made with lard
   (see Basics, page 335)
9 cups sliced apples, such as Greening, Cortland,
   Winesap, or other hard cooking apples
   (8 to 10 apples)
Juice of 1 lemon
1 tablespoon flour
$1/3$ cup sugar
$1/2$ teaspoon cinnamon
3 tablespoons unsalted butter, cut into bits
1 egg yolk beaten with 2 tablespoons cold water,
   for egg wash
Cheddar cheese, sliced

METHOD
Preheat the oven to 425° F.
Prepare the pie dough and line a 10-inch deep
   dish pie pan with half the dough.
Peel and core the apples and slice into eighths.
In a bowl, toss the apples with the lemon juice. Mix
   the flour with the sugar and cinnamon and toss
   with the apples.
Turn the filling into the pie pan and dot with butter.
Roll out the remaining dough into a circle. Moisten
   the edges of the pie crust with water and set the
   top crust in place. Seal and crimp.
Brush the crust evenly with the egg wash.
Cut vents in the top crust by inserting a paring
   knife $1/4$ inch through the dough.
Bake in the center of the oven for 20 minutes.
Reduce the heat to 350° F and continue baking for
   45 minutes more.
Cool for 1 hour before serving.
Serve with cheddar cheese.

Serves 8 to 10

Red Flannel Hash

RED FLANNEL HASH WITH POACHED EGGS AND KETCHUP ○ INDIAN PUDDING SOUFFLÉ AND WHIPPED CREAM ○ BLOODY MARYS ○ The Shipyard Old Thumper Extra Special Ale, ME

The name "Red flannel" originated when red beets were chopped into the corned beef hash, along with whatever leftover vegetables were handy. Although frugal and fast, this leftover meal is an all-time favorite, brightened up with a hot poached egg. Homemade ketchup, neither sweet nor tart, and the ever-present jar of relish or pickles were served alongside. "Come at pudding time" was an invitation to dinner, because the pudding opened the meal. Puddings were based on old English recipes. There's nothing Indian about this pudding at all, although the name was derived from the commonly used term "Indian cornmeal."

RED FLANNEL HASH

INGREDIENTS

2 cups diced corned beef
2 cups boiled potatoes
1 cup chopped scallions
1 cup diced, cooked carrots
1/2 cup diced, cooked parsnips
1 cup diced, cooked red beets
Salt and freshly milled black pepper
1/4 pound unsalted butter
2 to 3 tablespoons heavy cream
Ketchup (see Basics, page 335)

METHOD

In a large bowl, mix together the meat and all of the vegetables, except the beets.

Lightly salt and pepper the mixture to taste. If the corned beef is salty, do not add any salt.

Over moderate heat, melt the butter in a large cast-iron or other heavy skillet.

Fold the beets into the hash mixture and turn the mixture into the skillet.

Pack firmly, cover, and cook for 10 minutes.

Uncover and drizzle the cream over the hash.

Cover and continue cooking for an additional 10 to 15 minutes, until crusty and well browned.

Turn the hash over with a spatula and pack firmly again.

Continue to cook for another 15 minutes.

Serve the hash with a poached egg for each guest, and ketchup as a condiment.

Serves 5

INDIAN PUDDING SOUFFLÉ

INGREDIENTS
Butter and sugar for the mold
1/2 cup yellow cornmeal
4 cups milk, scalded
2 tablespoons melted butter
1/2 cup molasses
1 tablespoon cinnamon
1/2 teaspoon ground ginger
1 teaspoon salt
2 eggs, separated
Whipped unsweetened heavy cream, for serving

METHOD
Preheat the oven to 350° F.
Butter and sugar a medium-sized soufflé or
    baking dish.
Place the cornmeal in the top of a double boiler,
    and gradually add the scalded milk, stirring
    constantly for 20 minutes.
Remove from the heat and stir in the butter,
    molasses, spices, salt, and egg yolks. Set aside to
    cool slightly.

In a clean bowl, beat the egg whites until stiff but
    not dry. Fold into the pudding mixture.
Turn the batter into the prepared mold and bake
    for 40 to 45 minutes, until puffed and brown.
Serve with whipped cream.

Serves 4 to 5

Steak on the Rocks

An old Maine islander told me how generations of
people had been cooking meat out of doors. They
pulled a flat rock from the sea, and heated it in a
roaring fire. The rock was then pulled out with a
board or shovel and dusted off. A steak was set on
top to quickly sizzle, the fat from the meat
providing natural grease. The rock actually imparts
a sea flavor to the meat. He said he knew about
this from his grandfather, and his grandfather
before that, and so on, putting it back a dozen or
so generations. In all probability this method came
from the American Indians. After the steak is
cooked, and after you've had your meal, the rock
is thrown back into the sea.

Yankee Fourth of July

CHILLED BEET SOUP ○ POACHED SALMON WITH HOLLANDAISE SAUCE ○ SWEET SNAP PEAS AND RED POTATOES WITH DILL, KOSHER SALT, AND BUTTER ○ STRAWBERRY ICE CREAM ○ Sakonnet Vineyards Vidal Blanc, RI or Schneider Vineyards Cabernet Franc, NY

The Fourth of July heralds summer throughout New England, and it was at this time of year when salmon, in their heyday, began to spawn. Before pollution, some of the great salmon catches were from rivers in the East; most salmon today is farm-raised It was the custom to serve salmon on the Fourth of July with new peas and potatoes. Eastern salmon is best when poached. It is a rather delicate fish, unlike the King Salmon of the Pacific Northwest which is bigger and gamier. Oddly enough, Easterners, unlike American Indians of the Northwest, never planked their salmon as they did their shad. Sugar snap peas should be treated like any good variety of pea: thrown in salted water, cooked until tender, and not tinkered with beyond that. Hollandaise was a later accompaniment—thanks to Fannie Farmer—and became one of the preferred sauces with many fish dishes. In the summer, New Englanders suffer from berry fever. From strawberries and blueberries to huckleberries and gooseberries, they do everything with berries, through one perpetual berry season, ending with cranberries.

CHILLED BEET SOUP

INGREDIENTS

3 pounds small beets with their leaves
1 bunch scallions, including some of the green, halved lengthwise
2 lemons, cut into eight wedges
5 stems fresh dill
2 quarts chicken stock (see Basics, page 332) or canned low-sodium chicken broth
Salt and freshly milled black pepper
Sour cream, chopped fresh dill, and grated lemon zest

METHOD

Clean the beets, leaving 2 inches of the stems and the roots ends attached to prevent bleeding. Set aside the leaves.

Place the beets and leaves in a soup kettle and add the remaining soup ingredients. Pour in the stock and 2 cups of water.

Bring to a boil over high heat and reduce the heat to low. Simmer until the beets are tender.

Remove the beets and continue to cook the liquid at a low simmer.

Under cold running water, slip off the skins and stems.

Dice the beets.

Strain the broth, discarding the solids, and add the diced beets to the soup. Refrigerate until thoroughly chilled.

Serve with a spoonful of sour cream with a little chopped dill and grated lemon zest.

Note: This soup can be made one day ahead of time.

Serves 8

POACHED SALMON WITH HOLLANDAISE SAUCE

INGREDIENTS
1 whole salmon (5 to 6 pounds), gutted, gills
   removed with head and tail intact
2 sprigs fresh tarragon
Court bouillon (see Basics, page 332, double the
recipe but do not double the quantity of wine)
Vegetables (see Note)

SPECIAL TOOLS
Fish poacher large enough to hold the fish
   comfortably

METHOD
Wash the fish thoroughly and place the tarragon in
   the cavity.
Wrap the fish tightly in lengths of plastic wrap.
Place the fish in a poacher. Add the court bouillon
   and enough water to cover.
When the liquid begins to bubble, reduce the heat
   to low and simmer slowly for 20 to 25 minutes.

Remove from the heat and allow the fish to cool.
Remove the fish, place on a platter, and carefully
   remove the plastic wrap.
Peel away the skin and dark flesh to reveal the
   salmon flesh. Arrange the vegetables on either
   side of the fish and serve with Hollandaise Sauce.

Note: Fresh garden peas with butter and a
sprinkling of mint are a traditional accompaniment
to this festive dish. Sweet snap peas are a simple
vegetable to serve. Remove the stems, cook until
tender, and toss with melted butter, salt, and freshly
milled pepper. Culls are the tiny potatoes left
behind in the fields after harvesting. Some farmers
grow tiny potatoes approximately the size of
shooting marbles. They should be cooked in their
skins until tender, a matter of 5 minutes after the
water comes to a boil. Serve with melted sweet
butter, kosher salt, a little chopped dill, and grated
lemon zest.

Serves 6 to 8

HOLLANDAISE SAUCE

INGREDIENTS

3 egg yolks, at room temperature
1 tablespoon fresh lemon juice
Salt and freshly milled white pepper
Pinch of cayenne pepper
1 tablespoon cold, unsalted butter
1/4 pound plus 4 tablespoons unsalted butter,
    clarified (see Basics, page 333)

METHOD

Whisk the egg yolks in a saucepan until they
    become thick and lemony in color. Add the
    lemon juice and seasonings.
Add the cold butter and place the saucepan over
    very low heat, whisking constantly until the
    mixture thickens and becomes creamy.
Remove from the heat.
Beat the mixture with the whisk, adding the melted
    butter in droplets. When the sauce begins to
    take on the thickness of heavy cream, start
    adding the butter in a steady stream.
Taste for seasoning and reserve on a warm corner
    of the stove.

Note: Hollandaise is easily made in a blender
or food processor. Egg yolks, lemon juice, and
seasonings are blended and the clarified butter
is incorporated in a slow steady stream. This is a
fail-safe method; however, the flavor of the lightly
cooked yolks and the whisking in of the butter
result in a fluffier and richer-tasting sauce.

Makes approximately 1 cup

STRAWBERRY ICE CREAM

INGREDIENTS

1 quart cold English Cream (see Basics, page 336)
1 quart cold ripe strawberries, hulled and crushed

SPECIAL TOOLS

Ice cream maker

METHOD

Combine the English Cream and the strawberries.
Place the mixture in the ice cream maker and
    freeze according to the manufacturer's
    directions.

Makes 1 3/4 to 2 quarts

Fish Fry

CORN AND CLAM CHOWDER ○ FRIED WHITEBAIT ○ PAN-SAUTÉED OYSTERS ○ FRIED CLAMS ○ TARTAR SAUCE (See Basics, page 334) ○ COLESLAW (See page 122) ○ RASPBERRIES AND CREAM ○ Peconic Bay Riesling, NY or Ipswich India Pale Ale, MA

Corn and clam chowders are native to New England. Fresh corn is tender and creamy, and with the addition of fresh clams this chowder is irresistible. The fish fry that follows the chowder begins with tiny whitebait, which is baby herring, dusted with flour and thrown into hot oil—a lilliputian fish fry. Whitebait should be consumed on the spot and eaten with your fingers like potato chips, with perhaps a sprinkle of fresh lemon. Generally speaking, New England shellfish is dusted with flour and cooked in butter, while Southern shellfish is tossed with cornmeal and fried in oil. Here I've done one of each. The standard seashore accompaniments are tartar sauce and creamy coleslaw.

CORN AND CLAM CHOWDER

INGREDIENTS

8 ears fresh sweet corn
3 cups milk
3 cups chicken stock (see Basics, page 332)
   or canned low-sodium chicken broth

1 tablespoon unsalted butter
1 tablespoon all-purpose flour
Freshly milled black pepper
1/8 teaspoon cayenne pepper
1 1/2 cups chopped cherrystone clams
   (reserve 1/2 cup clam juice)
Salt to taste
2 tablespoons chives, snipped

METHOD

With a sharp knife, cut the kernels away from the
   cob and place them in a soup kettle.
With a small spoon, scrape the pulp and milk from
   the cobs into the kettle.
Add the milk and stock and bring to a simmer.
In a small bowl, blend the butter with the flour to
   form a smooth paste.
Whisk the paste into the kettle and season with
   black and cayenne pepper. Simmer for 15
   minutes, stirring occasionally.
Add the chopped clams and the reserved juices
   and bring to a simmer.
Add salt and seasonings to taste and ladle into
   heated bowls.
Sprinkle with snipped chives and serve.

Serves 5 to 6

FISH FRY

INGREDIENTS
1 quart whitebait, rinsed
Vegetable oil for frying
All-purpose flour for dusting
Salt
24 oysters, shucked
24 littleneck clams, shucked
Cornmeal for dusting
Lemon wedges for serving

SPECIAL TOOLS
Deep-fat frying thermometer

METHOD
Drain the whitebait and pat dry.

In a deep, heavy pot, heat 3 cups of vegetable oil
until it reaches 350° F when tested with a frying
thermometer.

Working in small batches, toss the whitebait in flour.

Place them in a mesh strainer and shake away the
excess flour.

Add the floured whitebait to the hot oil and cook
until crisp and golden.

Remove with a flat-slotted skimmer and place on
paper towels to drain. Salt lightly.

Continue until all whitebait have been fried,
drained, and salted.

Serve immediately.

Oysters:
Drain the liquor from the oysters. Discard it or save
for another use.

Dredge the oysters lightly through flour, shaking to
remove any excess.

Follow the method above and fry the oysters.

Serve immediately with lemon wedges.

Clams:
Drain the juice from clams. Discard it or reserve for
another use.

Dredge the clams lightly with cornmeal, shaking to
remove any excess.

Following the method above, fry the clams until
crisp and golden.

Serve immediately with lemon wedges.

Note: Oysters and clams can be dipped in beaten
egg and then coated with flour or bread crumbs.
They may be sautéed in clarified butter or
vegetable oil. Serve with White Remoulade (see
page 164) or Tartar sauce (see Basics, page 334).

Serves 6 to 8

Swordfish Dinner

GRILLED LITTLENECK CLAMS ○ THE BENCHLEY'S GRILLED SWORDFISH WITH SALT CRUST AND GIN-LIME BUTTER ○ DILLED KIRBY CUCUMBERS ○ BRAN POPOVERS ○ BLACK PLUMS, CURRANTS, AND GOOSEBERRIES ○ Channing Daughters Scuttlehole Chardonnay, NY

Swordfish adapts itself to the grill perhaps better than any other fish. Though usually swordfish is cut one-half to one-inch thick, this recipe works only if it is cut 2-inches thick and thinly sliced at the table as one would cut a steak. The salt crust doesn't penetrate the flesh but rather seals in the juices before it burns off during cooking. Cucumbers are a wonderful foil for fish, and seeds of the kirby are so tiny that they don't need to be removed. The common popover is best served with meat and gravy, but wouldn't make sense with this meal. The bran makes it more grainy and gritty, a nice complement in texture and taste.

GRILLED LITTLENECK CLAMS

INGREDIENTS
4 dozen small littleneck clams, scrubbed
For the sauce:
1 cup clarified butter (See Basics, page 333)
2 cloves, garlic, minced
2 tablespoons finely chopped fresh parsley
1 tablespoon snipped fresh chives
1 tablespoon chopped fresh tarragon leaves

METHOD
Scrub the clams under cold running water. Place in a colander and allow to drain. Chill.
In a small saucepan, warm the clarified butter and add the garlic and herbs. Set aside.
Prepare a fire using hardwood charcoal (not briquettes or lighter fluid).
When the coals are dusty and glowing, place the clams on the grill.
As they open, use the tongs to transfer them to a large bowl.
Discard any that do not open. While the clams are grilling, set the butter on the side of the grill to keep warm.

Transfer the clams to warm soup bowls.
Strain the collected clam juice from the bowl into the herb butter, leaving any sand in the bottom of the bowl. Ladle the sauce over the clams and serve.

Serves 6

THE BENCHLEY'S GRILLED SWORDFISH WITH SALT CRUST AND GIN-LIME BUTTER

INGREDIENTS

1 cold swordfish steak, cut 2-inches thick
   (approximately 4 pounds)
1/4 pound unsalted butter, melted
1 cup or more Kosher salt

For the Gin-Lime Butter:
1/4 cup dry gin
3 tablespoons fresh lime juice
1/4 pound plus 4 tablespoons (1 1/4 sticks) chilled,
   unsalted butter, cut into pieces

METHOD

Brush one side of the cold fish with some of the
   melted butter.
Dredge liberally with the kosher salt.
Refrigerate for 20 minutes, or until the butter
   has congealed.
Turn the fish over and butter and salt the other side.
Refrigerate for another 20 minutes, or until ready
   to cook.
Build a hardwood charcoal fire in an outdoor grill.
   (If grilling clams first, add more wood charcoal
   to the fire.)

For the sauce:
In a small saucepan, carefully bring the gin and
   lime juice to a simmer over medium heat. Cook
   until reduced to a thick glaze, about 7 minutes.
Remove from the heat and whisk in 2 tablespoons
   of the chilled butter, piece by piece. Return to
   the heat and, whisking constantly, add the
   remaining butter, piece by piece. The sauce
   should have the texture and consistency of a
   thick, creamy hollandaise.
Remove from the heat. Set aside until ready to
   serve with the fish.
When the coals are dusty and glowing, spread
   them out in the grill, banking them slightly
   against the sides. Place a sheet of heavy foil in
   the center. (This will prevent the melting butter
   from dripping onto the coals, flaring up, and
   burning the fish.) Place the grill over the fire.
Place the fish on hot grill and cook for 10 minutes
   on one side and 7 on the other, turning only
   once. The fish will be moist and tender.
Serve with Gin-Lime Butter Sauce and Dilled
   Kirby Cucumbers.

Serves 6 to 7

DILLED KIRBY CUCUMBERS

INGREDIENTS

18 small Kirby cucumbers, peeled and
quartered lengthwise
Salt
4 tablespoons unsalted butter
2 tablespoons chopped fresh dill

METHOD

Preheat the oven to 350° F.
Lightly salt the cucumbers and let stand in a
colander for 20 minutes.
Place the cucumbers in a small ovenproof
casserole and dot with butter.
Cover tightly and bake for 25 to 30 minutes or until
the cucumbers are limp but not soft, tossing
once or twice while they cook.
Toss the cucumbers with the dill and serve.

Serves 6

BRAN POPOVERS

INGREDIENTS

Bacon fat or butter, to grease the muffin tins
Unprocessed bran, to dust the tins
1 cup all-purpose flour less 1 tablespoon
$1/4$ teaspoon salt
2 tablespoons unprocessed bran
1 cup milk
2 eggs, lightly beaten
1 tablespoon unsalted butter, melted

METHOD

Preheat the oven to 450° F.
Grease a 12-cup muffin tin and dust with bran.
Sift the flour into a mixing bowl. Add the salt and
the bran.
Whisk in the milk, eggs, and melted butter.
Fill the muffin cups $3/4$ full and dust the
top of the batter with additional bran.
Bake for 15 minutes. Reduce the heat to 350° F
and continue to bake for 20 minutes.
Serve immediately.

Makes 8 to 10 popovers

Long Island Fish Dinner

SCALLOP STEW ○ STEAMED BASS WITH CIDER AND GINGER ○ STEWED RUM PLUMS ○ MAPLE WAFER COOKIES ○ Jamesport Vineyards Sauvignon Blanc, NY

Mid-autumn opens the scallop season. The sweetest are the bay scallops harvested by the fishermen from the eastern shore of Long Island north to Nantucket and Maine. Scallopers put on high-waisted waders and move slowly into the water with a rake and a metal basket supported by a rubber tube, attached to their waist by a cord. Scallops are elusive creatures, difficult to harvest, as they move quickly both through the water and in the sand. Their price is exorbitant due to their scarcity. The brown tide that hit the bays of the Eastern Atlantic in the 1990s, hurricanes, and coastal development have contributed to their decline. This beautiful mollusk is too fragile to be shipped live and is shucked immediately before being sent to market. This luscious, pearly shellfish should be eaten as fresh as possible, and cooked as briefly as possible.

The fish is steamed in cider. Cider was used in a variety of dishes, much in the way wine is used today. Trade routes had opened beyond anyone's expectations, and with the discovery of this country, an abundance of new items. Bass with cider and ginger may sound like a modern interpretation, but vanilla, rums, ginger, and other spices were a novelty of the seventeeth century, when these luxuries were carried into American harbors.

Both wild American and established European plums have been cultivated here since the early seventeenth century. P. americanus is a golden plum, varying in hue from burnished yellow to almost red. In early years, colonial women didn't poach twelve plums for guests, they poached a barrelful. When the plums were ripe, they had to be preserved: put up or dried to help get a family through the winter.

SCALLOP STEW

INGREDIENTS

3 cups heavy cream, reduced over moderate heat to 2 cups
2 cups fish stock, reduced over moderate heat to 1 1/2 cups (see Basics, page 333)
1 quart bay scallops
Worcestershire sauce
Cayenne pepper
Salt
1/4 cup fresh chives, snipped

METHOD

In a large saucepan, combine the reduced cream with the reduced fish stock over moderately low heat. Add the scallops and seasonings to taste and simmer for about 4 minutes, until the scallops are just turning opaque. Do not overcook or the scallops will toughen.

Season with cayenne pepper and salt to taste and pour into heated soup plates. Garnish with snipped chives.

Makes 4 large or 6 medium servings

STEAMED BASS WITH CIDER AND GINGER

INGREDIENTS

Vegetable oil

1 whole bass (approximately 5 pounds), spine removed with head and tail intact

Salt

2 ripe tomatoes—peeled, seeded, and chopped

3 small carrots, cut into 2-inch julienne and blanched for 1 minute (approximately 1 cup)

1-inch piece fresh ginger, peeled and cut into fine julienne (approximately $1/4$ cup)

1 small hot red chile pepper, seeded and cut into fine julienne

2 medium leeks—halved lengthwise, washed, cut into 2-inch julienne, and blanched

$1/4$ cup lightly chopped Italian parsley

$1/2$ cup apple cider

METHOD

Preheat the oven to 400° F.

Place a sheet of foil, large enough to envelop the fish, on a large baking sheet or baking pan. Line it with parchment paper.

Brush the parchment lightly with oil so the fish will not stick after cooking.

Set the fish on the parchment, lightly salt the cavity, and scatter some of the tomatoes, carrots, and ginger inside the fish.

Scatter the remaining ingredients over the fish and pour the cider over the fish.

Tightly close the foil and bake the fish for 20 to 25 minutes, or for 10 minutes per inch of thickness.

Serves 4 to 5

STEWED RUM PLUMS

INGREDIENTS
2 dozen golden plums
2 cups dark rum
2 cups sugar
1 vanilla bean, split
1 cinnamon stick
2 tablespoons peppercorns

METHOD
Place the plums in a single layer in a large
    shallow pan.
Add the rum, sugar, spices, and enough water to
    cover. Bring the liquid to a boil. Reduce to a
    simmer and poach until the fruit can be pierced
    easily with a knife.
Remove from the heat and let the fruit cool in
    the liquid.
Serve 2 plums per person with Maple Wafer Cookies.

Note: These stewed red plums can be put up in
sterilized jars or refrigerated for up to 5 days.

Serves 8 to 12

MAPLE WAFER COOKIES

INGREDIENTS
1 cup all-purpose flour
1/2 teaspoon baking powder
1/4 teaspoon baking soda
1/2 cup maple syrup
1/2 cup sugar
1/4 pound unsalted butter
1/2 cup chopped walnuts

METHOD
Preheat the oven to 350° F.
Fill a large saucepan with about 2 inches of water.
Place over high heat and bring to a simmer.
Sift the flour, baking powder, and baking soda into
    a mixing bowl and reserve.
In a heavy medium saucepan, bring the
    maple syrup, sugar, and butter to a boil.

Continue boiling for 30 seconds or until the sugar
    is dissolved.
Stir the dry ingredients into the sugar mixture and
    fold in the nuts.
Place the smaller saucepan over the saucepan
    filled with simmering water.
Remove from the heat (keeping the mixture warm
    will prevent it from hardening or seizing up).
With a large dessert or soup spoon, spoon the
    mixture onto ungreased or foil-lined baking
    sheets, spacing the spoonfuls 3 inches apart.
Bake for 7 minutes.
Allow wafers to cool before removing from the
    sheets. Store in an airtight container.

Makes 2 dozen wafers

Chowder Picnic

MANHATTAN FISH CHOWDER ○
GOOSEBERRY FOOL ○ LORNA DOONES
○ Corey Creek Vineyards Rosé, NY or
Brooklyn Lager, NY

Tomato-based clam chowder was being served up at the beginning of this century from Coney Island to Delmonico's. How it came to be called "Manhattan" no one really knows, but it was a distinct departure from the creamy chowders of New England. Manhattan, or Long Island, clam chowder is prepared with the addition of herbs, specifically thyme, tomatoes, and potatoes. All of the ingredients—especially the herbs and fish—should be as fresh as possible. Avoid taking shortcuts, such as using clam broth. The addition of several types of fish makes this chowder a heartier meal.

By the eighteenth century, there were more than 400 varieties of gooseberries, as well as numerous cultivated and wild currants. The berries never appealed to the American eating public much beyond New England. Affected by a blight that attacked the American white pine, both gooseberries and currants were outlawed and fell almost entirely from popular use. The berries are once again beginning to capture the fancy of home gardeners. Gooseberries give off an enormous amount of pectin and the fruit is jelly-like—ideal for a fool, that most English of desserts. For many of us, the Lorna Doone cookie was our first encounter with shortbread.

MANHATTAN FISH CHOWDER

INGREDIENTS

1 quart shucked large cherrystone clams,
  with their liquor
1/4 pound salt pork or slab bacon, diced
1 large onion, minced (approximately 1 cup)
4 ripe tomatoes—peeled, seeded, and chopped
  with juices reserved (approximately 3 cups)
2 cups cold water
1 teaspoon fresh thyme leaves
1 teaspoon fresh rosemary leaves, chopped
1 teaspoon fresh tarragon leaves
Freshly milled black pepper
1 1/2 cups small new potatoes, peeled and
  quartered
3 small carrots, diced (approximately 1 cup)
2 dozen small littleneck clams, washed, drained,
  and chilled
1 pound firm white fish fillets, such as weakfish
  or bass, cubed
1/4 cup fresh parsley, chopped
Oyster crackers

METHOD

Strain the clam liquor into a small bowl.
Chop the shucked clams with a sharp knife, or put
  through the medium disk of a food mill.
Cover and set aside.
In a large soup kettle, render the salt pork over
  moderate heat until the cracklings are golden.
Remove the cracklings with a slotted spoon and
  set aside.
Add the onions and sauté in the fat until translucent.
Add the tomatoes and their juices.
Add 2 cups cold water, herbs, and seasonings.
Add the reserved clam liquor, potatoes, and carrots.
Cover and simmer for approximately 8 minutes.
When the potatoes are cooked, add the reserved
  chopped clam meat and cook for 5 minutes.
Remove from the heat, cool and refrigerate,
  covered overnight.
To assemble:
Place the littlenecks in the freezer for 10 minutes to
  facilitate quick opening.
Meanwhile, skim off any fat that has congealed on
  the surface of the stew.

Bring the stew to a simmer over moderately
  low heat.
When the chowder bubbles lightly and is hot, add
  the littlenecks. Cover and continue to simmer.
When the clams begin to open, add the cubed
  fish and simmer until the fish becomes tender,
  about 5 minutes.
Add the reserved cracklings and parsley and serve
  with oyster crackers.

Note: This chowder is best when allowed to ripen in
the refrigerator for one day before serving. The
chowder freezes well before the addition of the
littlenecks and fish.

Serves 6

GOOSEBERRY FOOL

INGREDIENTS

1 quart fresh gooseberries
1 pint fresh red, pink, or black currants
About 1/2 cup sugar
1 cup heavy cream, lightly whipped

METHOD

Separately wash and drain the fruits.
In a saucepan, toss the gooseberries with 1/2 cup
  sugar or more, depending on the tartness of
  the fruit.
Warm the gooseberries over moderate heat until
  they begin to collapse and give off their juices.
Turn the gooseberries and juices into a bowl and
  refrigerate until completely chilled.
Repeat this method with the currants, adding 1 to
  2 tablespoons sugar and warming the berries
  until the sugar dissolves. Place the berries in a
  bowl and refrigerate until completely chilled.
When ready to serve, place layers of gooseberries,
  currants, and cream in a glass serving bowl,
  alternating layers until all of the fruits and creams
  are used.
Swirl the mixture slightly before serving with
  Lorna Doones.

Serves 6

Street Food

The Lobster Roll

All good cooks treat the lobster with reverence. Even when served cold in a salad on a toasted frankfurter roll, lobster is always a luxurious treat. One of life's simple pleasures, the lobster roll started in the lobster shacks and fish houses that dot the coast from Maine to Montauk and is New England's version of the hot dog.

INGREDIENTS
2 cooked lobsters, each approximately
    1 1/2 pounds, shelled and chilled
    (see page 36)
1/2 teaspoon dry mustard
Lemon juice to taste
About 3/4 cup mayonnaise (see Basics, page 334)
    or Hellman's
A few dashes of Tabasco sauce
2 celery ribs, stringed and finely diced
4 hot dog rolls
4 tablespoons unsalted butter, melted

METHOD
Remove the lobster meat from the tails and claws
    and cut into 1/2-inch pieces.
In a small bowl, whisk together the dry mustard
    and lemon juice. Add the mayonnaise and
    season with Tabasco.
Combine the lobster and celery with the
    mayonnaise mixture.
Cover and chill for 30 minutes.
Preheat the broiler.
Open the hot dog rolls and brush them with the
    melted butter.
Place the rolls, buttered side up, in a hot broiler
    and toast lightly, until golden.
Fill each roll with the lobster salad and serve
    immediately.

Serves 4

Rum Punch

In the early 1800s, there was a wonderful drink called "yard of flannel," made with steaming ale, lemons, eggs, sugar, spices, and rum. Over the years, our taste in drinks has become simpler. We drink eggnog once a year, our syllabub has become a dessert, and wine has become a cocktail. In the cold of winter, hot drinks are a satisfying pick-me-up that warm the spirit, the head, and the belly.

HOT BUTTERED RUM

INGREDIENTS
1/4 pound unsalted butter, at room temperature
3 tablespoons brown sugar
Pinch of ground cloves
4 navel oranges
8 small cinnamon sticks
2 cups dark rum
Boiling water, hot tea, or hot cider

METHOD
In a small bowl, cream the butter, brown sugar,
    and ground cloves and set aside. Remove
    the zest from each orange in one spiral strip.
    Cut each strip in half.
In each glass or mug, place one spoon, a strip of
    zest, 1 cinnamon stick, and 2 ounces of rum.
Pour 4 to 5 ounces of boiling water, tea, or cider
    into each glass or mug and float 1 tablespoon
    of the softened butter mixture on top.
Serve warm.

Makes 8 drinks

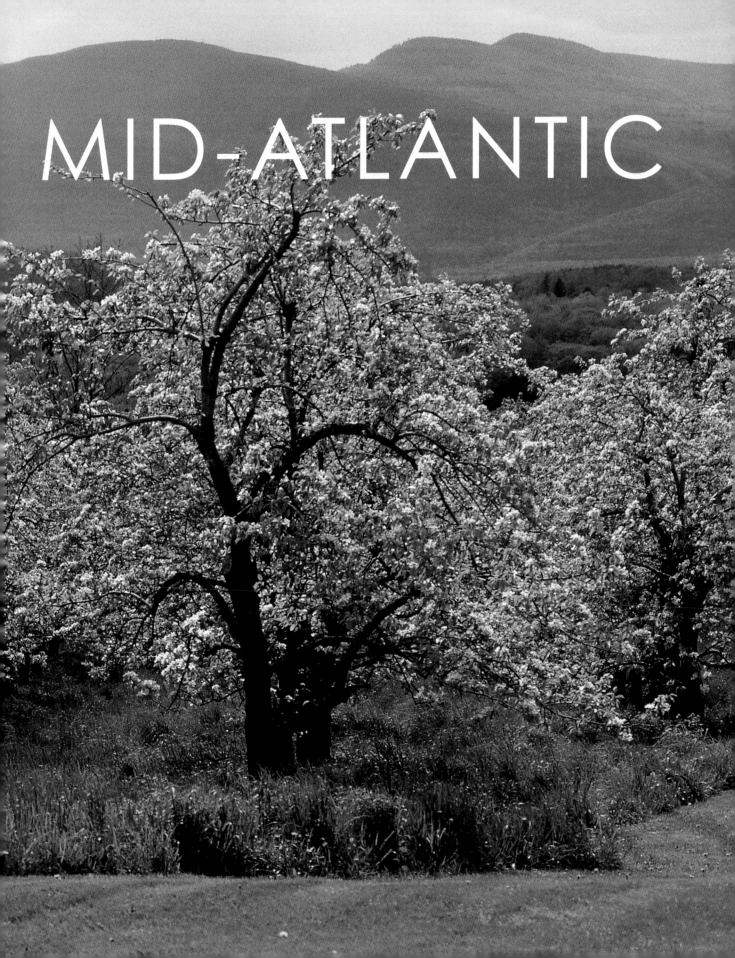

MID-ATLANTIC

MID-ATLANTIC

In a land of valleys jeweled with orchards from the Hudson west to Pennsylvania, carefully tended hothouses and sheltered gardens glowed with delicate cuttings and seeds brought by settlers from plants as varied as the apple, peach, plum, cherry, apricot, fig, and wild persimmon. The myth of Johnny Appleseed grew from tales of a vagrant horticulturist named John Chapman, who wandered from the Alleghenies to Ohio, planting and tending nurseries. Apples were important food, especially considering their storage life, for an apple barrel could be kept year-round. Apples were sliced in rings and dried for winter use. A child's thirst was quenched with cider, and a man's slaked with hard cider, rather decent brandy, and potent applejack. Expatriate Europeans missed their clarets, but these apple beverages kept many an Englishman and Dutchman happy. Settlers were remarkably self-sufficient, and a newcomer was quick to clear a field and sow an acre or two with corn, potatoes, and gardens of vegetables. The hills were cleared to provide pasture for dairy cows that yielded milk, rich cream, butter, and even cheddar that rivaled that of Vermont and England. Streams and lakes were filled with trout and bass, and the Hudson provided much of the East Coast with sturgeon and shad, and delicate shad roe in the springtime. Traditionally, buck shad was smoked to juicy perfection, and the roe-heavy females still sell briskly throughout the Eastern seaboard. Eel was packed in great quantities and shipped to Holland for smoking; early Dutch farmers considered it more valuable for export than for local markets.

Frugality was the watchword of the prosperous small farm. The larder was stocked with basics—pork and apple barrels, dried corn, and a root cellar—to stave off hunger over winter's long course. The home cook put up preserves, jams, vegetables, and pickles, and a smokehouse filled with wild game, fish, ham, and bacon provided peace of mind. These little farms survived because they wasted nothing; even corn cobs and apple tree prunings were used, infusing smoked pork, chickens, and wild game with their sweet flavors.

While the Philadelphia Germans ate pickled pig's feet, jellied pig's knuckles, hard-boiled eggs pickled in beet juice, and crunchy Reading pretzels, the Quaker Philadelphians preferred more luxurious tables. Lordly landowners, powdered and puffed to suit the style of their century, indulged themselves. The Quaker William Penn himself enjoyed living well, and was rarely inclined to forgo a social evening, typically dining on turtle from the West Indies, oysters from the Chesapeake, local game, syllabub, flummeries, trifles, and fools, all washed down with Madeiras, ports, and other imported wines. Philadelphia, hub of the colonies, hosted glittering evenings of mock Regency and was this country's capital until 1800, except for a brief year of glory for New York City.

Fried scrapple and eggs were everyman's breakfast. Hot pepper pot—a filling bowl of tripe, veal, vegetables, herbs, and whole spoonfuls of pepper, reportedly tossed together by Pennsylvania Dutchmen for Washington's troops at Valley Forge—appeared on menus in Philadelphia and around the countryside. By the nineteenth century it was hawked from

steaming cauldrons in the city streets. The formal dinners attended by our Founding Fathers were staggering two-course affairs: soups and fishes, served with game, poultry, roasts of beef and mutton, chops, and vegetables and sweets with the second course. Fifty dishes might ornament such a function, attended by gallons of wines, beer, cider, and rum. When Mr. Washington ran for the legislature in 1758, his agents doled out three Imperials, or three-and-a-half gallons, to each voter, and worried that the quantity might be stingy! Penn, whose Philadelphia was as German as it was English Quaker, established that city's first brewery, which succeeded where the New England ones had failed. Yeasty brews made from pure local water met with approval, and dark Bock or "Easter beer" was the companion drink to the Lenten weisswurst flecked with spring chives. Bock was left behind in favor of a lighter and more sparkling beer brewed here in the eighteenth century by German refugees of the European potato famine who later immigrated to Ohio, Minnesota, and Wisconsin.

The rising cities of Boston, New York, and Philadelphia could boast restaurants with services of silver, fine china, and crystal, in proud imitation of European custom and the luxury enjoyed by owners of local estates. Dining clubs became havens of the select. The oldest of these, the Schuylkill Fishing Company, was established in 1732 and is further renowned as the birthplace of the infamous Fish House Punch, a fairly lethal combination of rum, Cognac, peach brandy, citrus juices, and sugar. Indoctrination into the club required a new member to carefully fry a half dozen perch in a long handled skillet and to flip the fish perfectly in the air.

From early days, land in New York was expensive. The Pennsylvania government, on the other hand, offered some of the richest farmland in the east for 10 cents an acre. This was particularly fortunate for Germans seeking relief from religious persecution. Penn's royal grant was open to oppressed societies from other countries, and soon such sects as the Moravians, Amish, Shakers, and Schwenkfelders arrived. These groups joined the company of thirteen Mennonite and Crefelder families already here, who had left their native Rhine Valley which was still in ruins some thirty-five years after the Thirty Years' War.

The character of these people set standards for this country. The Shakers spread across the Mid-Atlantic as far as Ohio, Indiana, Illinois, and Iowa, their celibate communities always tiny and on the verge of extinction. For all the Shakers' austerity, their cooking is brilliant, coupling asparagus with mint, spinach with rosemary, omelets with blue chive blossoms, and apple pie with rose water. Their most influential innovation, pearl-ash, became a staple colonial leavening for dough: modern baking powder. It might almost be said that the Shakers—with their elementary formulas for muffins, cakes, biscuits, and pancakes (consisting of flour, salt, sugar, and baking powder)—were the originators of packaged baking mixes.

Unlike some other sects, the Mennonites did not travel far west, and together with the Amish greatly influenced American cookery

throughout the middle and northern regions of this country. Like the Shakers, they maintained an austere way of life, refusing to this day to use electricity or automobiles. They became known as the "Pennsylvania Dutch" (a corruption of "Deutsche," meaning German). Their lives are ruled by simplicity: their children run barefoot in fine weather. Mothers and daughters wear hand-sewn buttonless dresses, with their hair in neat white caps; fathers and sons go about their farm chores in white shirts and black trousers with suspenders, usually sporting flat-topped straw hats. They grind their flours and meals, buckwheat and rye-barley, in the eighteenth-century way. Their larders are full and their kitchens pleasantly perfumed with the smells of yeast, onion, honey and baking bread. Jersey and Guernsey cows are free to graze on the grasses of rolling soft hills, but the pig, which can quite happily eat anything and still turn into pork, is fussed over and fattened with apples to perfume his tender flesh. A Pennsylvania Dutch table is not properly set without an assortment of "seven sweets and seven sours"—chowchow, corn relish, spiced cantaloupe, bread-and-butter pickles, coleslaw, crab apple jelly, creamy cottage cheese, and apple butter.

Pennsylvania Dutch cooking is famous for its dumplings and noodles. Chicken pot pies and stews were laced with threads of aromatic saffron that enhanced game sauces in this region as early as 1683. Saffron-scented chicken broth comes with chunks of chicken, fresh corn, and popcorn floating on top. Hickory smoke flavored their meats, sweet hams, and sausages; sometimes they served their bologna sliced with apple pie, as the New Englanders did with cheese. Later their ring bologna would develop into the hot dog. Typically pot roasts and sauerbraten were spiked with cloves, cinnamon, and ginger, and set to bake in Dutch ovens in a bath of beer or wine. And surely most representative of their farmhouse sweets is the shoofly pie, a sticky concoction of molasses, brown sugar, spices, and sweet crunchy crumbs. Americans have always been fond of sweets, and marble cake and sweet chocolate sauces were riches of the Mennonite table, satisfying their passion for this devilish sweet. As early as 1765, their first chocolate mill, in Lansdale, Pennsylvania, combined cocoa and milk in the Swiss fashion. By 1780 New England's Walter Baker Cocoa and Chocolate Company was supplying chocolate to all of the original colonies. It was the only packaged and advertised item in the store operated by Abraham Lincoln and his partner in Illinois in 1833. (The Baker Company even went so far as to ship their products around the Horn to early California outposts.) And of course the town of Hershey, Pennsylvania, has long been renowned for chocolate. It would be almost 100 years before the first book of confections would be published in America, but the tradition of sweets continued across the plains with the pioneer woman's memories of her grandmother's favorite recipes.

Farmhouses still sell preserves, pickles, pies, and scrapple along country roads, and homemade jams are sold at the Lancaster Farmers' Market.

This market, set up in perpetuity by Royal Charter during the reign of George II in 1742, is a reminder of how little the cooking of the region has changed. The bottled, freshly grated horseradish, prepared by local Mennonite and Amish women is not to be missed.

It is still in recent memory that these "market" or "truck" farms supplied the large city wholesale markets, which in turn sold to the small grocery stores. This was a time when the baker sold his own bread, and one visited the butcher for meats and poultry, the fishmonger for fish, and the cheese shop for eggs, cream, and cheese. But the small groceries and markets have fallen away just as the small farms have succumbed to new technology. The great urban sprawl, begun in the 1950s, has inexorably encroached on our farmland, and at this writing some three million acres of farmland are lost every year. Our produce, once brought to town by pickup truck, is now shipped in bulk from national and international producers, much of it packed even before it has ripened.

Some of the old family farmers managed to hold on, surviving long enough to be joined by younger generations with a desire to return to the land. It is this new blood, coupled with the sophisticated urbanite's demand for high-quality produce, free-range chickens and sustainably raised pork, that has become a boon to the local farmer. For more than a decade, towns and cities have given over public squares and empty lots for farmer's markets, and both the farmer and the community have benefited.

Breakfast

ASPARAGUS ○ SHAD ROE ○ RHUBARB PIE ○ Clinton Corners Seyval Blanc, NY

Shad roe is the caviar of the East. The Hudson River continues to be cleaned up, which is an encouraging sign, and shad once again thrive to such a degree that they are being used to stock other depleted rivers in the East. Shad roe is too often broiled or fried, overwhelmed with rashers of bacon, and served so tough that understandably few people are enthusiasts of the dish. Shad roe should be submerged in melted butter and gently poached, so that the grains of eggs are gossamer forkfuls of spring's first treat. To complete the celebration, I choose crisp young stalks of asparagus and sour sorrel. Rhubarb grew wild in the East and was a favorite of the Dutch and English before they settled here. These foods are natural complements, and together create a regional meal.

ASPARAGUS

INGREDIENTS
Salt
1 1/2 bunches asparagus spears (approximately
   8 per person), trimmed and peeled
1 stick unsalted butter, melted
Freshly squeezed lemon juice
2 tablespoons parsley, chopped

METHOD
Bring 1 1/2 inches of lightly salted water to boil in a
   large shallow pan.
Add the asparagus and bring to a boil. Reduce
   the heat and simmer for 5 to 6 minutes, or when
   the thickest part can be easily pierced with a
   sharp pairing knife. Using kitchen tongs, remove
   asparagus and drain on paper towel.
Divide the asparagus among 4 warm plates.

Spoon about a tablespoon of butter over the
   asparagus and sprinkle with lemon juice
   and parsley.

Serves 4

SHAD ROE

INGREDIENTS
Roe:
1 pound unsalted butter
2 pairs shad roe, washed in cold water and
   dried carefully
Sauce:
3 tablespoons unsalted butter
3 tablespoons all-purpose flour
1 1/2 cups half-and-half
Salt and freshly milled pepper
1 cup sorrel leaves, washed and cut into ribbons

METHOD

In a medium deep saucepan, melt the butter and
bring it to a mild simmer over moderate heat.

Set the shad roe in the butter, cover, and poach
gently for 10 to 12 minutes turning once.

Meanwhile, prepare the sauce. Melt the butter in
the saucepan set over moderate heat.

When the foam subsides, remove the pan from the
heat and whisk in the flour.

Return the roux to the heat, gradually pour in the
half-and-half, and whisk vigorously. Continue to
cook, whisking, until the sauce thickens,
approximately 8 to 10 minutes.

Season to taste with salt and pepper and fold
in the sorrel.

When the roe are cooked, slide a slotted spoon
under them, and move to a heated serving plate.

Set aside and keep warm.

Continue cooking the sauce for 2 to 3 minutes,
stirring with a wooden spoon, until the sorrel wilts.

Spoon the sauce over the shad roe.

Serve with steamed or boiled new potatoes,
sprinkled with a combination of finely chopped
lemon zest and parsley.

Note: This amount of roe will serve two handsomely
but, due to its richness, is adequate for four.

Serves 2 to 4

RHUBARB PIE

INGREDIENTS

$^1/_2$ recipe pie dough, made with butter
(see Basics, page 335)

1 $^1/_2$ pounds young rhubarb stalks, cut into 1-inch
pieces (approximately 5 cups)

$^1/_2$ teaspoon grated orange zest

$^3/_4$ cups sugar

2 tablespoons quick-cooking tapioca

Meringue:

2 egg whites, at room temperature

$^1/_4$ cup sugar

SPECIAL TOOLS

Pastry bag fitted with a star tip

METHOD

Preheat the oven to 425° F.

Bake the piecrust in a 9-inch pie pan until golden,
following the directions in Basics, page 335.

Move to a cooling rack. Reduce the oven
temperature to 350° F.

Wash the rhubarb pieces and drain.

In a saucepan, combine the rhubarb, with the
orange zest, sugar, and tapioca.

Cover and simmer over moderately low heat until
the rhubarb is tender, approximately 12 minutes.

Turn the mixture into a bowl and cool to
room temperature.

When cooled, spread the rhubarb filling evenly in
the pie shell.

Prepare the meringue.

With an electric mixer, beat the egg whites
until foamy.

Gradually add the sugar, and beat until the whites
are stiff and glossy.

Place the meringue in a pastry bag fitted with a
star tip and pipe the meringue in lattice fashion
over the rhubarb mixture.

Bake the pie for 10 minutes, or until the meringue
is golden.

Serve at room temperature.

Serves 6

Pig Roast

ROAST SUCKLING PIG ○ WILTED GREENS AND CORN BREAD ○ TURNIP AND RHUBARB KRAUT ○ SPICED PEACHES ○ CHERRY PIE ○ Chaddsford Winery Pinot Grigio, PA or Victory Hop Devil Ale, PA

The Pennsylvania Dutch feast on roast suckling pig for any occasion. It is usually stuffed, spitted and roasted, and served with sauerkraut, apples, and the perpetual accompaniment of seven sweets and seven sours. Shreds of turnip can be brined just like cabbage and, with the addition of rhubarb, results in a seasonal kraut. Likewise, the customary onslaught of relishes is replaced by spiced peaches. Wild greens are picked from nearby fields, and are wilted with hot pan juices from the pig, making this field green salad into a pot liquor. Most of the early settlers depended on wild vegetation and today handfuls of these wild greens make a delightful addition to a meal. The greens, with their hot dressing, should be served on fresh baked cornbread following the recipe on page 246, omitting the vegetables.

ROAST SUCKLING PIG

INGREDIENTS
1 suckling pig (14 to 16 pounds)
Salt and freshly milled pepper
6 tart apples, quartered
2 sprigs fresh thyme
2 sprigs fresh rosemary
2 lemons, halved
Vegetable oil
Wild flowers or fresh herbs, for serving

Larding needle or skewers and string
Meat thermometer

METHOD
Preheat the oven to 450° F.

Remove the liver, kidneys, heart, and other organs from the cavity of the pig and thoroughly scrub the pig.

Towel dry thoroughly, inside and out.

Salt and pepper the cavity, and stuff it with apples, herbs, and lemon halves. Sew the cavity shut with a larding needle or close it with skewers and string.

Place the pig in a large roasting pan in a sitting position with its back legs folded under its rump and its front legs forward.

Brace the mouth open with a 2-inch ball of foil.

Cover the ears with foil to protect them from burning.

If the pig is too large for the roasting pan, surround the pan with a double thickness of heavy-duty foil.

Roast the pig for 30 minutes.

Brush on vegetable oil to coat the skin, and reduce the temperature to 350° F.

Roast for 30 minutes and baste again.

Continue roasting for 2 1/2 hours, basting every 30 minutes with the pan juices.

Insert a meat thermometer into the fleshiest part of the thigh. When the internal temperature reaches 185° F, the pig is roasted.

Remove the pig from the oven and let it rest for 30 minutes.

Transfer the pig to a serving board or platter and remove the foil.

Fill the mouth with wild flowers or fresh herbs, and surround the roast with more flowers or herbs.

Meanwhile, skim off as much fat as possible from the pan juices and pour the liquid into a small saucepan.

Cook the juice until heated through and reserve 3/4 cup to wilt the salted greens.

Serve the remaining juices with the roast.

Serves 8 to 10

TURNIP AND RHUBARB KRAUT

INGREDIENTS
3 pounds small, white turnips
3 tablespoons salt
1 cup cider vinegar
2 pounds fresh rhubarb stalks
3/4 cup sugar

METHOD
Peel the turnips and coarsely grate them into a bowl.

Toss with salt and vinegar.

Cover and set aside at room temperature for 1 hour.

Cut the rhubarb into 2-inch pieces. Cut each piece lengthwise into 3 strips.

Wash in cold water and drain.

Place the rhubarb in a large saucepan and toss with the sugar.

Cook the rhubarb over moderate heat for 5 minutes, or until the rhubarb begins to wilt but is still slightly crisp.

Drain the grated turnips in a colander or strainer, pressing out as much liquid as possible.

Fold the turnips into the rhubarb and cook until heated through.

Serve immediately.

Serves 8 to 10

SPICED PEACHES

INGREDIENTS
12 firm, ripe peaches, blanched and peeled
1 bottle dry white wine
1 cup white wine vinegar
3 small cinnamon sticks
6 whole cloves
8 peppercorns
1 lemon, halved and squeezed
Approximately 2 cups sugar, depending on the sweetness of the fruit

METHOD
In a large kettle, combine the peaches with all of

the other ingredients.

Bring to a simmer over moderate heat and poach until the peaches can be pierced easily with a sharp knife, 10 to 15 minutes. Discard the lemons.

Let the peaches cool in their liquid, and serve at room temperature.

Note: The peaches can be put up in sterilized jars according to manufacturer's directions, or be kept refrigerated for up to 3 months.

Serves 8 to 12

CHERRY PIE

INGREDIENTS

1 recipe pie dough (see Basics, page 335)
1 quart sour cherries, pitted (approximately 4 cups)
1 cup sugar
2$^1/_2$ tablespoons quick-cooking tapioca
Zest of $^1/_2$ lemon
1 egg, beaten with 2 tablespoons water, for egg wash

METHOD

Preheat the oven to 350° F.

On a floured board, roll out half of the dough to approximately $^1/_4$-inch thick.

Fit it evenly into a 9-inch pie pan, pressing gently against the bottom and sides.

In a bowl, toss the cherries with the sugar, tapioca, and lemon zest.

Pour the mixture into the piecrust.

Roll out the remaining dough and set the top crust in place.

Trim the dough and crimp and seal the edges.

Cut 3 small steam vents in the center of the piecrust.

Brush the egg wash over the top.

Bake the pie in the center of the oven for approximately 1 hour, until the crust is lightly browned and the filling inside is bubbling.

Let cool before cutting.

Serve slightly warm.

Serves 8 to 10

Dumpling Dinner

CHICKEN WITH DILL DUMPLINGS ○ MINTED PEAS ○ GLAZED CARROTS ○ STEAMED GINGER PUDDING ○ Herman J. Weimer Vineyards Riesling, NY or D.G. Yuengling Traditional Lager

The sects that settled in Eastern Pennsylvania brought with them an Epicurean style that was fascinating, intelligent, and wholly their own. The abandon with which they would spike their dishes with fresh herbs, and their cakes and desserts with spices is brilliant. Light, fluffy dumplings are refreshing with dill and elevate the simple farm chicken stew beyond the usual fricassee. Gingerbread and its variations were all-time favorites. Gingerbread cake came warm to the table in New England with whipped cream, here with sour cream and applesauce, and in the West with chocolate sauce. This variation is served steaming, with crystallized ginger and accompanied by poached pears.

CHICKEN WITH DILL DUMPLINGS

INGREDIENTS

Chicken:
2 whole chickens (each approximately 3 1/2
   pounds), cut into small serving pieces with breast
   and thigh boned and bones reserved
Salt and freshly milled black pepper
3 tablespoons unsalted butter
2 celery ribs, chopped
1 medium onion, chopped
3 tablespoons all-purpose flour
2 1/2 cups chicken stock (see Basics, page 332)
   or canned low-sodium chicken broth
2 cups heavy cream
1/2 cup fresh dill, chopped

Dumplings:
2 cups all-purpose flour, sifted
1 teaspoon baking powder
1/4 teaspoon baking soda
1 teaspoon salt
3 tablespoons unsalted butter, melted
3/4 cup buttermilk
1/2 cup fresh dill, chopped
1 1/2 quarts chicken stock (see Basics, page 332)
   or canned low-sodium chicken broth

METHOD
Preheat the oven to 225° F.
Prepare the chicken:
Wash and dry the chicken pieces with
   paper towels.
Lightly salt and pepper the chicken.
In a large, heavy skillet, melt the butter and brown
   the chicken pieces skin-side down over
   moderate heat until golden brown.
Turn the chicken, and cook for another 7 minutes
   or until golden.
Move the chicken to an ovenproof dish and
   reserve in the preheated oven.
Add the reserved bones to the skillet and cook,
   stirring until browned.
Add the chopped celery and onions, and cook
   until they wilt.
Add the flour and cook, stirring, for 5 minutes.
Add the chicken stock and cream, and reduce
   the heat to low.
Simmer for 30 minutes.
Strain the sauce into a serving tureen, discarding
   the solids.
Fold the dill into the sauce and check for seasoning.

Add the chicken pieces to the sauce and place in the warm oven.

Prepare the dumplings:

Sift the dry ingredients into a large mixing bowl.

Add the melted butter and buttermilk and blend until smooth.

Fold in the chopped dill.

In a large pot, bring the stock to a simmer.

Drop the dumpling mixture by soup spoonfuls into the simmering stock.

Cover and cook for 5 minutes.

Turn the dumplings over with a slotted spoon.

Cover and cook 5 minutes more.

Continue poaching the dumplings until they have puffed and are cooked in the center.

Place the dumplings on top of the chicken and sauce and serve with glazed carrots and minted peas.

Serves 6 to 8

MINTED PEAS

INGREDIENTS

3 pounds fresh shelling peas, shelled (3 1/2 to 4 cups)

1/4 teaspoon sugar

3 tablespoons unsalted butter

Salt and freshly milled black pepper

8 fresh mint leaves, cut into thin ribbons

METHOD

In a saucepan, bring 2 cups of lightly salted water to a boil.

Add the peas and the sugar.

Simmer for 8 to 10 minutes, or until tender.

Drain.

Fold in the butter, salt and pepper to taste, and the mint.

Serve immediately.

Serves 6 to 8

GLAZED CARROTS

INGREDIENTS
8 to 10 medium carrots
3 tablespoons unsalted butter
1 tablespoon sugar
Salt and freshly milled black pepper

METHOD
Peel and trim the ends off of the carrots.
Cut the carrots into thirds. Cut each third
  lengthwise into 1/2-inch sticks.
In a pot of boiling water, cook the carrots until
  tender, but not mushy.
Drain and set aside.
Melt the butter in a skillet over moderate heat.
Add the sugar and stir until dissolved.
Add the carrots and toss in the butter and sugar
  until thoroughly coated.
Season with salt and pepper and cook until
  heated through.

Serves 6 to 8

STEAMED GINGER PUDDING

INGREDIENTS
2 tablespoons softened unsalted butter, to grease
  the mold
3 cups all-purpose flour
1 teaspoon baking soda
1 tablespoon ground ginger
1 tablespoon ground cinnamon

1/2 pound unsalted butter, at room temperature
1 cup dark brown sugar, packed
4 eggs
1 cup molasses
1 cup heavy cream, lightly whipped
4 pieces crystallized ginger, cut into fine julienne

SPECIAL TOOLS
2-quart steamed pudding mold with cover or
  2-quart pudding basin

METHOD
Use the 2 tablespoons butter to coat the pudding
  mold and its cover. Set aside.
Sift together the dry ingredients and set
  them aside.
Using an electric mixer, cream the butter with
  the sugar.
Add 2 of the eggs and blend thoroughly.
Add half of the sifted dry ingredients and blend.
Add the remaining 2 eggs and mix well.
Add the remaining dry ingredients and blend.
Stir in the molasses and mix thoroughly.
Turn the batter into the prepared mold, and tap
  on a hard surface to settle the batter.
Cover the mold tightly with the buttered cover.
Place the mold in a large pot.
Fill the pot with boiling water to reach 2/3 of
  the way up the sides of the mold.
Cover the pot and steam over moderate heat for
  1 3/4 hours, adding additional boiling water after
  30 to 45 minutes, if necessary.
Remove the pudding from the mold.
Serve with crystallized ginger and poached pears.

Note: Pudding may be made ahead. Leave the
pudding in the mold and refrigerate up to 3 days.
To serve, steam until heated through and proceed
as directed.

Serves 8

Dutch Brisket Dinner

DUTCH BRISKET WITH BRAISED ONIONS ○ HORSERADISH BEET SAUCE ○ SPAETZLE ○ SAUTÉED RED AND WHITE CABBAGE ○ SPICED CANTALOUPE ○ DILL PICKLES ○ APPLE CAKE ○ Penn Dark Munich Dunkel Lager, PA

Throughout history, spices have been used to disguise the flavor of meat that was beginning to turn. Sauerbratens and marinated meats were a German custom and an extender meal that was served both hot and cold. The marinade is pungent, but the spices give an illusion of sweetness. The cabbage is a fresh hot slaw served up with caraway, a seed favored in the breads, dumplings, and cheeses of the area. The cantaloupe, briefly sautéed and spiced, plays the part of a glorified pickle. The deep-dish apple cake was just one of countless filling desserts quickly thrown together by the competent farmwife.

DUTCH BRISKET WITH BRAISED ONIONS

INGREDIENTS

1 beef brisket (6 to 7 pounds)

Marinade:

1 bottle dry red wine

1 cup white wine vinegar

4 celery ribs, coarsely chopped

1 large onion, coarsely chopped

6 peppercorns, crushed

Kosher Salt

1 bay leaf

2 sprigs fresh thyme

Flour for dredging

Onions:

4 tablespoons butter

4 pounds yellow onions, thinly sliced

Salt and freshly milled black pepper

$1/4$ teaspoon ground cinnamon

$1/2$ teaspoon ground cloves

METHOD

In a bowl or pan, combine the brisket with the marinade ingredients. Refrigerate for 24 hours, turning once.

Preheat the oven to 400° F.

Remove the brisket from the marinade and dry with paper towels.

Reserve the marinade.

Rub the salt and pepper into the brisket.

Lightly dredge with flour.

In a large, heavy skillet, brown the brisket, fat side down, over moderate heat. Turn and brown all over.

Move the meat to a large ovenproof casserole or Dutch oven.

Strain the marinade, discarding the solids.

Pour the liquid into the skillet and deglaze over moderately high heat, scraping up the brown bits that cling to the bottom of the skillet. Simmer for 5 minutes.

Pour the liquid over the meat and set aside.

Add the butter to the skillet, toss the onions with salt and pepper and cook over medium heat until browned.

Add the onions and their juices to the casserole and spread over the meat.

Cover the casserole and bake for 30 minutes.

Remove the cover and continue cooking for 1 hour.

Cover again and cook for 1 to $1 1/2$ hours more, until the meat is fork-tender.

Let the brisket rest for 10 to 15 minutes.

Serve with the onions and pan juices.

Serves 12

HORSERADISH BEET SAUCE

INGREDIENTS

3 small raw beets, peeled and finely grated
1 cup freshly grated horseradish
$^1/_4$ cup sour cream
$^1/_4$ cup heavy cream, whipped

METHOD

In a small serving bowl, fold together all of
    the ingredients.
Chill and serve.

Makes 2 cups

SPAETZLE

INGREDIENTS

4 cups all-purpose flour
6 eggs
1 $^1/_2$ teaspoons salt
3 to 4 gratings fresh nutmeg
1 $^1/_2$ cups cold milk
$^1/_4$ pound unsalted butter
Salt and freshly milled black pepper

SPECIAL TOOLS

Spaetzle-maker (see Note)

METHOD

Combine the flour, eggs, salt, nutmeg, and cold
    milk in a large bowl. Mix with a wooden spoon
    and set aside. The dough will be quite stiff.
Bring a large pot of salted water to a boil.
Pick up small amounts of dough with a teaspoon
    and push the dough into the water with another
    teaspoon or use a spaetzle maker if you want
    smaller pieces. Dip the spoons in the boiling
    water to prevent them from becoming sticky
    and unmanageable.
Using a wooden spoon, stir the spaetzle off the
    bottom of the pot and cook for 2 minutes.
With a slotted spoon, transfer the spaetzle to a
    bowl of ice water.
Repeat the process until all of the dough
    has been used.

Rinse and drain well.
Refrigerate until ready to serve.
In a large skillet, melt the butter over
    moderate heat.
Add the spaetzle and lightly sauté until
    warmed through.
Season with salt and pepper and serve warm.

Note: A spaetzle-maker, while not essential, is an
extremely useful and efficient tool which we highly
recommend.

Serves 12

SAUTÉED RED AND WHITE CABBAGE

INGREDIENTS

1 small head red cabbage, outer leaves removed
1 small head white cabbage, outer leaves
    removed
$^1/_2$ pound lean slab bacon, cut into $^1/_4$-inch slices
    and cubed
1 teaspoon caraway seeds
$^1/_2$ cup sour cream
Salt and freshly milled black pepper

METHOD

Halve the cabbages and core them.
Slice into thin strips.
In two separate pots of boiling water, blanch
    each type of cabbage for 5 seconds and
    drain immediately.
In a large skillet, render the bacon until
    golden brown.
Drain the bacon on paper towels, and set aside.
Add the cabbage to the skillet and cook, tossing
    over moderate heat, to coat it with the
    rendered fat.
Add the caraway seeds.
Fold in the sour cream and season to taste.
Toss and cook until the cabbage is tender.
Fold in the bacon pieces and serve.

Serves 12

SPICED CANTALOUPE

INGREDIENTS
2 small ripe cantaloupes
2 small cinnamon sticks
2 tablespoons sugar
Juice of $1/2$ a lemon
1 teaspoon curry powder

METHOD
Halve the melons and seed them.
Cut each half into $1/2$-inch-wide strips and remove
    the rinds with a paring knife.
Place the melon in a saucepan and add the
    cinnamon sticks, sugar, and lemon juice.
Cover over moderate heat, stirring gently until all
    of the sugar melts, about 5 minutes.
Add the curry powder and cook for another
    5 minutes.

Serves 12

DILL PICKLES

INGREDIENTS
$1/2$ cup pickling salt or kosher salt, for brining
2 quarts cold water
4 pounds Kirby cucumbers, freshly picked and
    washed thoroughly
3 cups good quality distilled white vinegar

1 tablespoon sugar
6 large cloves, garlic, blanched in their skins for
    3 minutes and peeled
3 whole allspice berries
6 peppercorns
1 bunch of fresh dillweed with flowers

SPECIAL TOOLS
Deep kettle, preferably with a canning rack
Canning tongs
3 quart-sized or 6 pint-sized sterilized canning jars
    and lids

METHOD
In the stoneware crock, combine the pickling salt
    with 2 quarts cold water.
Add the cucumbers and soak for 24 hours.
When ready to jar:
Bring a large kettle of water to a boil.
In a large saucepan, combine the vinegar, sugar,
    and 3 cups of water.
Bring to a boil over high heat, then lower to
    a simmer.
Remove the Kirbys from the brine with a slotted
    spoon and drain.
Plunge the cucumbers into the pot of boiling water.
Drain immediately and pack the Kirbys into
    sterilized jars.
Divide the garlic, spices, and dillweed equally
    among the jars, filling to within 1 inch from
    the top.
Pour in the hot vinegar liquid to reach $1/2$ inch
    from the top of each jar.

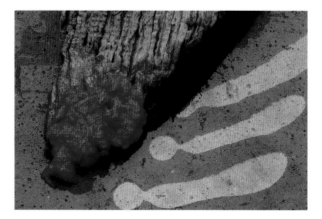

Tightly seal the jars.

Place the jars on a rack in the kettle, making sure they do not touch.

Add enough hot water to cover the lids by 2 inches.

Cover and bring to a boil. Continue to boil for 15 minutes if using pint-sized jars, or 20 minutes, if packed into quarts.

Remove the jars from the water bath with the canning tongs and set on a rack to cool.

Store in a cool place.

Note: Kirby cucumbers are small, firm 3 1/2- to 4-inch cucumbers. Vegetables and fruits used for canning should be fresh-picked and put up within 24 hours.

Makes 3 quarts

APPLE CAKE

INGREDIENTS

2 to 3 tablespoons unsalted butter, for greasing the pan

10 large apples (such as Cortland, Matsu, or Pippin), peeled and cored

1/2 pound unsalted butter, at room temperature

2 cups sugar

2 eggs

3 cups all-purpose flour

2 teaspoons baking soda

1/2 teaspoon ground cinnamon

1 teaspoon freshly grated nutmeg

1 teaspoon ground allspice

1 cup heavy cream, whipped, for serving

METHOD

Preheat the oven to 350° F.

Butter a large, deep baking dish.

Roughly chop the apples.

Reserving 1 cup, place the apples in a large pot with 1/2 cup water.

Simmer over moderately low heat until the apples begin to soften, but do not turn to sauce.

The mixture should be very chunky.

Remove from the heat and set aside.

In a mixing bowl, cream together the butter and sugar.

One at a time, add the eggs.

In a large bowl, sift together the dry ingredients.

Fold in the apple mixture with a rubber spatula.

Turn the batter into the prepared baking dish.

Sprinkle the reserved apples over the dough and pat down with a spatula.

Bake for 1 hour, or until golden brown.

Serve warm with unsweetened whipped cream.

Serves 12

Street Food

Hot Dogs

There is nothing like a "dirty," in-the-street, New York City, out-of-the-steam-wagon hot dog. We eat them everywhere—in arenas, in parks, at concerts, and at ball games.

Deli Food

The Jewish Deli is quintessentially New York. It's as much a part of the visitors' eating experience as eating pasta in Little Italy and dumplings in Chinatown. New Yorkers still hanker for a good pastrami on rye or blintzes bursting with farmers cheese and sour cream. We think twice and then succumb. The best delicatessens have always been in New York City and the best of the best have managed to survive.

MATZO BALL SOUP

INGREDIENTS

Stock:

2 quarts chicken stock (see Basics, page 332) or canned low-sodium chicken broth

1 chicken (about 3 pounds)

2 celery ribs, cut into 2-inch pieces

1 medium carrot, cut into 1-inch pieces

3 parsley sprigs

Salt

Matzo Balls:

3 eggs

$1/4$ cup plus 2 tablespoons seltzer or soda water

3 tablespoons chicken fat (skimmed from the chilled chicken stock or store-bought, called "schmaltz")

$2/3$ to $3/4$ cup matzo meal

1 tablespoon fresh parsley, finely chopped
Salt and freshly milled white pepper
$1/4$ cup fresh parsley, minced, for serving

METHOD
Prepare the stock:
Place the stock ingredients in a soup kettle and
    bring to a simmer over moderate heat.
Partially cover the kettle and poach the chicken
    for 30 to 40 minutes, or until the thigh juices run
    clear when pierced with a kitchen fork.
Remove and discard the vegetables from the soup
    and let the chicken cool in the stock.
When the stock is cool, remove the poached
    chicken and refrigerate the stock and the
    chicken separately.
Reserve the chicken for sandwiches and
    chicken salads.
Prepare the matzo balls:
In a bowl, lightly beat the eggs and combine with
    the seltzer.
Add the chicken fat and blend.
Gradually add the matzo meal, stirring until the
    mixture is spongy and lightly thickened.
Add the parsley and seasonings and blend.
Cover and refrigerate for at least 30 minutes.
Remove the mixture and the stock from the
    refrigerator 30 minutes before preparing the soup.
Skim all the fat off the stock and bring to a simmer
    over low heat.
Shape the matzo mixture into 1-inch balls, wetting
    your hands in cold water from time to time to
    prevent sticking.
Increase the heat to produce a gentle boil and
    add the matzo balls to the soup. Partially cover
    the kettle and poach the matzo balls for
    20 to 25 minutes, until cooked through.
Test one to be sure it is cooked in the center.
Ladle 2 matzo balls and broth into each heated
    bowl and sprinkle with the additional parsley.

Serves 5 to 6

Martini

A good cocktail must be made with the finest
liquor. It should be made with care; the
overzealous can just as easily ruin the drink as the
careless. The martini is a drink I associate with
Manhattan, its finest bars and restaurants. My
advice to you is to end your day with a perfect
martini. A good bartender can set you up for a
marvelous evening.

GIN MARTINI

INGREDIENTS
Ice cubes
Splash of imported dry vermouth
$2 1/2$ ounces of gin, chilled
Small strip of lemon zest or 1 large green olive

SPECIAL TOOLS
Cocktail pitcher and stirrer
4-ounce martini glass, chilled
Cocktail strainer

METHOD
Fill the pitcher with 6 to 8 ice cubes.
Add the vermouth and gin and stir briskly.
Strain the martini into the chilled glass and twist
    the lemon zest over the top of the liquor or add
    the olive.
Serve and sip.

Serves 1

SOUTH

SOUTH

Thomas Jefferson, who returned to Monticello to resume life as a gentlemen farmer after his eight-year presidency, called himself the most "ardent farmer in the state." William Byrd, founder of Richmond, called Virginia the "Garden of Eden," and recorded in his 1737 *Natural History of Virginia* that the colony was growing all manner of European produce—artichokes, cauliflower, peaches, pears, quince, figs, cherries, pomegranates, as well as olives and wine grapes. It was really Jefferson who cultivated this garden. Jefferson, America's first man of style, took advantage of his duties at the court of Louis XVI to travel Europe widely. So delighted was he with the olive oil he found there that he sent cuttings from Provence to North Carolina to plant, where he hoped they might thrive. He rhapsodized about this oil, for him a necessary luxury, and attributed his long life to a diet largely of vegetables and salads bathed in it. (When the olive tree did not take to the southern climate, Jefferson experimented with the oil from benne seeds, known also as sesame). Long a staple of the southern kitchen, sesame is not native to our soil. According to legend, it was brought here by slaves from Africa, who hid the seeds in their ears and carried them across the ocean to southern America where they flourished, a melancholy reminder of their native land. How tragically different from the New England settlers, who enthusiastically tucked apple pips into their baggage and sacks, looking forward to their life in the New World.

Jefferson was the model of a southern host, hospitable and ebullient. Frugal New Englander John Adams was driven to remark, "I dined a large company once or twice a week. Jefferson dined a dozen every day. I held levees (receptions) once a week. Jefferson's whole eight years was a levee!" Jefferson held wine to be one of the table's great merits, and once remarked, "No nation is drunken where wine is cheap: and none sober, when the dearness of wine substitutes harder spirits as a common beverage." Relentlessly inquisitive, he studied the wine country of France, Germany, Italy, and Spain, and sent vine cuttings to Virginia in attempts at viniculture. He took frequent notes and kept meticulous accounts, calculating that a bottle of champagne served $3\frac{1}{7}$ guests. His own consumption of champagne numbered more than 500 bottles annually, and his notorious Washington cellar at one time held 400 bottles of claret, 540 of Sauternes, and casks of Madeira and port. (During his first year as president, he frightfully exceeded the wine budget, spending nearly $3,000, the equivalent of about $62,000 today.) His unfailing good taste was well known, and he was not reticent to share it. He advised President George Washington on what wines to buy (ordering 65 dozen bottles in 1790). Even his congratulatory letter to President James Monroe offered only a few formalities, and rushed to a discourse recommending which wines are best served at which occasions. In the White House Jefferson brilliantly entertained foreign ministers, congressmen, and assorted dignitaries and citizens, undoubtedly to the enjoyment and great admiration of some and to the rankling envy of others. The elements of Jefferson's kitchen were Virginian and French: velvet brown sauces, clear soups, custards, meringues, macaroons, blancmange, wine jellies, trifles, bread puddings, even floating island in a pool of syllabub. He treasured the recipes of his best cooks, as did his daughter Mrs. Randolph, who added greatly to the repertoire of local dishes. She compiled a cookbook and created the dish macaroni and cheese for her father using Parmesan. Jefferson had particular fondness for local foods: sweet potatoes, black-eyed peas, turnip greens, ham, and crab. He deserves much credit for the endive, cress, cucumbers, asparagus, tomatoes, and almond trees that flourish here. In his own gardens, he enthusiastically planted more than 30 varieties of peas. At the time, the potato was newly vindicated in Europe as an acceptable, if plebian, food, and its blossom was sported at

the elegant French court by the king himself. Although Jefferson is said to have personally preferred the potato to corn, he nevertheless took pains to introduce maize to his French hosts, which he grew in his Paris garden. Always Jefferson's interest and loyalty lay with an agrarian nation, moving him to pronounce that "the introduction of anything which will divert our attention from agriculture must be extremely prejudicial if not ruinous to us."

A southern plantation was society in miniature. Self-sufficient, its success depended wholly on slaves and servants. Plantations raised cash crops for trade, most notably tobacco and cotton destined for England. Their own blacksmiths made the ploughs, wagons, tools, gates, and fancy ironwork. Their cattle filled the larder and supplied skins for the plantation tanner to make shoes and saddles. Their sheep furnished wool and the fields produced cotton. Their carpenters repaired the houses, barns, and stables; no one was idle.

From the early days in the southern colonies, hospitality was a custom of both the wealthy and the poor. Friend or stranger was invited to dine and to stay for a night, a few days, a few weeks—some abused the privilege and stayed a month here and a month there! Balls and parties brought the gentlefolk from far and near. Lavish picnics were held in cool woods, and barbecues and fish feasts were held on the riverbanks. Prosperous plantations dotted the banks of rivers running inland from Charleston to Virginia.

Pig raising would become a major industry. So sweet and tender were these porkers, fattened

on peanuts and corn, that Queen Victoria had them sent to her, along with her favorite Belon oysters from Maine. The South was a congenial home for the pig, the southern larders were so near to bursting with pork and hams that William Byrd wrote in 1720 that he found "the people extremely hoggish in temper and prone to grunt rather than speak." Hog killing was an event that brought out the full platoon of servants, slaves, and family. "Kill your hogs when the wind is from the northwest" was heard from Kentucky through North Carolina, and all at once the hogs were killed, hung, scalded, and scraped. Butchered to use every morsel right down to the tail, the pig yielded heavy roasts, hams, and bacon (to be salted, hickory-smoked, or sugar-cured). Mounds of snow-white lard, chitterlings, sausage-skins, masses of rendered fat, and the tripe, backbones, and livers sent straight into the kitchen for the traditional "hog-killing day" dinner, complete with cracklings.

The black help ate differently from their masters. In the evenings when the manor slaves and the field slaves got together, they would make do with the chitterlings, jowls, ears, tails, maws, snouts, hocks, or whatever else from the pig might be given to them. They gathered wild greens, beet tops, and turnip and mustard greens to be cooked slowly with a hock or jowl until nearly soup. This "mess o' greens" or "pot licker" was served up with hot pones and black-eyed peas. It was the beginning of "soul food." The black cooks who ran the kitchens of the manor houses combined soul food with the French and English preferences of their masters, creating a unique style that is quintessentially what we think of as southern cooking today.

By southern tradition, grits and hominy were set at almost every table, with some sort of cornbread (pones, hoe cakes, corn cakes), biscuits, crackling bread, and "oyster cakes" (a paste of grated green corn mixed with egg, wheat flour, and butter, fried to simulate an oyster).

Throughout the South, the hog was considered to be the only meat. The favored method of preparation in the North Carolina backcountry was to dry-roast the hog in hickory coals for 8 to 12 hours. Nowadays, it's still to be found cooked in the same way, then hacked with a cleaver, seasoned with salt, pepper, and vinegar, and served on good, reliable packaged white bread. This type of cooking, long known as "barbecue," came to the South through the Caribbean. This is a method of cooking meat on a grid of sticks raised on forks above the coals. This typically southern barbecue is at odds with the spicy tomato and sweet-sour sauces found from Texas to Kansas. (Just off the highway on the Maryland–D.C. border is a shack with a painted sign advertising "RIBS," half a dozen of them slapped between slices of Wonder bread. Getting this down is one of the miracles of the human mouth.)

At the end of the eighteenth century, the region west of the Appalachian Mountains was referred to as the "western country." The inhabitants, many of them Irishmen and Scotsmen, were skilled hunters by reputation. Fall was the season there to trap bears for their valuable warm pelts and nourishing fat flesh: the hind legs when smoked made delicious hams. Squirrel hunts were also a popular pastime, and sporting parties would roast hundreds of these exceedingly tender, lean-fleshed rodents. Dishes here were somewhat influenced by the South, but there were other additions to the menu, such as rabbits, brains, sweetbreads, possum, and the especially choice wild turkey and quail. Squirrel was baked, fried, fricasseed, coupled with dumplings or rice, and served in a rich stew-like soup they called burgoo. They also cultivated corn, but most of it was destined for the city ports of Charleston and Savannah. Their rustic bread was ground Indian meal, shaped into heavy loaves and baked in ovens, or baked as small cakes on a board before a fire. Peaches were cultivated (especially around Lexington), and often made into a popular brandy.

It was these same Scots and Irish settlers who introduced whiskey. The prevailing spirit of the day was rum, but transporting it across the colonies was too expensive, and so they distilled corn and rye. Moonshine was widely enjoyed and is by no means forgotten today.

The frontier folk were a poor lot who managed to get by with little. The countryside was speckled with tree stumps and peppered with rude wood cabins. But a young visiting Frenchman, Francois Michaux, recorded that

there was not "a single family without milk, butter, salted or dried meats, and Indian corn generally in the house."

Smithfield-style, country-cured hams of Virginia and the Carolinas are salted, cured, and smoked, and then require soaking, simmering, and baking before they can be eaten. On Derby Day, a luncheon is made of silver dollar–sized biscuits with paper-thin slices of ham (the way prosciutto is sliced), served with corn pudding and frequently freshened mint juleps.

So much southern cooking has depended on the sea's harvest. The York, Susquehanna, Potomac, Rappahannock, and James Rivers all feed the Chesapeake Bay. Its backwash seeps into the swamps of North Carolina and reaches the barrier islands at the Atlantic. It is the largest estuary on the American continent, its shoreline a welcoming cradle for the settlers led by John Smith who discovered it in the early seventeenth century. This watershed supplied most of the Eastern seaboard with oysters, crabs, clams, herring, shad, bass (what locals call "blackfish"), perch, and an impressive amount of eel. The shoreline still teems with birds—herons, ospreys, swans, ducks, field birds and too many Canadian geese—filling the air with an incessant cacophony of chirping, honking, and trumpeting. From Tilghman Island to Cape Charles, this area known as the Eastern Shore is a poignant reminder of the beauty that met the new arrivals at Charlestown harbor 300 years ago. The South begins here.

The families who have fished these waters trace their beginnings to the stalwart Elizabethans who

crawled their way up to the Bay. Their language, spicy as a blue crab boil, still smacks of old English. These isolated watermen patiently crabbed from spring to fall and dredged and tonged for oysters when winter turned the bay's blue foamy peaks into murky black swells. A waterman did daily battle with the sea, a heritage that was passed from father to son, rewarded with a decent, hard-earned wage.

Skipjacks opened the oyster season with an annual meet. These beautiful hulls gleaming afresh can tack on a dime with their sails pressed to the wind. Their seemingly fragile brilliance was put to the test when their iron-spiked chain baskets dragged the bay floor and hauled in the oysters. The skipjacks were a far cry from the nearly 7,000 sailing canoes that worked these waters in the 1880s. The

nineteenth century was oyster-crazy, and the new railways sent the live oysters to the far west. The Wellfleet captains of Cape Cod indiscriminately ravaged their natural stock, starting in Buzzard's and Narragansett Bays in Massachusetts, working their way down the Atlantic Coast, and ultimately doing the same to the Cheseapeake. At one time the bay gave up millions of bushels every year—more than twice the amount of oysters eaten from coast to coast today.

A waterman's life remained pretty much the same up until the mid 1980s. Plundering nature was long thought to be this country's birthright, and by the late nineteenth century the environment's delicate balance was rarely considered. This was the beginning of the Cheseapeake Bay's dark future. Pollution,

development, and run-off from fertilizers turned the bay to sludge, killing the eelgrass where crabs burrow and mate, and poisoning the muddied silt floor where the oysters live. The fleet of hundreds of skipjacks dwindled to barely a hundred. In 2004, after more than 150 years of oystering, only two skipjacks still harvest these waters. (And more often then not, when you do see a skipjack on the Bay, it's a pleasure-boat for tourists.) Though some attempts are being made to protect and clean up the Bay, the once abundant breeding grounds will most likely never be fully restored. It's an unhappy tale, but one worth telling: how just a scant twenty years ago generations of baymen still hauled and crabbed the Bay's then fertile waters.

In spite of the diminished harvests, the natural cycles fight to continue. In the spring, when the crabs leave their burrows in the basins along the Atlantic and migrate to the Bay, the blue crab reddens and the sooks' (female crabs) claws turn bright red. The crabs journey up the grassy sea shoals at the sides of the bay to molt and spawn. Two or three days before the female molts, the hard-shelled jimmie (male) and the sook copulate from six to as long as twelve hours. He continues to cradle her for another two or three days while her new shell hardens. The jimmie goes on to mate again, but the sook, with her million eggs, is now fertile for the rest of her life.

This was once the time when the watermen set out their nets and baited their crab pots. The catch was sorted on deck or in long, narrow tubs in the crab shacks along the shore: the

greens molted in a couple of weeks, the pinks within a week, and the busters shedding within mere hours. Once they shed their shells they were boxed in eelgrass and ice. Huge quantities of soft-shells were sent live to the New York Fulton Fish Market, and made their first appearance just as the season for shad and shad roe was on the wane. The crabs had to be crawling and kicking to be worth the price, for a dead crab isn't worth cooking.

Back then, tidewater shores were lined with picking houses. Throughout autumn, the crab picking houses were staffed mostly by women, busy pasteurizing and packing the various grades of prized lump, special, regular, and claw meat. Picking was a difficult job, a skill paid by the pound. Today, shore residents and vacationers crowd the few remaining crab houses to dine on hard-shelled, hot-spiced red crabs piled on newspapers and served with wooden mallets to aid in the cracking, sharp knives to catch every flake, and pitchers of beer to reward the task. The voluptuous hot spices used in boiling the crabs permeates the flesh, and the residue, left on the claws and fingers alike, smarts the tongue. This was and is truly the flavor of the Bay, from the elegant large pincers packed with delicate meat and served with spicy remoulades to the baskets of hundreds of whole crabs unceremoniously steamed in huge cauldrons.

Soft-shell crabs are still available, although in much smaller quantities, making them expensive to buy. The Eastern Shore continues to celebrate the crab, hosting festivals every spring, but sadly what you often sample may not be local.

Breakfast

FRIED COUNTRY HAM WITH REDEYE GRAVY ○ FRIED EGGS ○ SPOON BREAD ○ NELL DILLOW THOMAS' PICKLED PEARS ○ BLACK COFFEE

To the uninitiated, the salty cured hamsteak of the South is a rude awakening. Making a "sauce" with coffee or water was an afterthought to juice up the sometimes dry, cured meat. The term "redeye" refers to the red flecks of fat that surface in the gravy. The spoon bread is the morning's grits. Southerners will pickle anything from peanuts to watermelon rind, and the pickled winter pears make the ham go down easier.

FRIED COUNTRY HAM WITH REDEYE GRAVY

INGREDIENTS
4 slices country ham, each ¹/4-inch thick
   (Smithfield type, preferably with the bone)
Milk
¹/2 to ²/3 cup black coffee
Eggs for frying

METHOD
Trim the skin off the ham, leaving as much of the
   fat as possible.
Soak the ham in enough milk to cover for
   approximately 20 minutes.

Drain and pat dry with paper towels.
In a large heavy skillet over moderate heat, brown
   the ham on each side, using a bacon press
   to keep the ham from curling and to help it
   cook evenly.
Move the ham to a warm plate.
To deglaze the skillet, add the black coffee and
   cook, scraping up the brown bits that cling to
   the bottom of the pan.
Reduce the mixture over high heat for
   approximately 1 minute.
Pour the redeye gravy over the ham and serve hot
   with fried eggs.

Serves 4

SPOON BREAD

INGREDIENTS
Butter for greasing the mold
2 cups milk
2/3 cup yellow cornmeal
1 teaspoon salt
1 tablespoon sugar
2 tablespoons butter
3 eggs, separated
2 teaspoons baking powder

METHOD
Generously butter a 2-quart soufflé or baking dish.
Preheat the oven to 350° F.
In a heavy medium saucepan, scald the milk. Do
   not let it boil.
Combine the cornmeal, salt, and sugar, and slowly
   stir into the milk.
Add the butter and stir constantly over moderate
   heat for 10 minutes. Remove from the heat and
   beat in the egg yolks and baking powder.
Let cool.
With an electric mixer, beat the egg whites in a
   clean bowl with a dash of salt until they form
   soft peaks.
Thoroughly blend approximately 1/2 cup of the
   egg whites into the cornmeal mixture to lighten it.
Gently fold in the remaining egg whites; do not
   over blend.
Pour the mixture into the buttered mold and bake
   for 30 to 35 minutes, until the top is golden.

Serves 4 to 5

NELL DILLOW THOMAS' PICKLED PEARS

INGREDIENTS
Approximately 16 Kiefer or other hard winter pears,
   peeled, cored, and cut into medium-thin slices
   (4 cups)
Juice of 1 lemon
1 cup cold water
4 cups cider vinegar
4 cups sugar
2 teaspoons pickling spices

SPECIAL TOOLS
3 quart-sized or 6 pint-sized sterilized canning jars
   and lids

METHOD
In a bowl, toss the sliced pears with the lemon juice
   so they do not discolor.
In a heavy kettle, combine the pears with the
   remaining ingredients and 1 cup of cold water.
Bring to a boil over high heat. Reduce the heat to
   low and simmer the pears for approximately 45
   minutes, or until almost tender.
Place the pears in sterilized jars, dividing the spices
   among the jars.
Add syrup to reach 1/2 inch from the top.
Seal the jars and process them following the
   manufacturer's instructions. If not preserving, the
   pears will keep up to 3 months refrigerated.

Makes 2 1/2 to 3 quarts

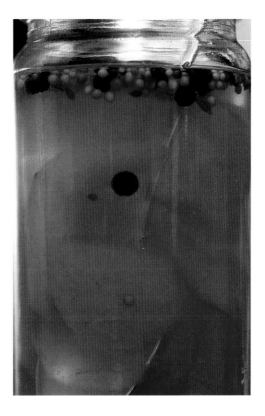

Oyster and Buckwheat Dinner

TOMATO SOUP ○ BEATEN BISCUITS ○ CREAMED OYSTERS AND HAM ○ BUCKWHEAT CAKES WITH MELTED BUTTER ○ LADY BALTIMORE CAKE ○ Boordy Vineyards Seyval Blanc, MD or Frederick's Extra Special Bitter, MD

Oyster and ham pie was very common along the Atlantic coast, but can be overly doughy. What makes the following recipe legitimate, I suppose, is the fact that they eat a lot of buckwheat down there; I've taken this traditional filling and poured it on top of a stack of buckwheat cakes. The infamous beaten biscuit is about as close as you can get to soft tack. The Lady Baltimore Cake was a specialty of a Charleston tearoom, but the recipe became popular up the Chesapeake and throughout that region. The leftover yolks inspired a Lord Baltimore cake, and the two together were often the bride and groom's cake at many southern weddings. The sweet, gooey meringue, for good or bad, foreshadowed the marshmallow.

TOMATO SOUP

INGREDIENTS

4 pounds very ripe tomatoes, coarsely chopped
3 fresh basil leaves
Salt and freshly milled white pepper
1 cup heavy cream, reduced over moderate
    heat by $1/3$

SPECIAL TOOLS

Food mill

METHOD

In a large saucepan, combine the tomatoes and their juices, the basil, and salt and pepper to taste. Bring to a boil, reduce the heat, and simmer for 30 minutes, or until the liquid begins to evaporate.

Puree the tomatoes using a food mill to remove the skin and seeds.

Return the tomato puree to a clean saucepan, add the cream, and bring to a simmer.

Check the seasonings and serve hot.

Serves 4

CREAMED OYSTERS AND HAM

INGREDIENTS

16 to 20 large oysters, shucked, with 1 cup of liquor reserved (4 to 5 oysters per person)
1 cup heavy cream, reduced over moderate heat by $1/2$
$1/8$ teaspoon cayenne pepper
$3/4$ cup cured Virginia-style ham, cut into long, thin slivers

METHOD

In a small saucepan, reduce the cup of oyster liquor by half over moderate heat.

In a medium saucepan, combine the reduced cream with the cayenne pepper.

Strain the reduced liquor into the cream. Set aside and keep warm while you make the buckwheat cakes.

To serve, fold the oysters into the warm cream mixture and cook over moderate heat until the edges begin to curl.

Stir in the ham. Keep warm.

Note: If using salt-cured ham, steep in milk and refrigerate overnight.

Serves 4

BUCKWHEAT CAKES WITH MELTED BUTTER

INGREDIENTS

1 cup buckwheat flour
1 cup sifted all-purpose flour
1 tablespoon sugar
2 teaspoons baking powder
1 teaspoon baking soda
1/2 teaspoon salt
2 eggs
2 cups buttermilk
1/2 cup Clarified Butter (see Basics, page 333)

METHOD

In a mixing bowl, sift together all of the dry
    ingredients.
In another bowl, lightly beat the eggs and mix in
    the buttermilk and 1/4 cup of the butter.
Fold the egg mixture into the dry ingredients and
    blend well.
Cook the cakes on a well-buttered griddle.
To serve, pour a little of the remaining clarified
    butter over each pancake and portion the
    creamed oysters and ham over the stacks.

Note: As the mixture sets, it thickens. You may want
to add additional buttermilk to thin the batter out.

Makes approximately 24 small pancakes

LADY BALTIMORE CAKE

INGREDIENTS

Cake Layers:
1/2 pound plus 3 tablespoons unsalted butter, at
    room temperature
2 1/4 cups sugar
5 cups cake flour
1 tablespoon plus 1 teaspoon baking powder
1/4 teaspoon salt
1 1/2 cups milk
1 tablespoon white rum
10 egg whites

Filling:
2/3 cup chopped dates
1/2 cup raisins
1/4 cup white rum
1/2 cup chopped walnuts

Frosting:
4 1/2 cups sugar
2 tablespoons light corn syrup
1 1/2 cups water
6 egg whites
Salt

Assembly:
Simple Syrup (see Basics, page 337)
1/3 cup white rum

SPECIAL TOOLS

Three 9-inch cake pans
Candy thermometer
Pastry brush

METHOD

The cake layers:
Preheat the oven to 350° F.
Using 3 tablespoons butter, grease the pans.
Using an electric mixer, cream together the
    butter and sugar in a large mixing bowl until
    lemon-colored.
Sift together the dry ingredients and gradually
    incorporate them into the butter mixture.
Slowly add the milk and rum. Set aside.
In a clean mixing bowl, beat the egg whites with a
    dash of salt until stiff and glossy.
Fold the whites into the batter.

Divide the batter evenly among the cake pans.

Bake for 25 minutes, or until the cake pulls away from the sides of the pan. Remove from the oven and cool for 10 minutes.

Unmold the cake layers and let cool completely on a wire rack.

The filling:

In a small bowl, soak the dates and raisins in the 1/4 cup rum for several hours.

The frosting:

In a heavy saucepan, bring the sugar, corn syrup, and 1 1/2 cups water to a boil and cook until it reaches a temperature of 232° F, or until the syrup threads 8 inches off the edge of the spoon without dripping.

In a bowl, beat the egg whites and a dash of salt with an electric mixer until the mixture is stiff and glossy. With the mixer running, gradually beat the hot syrup into the egg whites and whisk until cool.

Drain the dates and raisins, reserving the rum.

Combine the fruits and chopped nuts with 1/3 of the frosting to make the filling.

To assemble:

Combine 1 cup of Simple Syrup with 1/3 cup white rum and reserved rum.

Trim the tops and bottoms of the cakes.

Brush the bottom layer with some of the rum syrup.

Spread half of the filling over the bottom layer.

Place the second layer on top of the first. Brush it with syrup and spread with the remaining filling.

Set the top layer in place and brush with a little of the syrup. Frost the sides and top of the cake, using small circular motions to create swirling peaks.

Serves 8 to 10

Crab Lunch

SOFT-SHELL CRABS ○ SALAD ○ STRAWBERRY SHORTCAKE ○ ICED TEA ○ Catoctin
Vineyards Chardonnay, MD or Dogfish Head Shelter Pale Ale, DE

*Soft-shell crabs, a delicacy of the East Coast, are at their peak in May and early June. It is a must
to purchase crabs alive. The squeamish should have their crabs cleaned by the fishmonger. They
need no embellishment other than the juices they are cooked in, except perhaps thinly sliced bread
fried in sweet butter and a squeeze of lemon. The hot, buttery shortcake will be your bread for this
meal, covered with sliced strawberries and fresh cream. Iced tea is the perennial beverage of the
South, drunk throughout the meal. It is a refreshment every proper Southern lady has been
making ever since there were porches to sit on.*

SOFT-SHELL CRABS

INGREDIENTS
2 to 3 soft-shell crabs per person, depending
    on size
1/4 pound unsalted butter
1/4 cup slivered almonds (optional)
Juice of 1/2 lemon
1/4 cup fresh parsley, chopped

METHOD
To prepare the crabs, use a sharp paring knife to
    fold back the soft carapace and trim off the
    head of the crabs. Remove the gills.

Trim the apron from the underside of the crab.
Melt the butter in a large heavy skillet and sauté
    the crabs for 1 to 2 minutes on each side.
Remove to a heated platter, and keep warm.
If using the almonds, add them to the butter, and
    toss until the almonds are golden brown. Add
    the lemon juice and stir in the parsley.
Pour the butter-almond mixture over the crabs
    and serve.

STRAWBERRY SHORTCAKE

INGREDIENTS

Dough:

2 sticks plus 1 tablespoon cold unsalted butter

2 cups all-purpose flour

$1/8$ teaspoon salt

2 tablespoons baking powder

$1/2$ cup plus 1 tablespoon sugar

1 cup half-and-half

Filling:

2 generous pints strawberries (or any combination
of mixed berries)

$1/4$ cup sugar

2 cups heavy cream, whipped, for serving

METHOD

Prepare the dough:

Preheat the oven to 350° F.

Cut the 2 sticks of butter into small pieces and
keep refrigerated for 10 minutes or more.

In a large bowl, sift together the flour, salt, baking
powder and $1/2$ cup of sugar.

Add the butter. Using your fingers, quickly combine
the butter with the flour mixture until it reaches
the consistency of cornmeal.

Stir in the half-and-half using a wooden spoon to
form smooth, soft dough.

Lightly butter a baking sheet with the remaining
tablespoon of butter.

Divide the dough into 8 mounds on the baking
sheet, allowing at least 2 inches between
each one.

Sprinkle with sugar and bake 20 to 25 minutes or
until lightly browned.

The filling:

Wash, drain, hull, and slice the strawberries.

Mix with sugar.

Split the shortcakes and spoon the strawberries
and their juices onto the bottom half.

Replace the tops and serve with whipped cream.

Serves 4

Pan-Fried Quail Supper

PAN-FRIED QUAIL ○ BREAD SAUCE ○ FRIED CRUMBS ○ FRIED BAKED GRITS ○ PARSLEY-BUTTERED TURNIPS ○ GLAZED TOMATOES ○ SYLLABUB ○ CRYSTALLIZED GRAPEFRUIT ○ Barboursville Vineyards Cabernet Franc, VA or Legend Brown Ale, VA

More often than not, the eye-opener for a man was a brandy or a julep, while a lady sometimes began her day with a glass of syllabub. It was the custom of the guests at lordly plantations along the river into Savannah to go dove hunting in the fall and spring. Ladies and gentlemen were driven down oak-lined paths in their horse-drawn carts, while a couple of farmhands clapped their hands to startle the birds into flight. The gentlemen shot a covey, the slaves ran off to pick it up, and the cook later fried it for eating. Although dove hunting is still a tradition on a minor scale, I chose quail for this recipe because of their availability.

PAN-FRIED QUAIL

INGREDIENTS
8 quails split
Salt and freshly milled black pepper
1 tablespoon juniper berries, crushed
1/4 pound butter, clarified (see Basics, page 333)
2 tablespoons gin

METHOD
Lightly rub the quail with salt, pepper, and the juniper berries.

In a large, heavy skillet, warm the butter over moderately high heat.
Add the birds, skin-side down, and sauté for 4 to 5 minutes, until browned.
Turn the birds and cook another 5 minutes, until pink and juicy.
Sprinkle with the gin and ignite, shaking the pan until the flames subside. Serve at once.

Serves 4

BREAD SAUCE

INGREDIENTS

2 tablespoons butter
2 tablespoons all-purpose flour
2 cups milk
1/8 teaspoon ground mace
Freshly milled white pepper
1 cup day-old white bread, crusts removed, torn
    into small pieces (approximately 3 slices)
1/2 cup country cured ham (like Smithfield), diced

METHOD

In a small saucepan, melt the butter.
Remove from the heat and whisk in the flour.
Return to the heat and add the milk, mace, and
    pepper to taste.
Whisk constantly until the sauce thickens and is
    velvety-smooth.
Fold in the bread and ham and pour into a
    heated sauceboat.

Serves 4

FRIED CRUMBS

INGREDIENTS

1 tablespoon butter
1 cup dried breadcrumbs, made from stale bread
Salt and freshly milled pepper
Pinch of fresh or dried thyme

METHOD

In a medium skillet, melt the butter over
    moderate heat.
Add the breadcrumbs and the seasonings and
    sauté, tossing until golden brown.
Serve with the quail.

Serves 4

FRIED BAKED GRITS

INGREDIENTS

Butter, for greasing the baking dish

4 cups milk
2 cups water
1 1/2 cups quick-cooking grits
1/4 pound plus 4 tablespoons unsalted butter
1 1/2 teaspoons salt
Dash of hot pepper sauce
1 1/2 cups grated cheddar cheese
3 eggs, well-beaten
Butter, for frying

METHOD

Butter a large rectangular baking dish and
    set aside.
Preheat the oven to 350° F.
In a large saucepan, bring the milk and 2 cups
    water to a boil over high heat.
Pour in the grits, stirring constantly until moistened.
Remove from the heat and stir in the butter,
    seasonings, cheese, and eggs.
Pour into the prepared baking dish and bake for
    1 hour.
Let cool to room temperature and cut into
    diamond shapes.
In a large, clean skillet melt the butter and fry the
    diamonds until browned on both sides.

Note: These grits can be served hot, direct from
the oven, or made in advance and fried just
before serving.

Serves 6 to 8

PARSLEY-BUTTERED TURNIPS

INGREDIENTS

8 small turnips, trimmed and quartered,
    but not peeled
Salt
2 tablespoons butter
1 teaspoon sugar
1 tablespoon fresh parsley, chopped

METHOD

In a large pot of salted boiling water, cook the
    turnips until tender.

Drain.

Melt the butter in a large heavy skillet.

Add the turnips and sugar and cook, tossing, until coated with the butter.

Add the parsley, toss to coat, and serve.

Serves 4

GLAZED TOMATOES

INGREDIENTS

4 ripe tomatoes, cored, halved horizontally, and lightly squeezed of seeds

Salt and freshly milled pepper

1 teaspoon sugar

1 tablespoon fresh parsley, chopped

METHOD

Preheat the oven to 350° F.

Place the tomatoes on a lightly oiled baking sheet.

Sprinkle with salt, pepper, sugar, and parsley.

Bake for 10 minutes, until softened.

Remove and place under the broiler for a few seconds, until glazed.

Serves 4

SYLLABUB

INGREDIENTS

8 to 10 dried Amaretti cookies

1 cup confectioners' sugar

1 cup heavy cream

$1/2$ cup dark rum

$1/4$ cup fresh lemon juice

Cocoa powder for dusting

METHOD

In a food processor, pulse the Amaretti cookies until finely crumbled. Set aside or store in a closed container.

Place the sugar in the food processor and pulse for 1 minute.

Add the cream and pulse for another minute.

Slowly pour in the rum and lemon juice and pulse until smooth.

Scrape the mixture into a bowl; cover and refrigerate.

When ready to serve, fold in 1 cup of cookie crumbs.

Serve in small cups or glasses and dust with cocoa powder.

Serves 4

CRYSTALLIZED GRAPEFRUIT

INGREDIENTS

3 grapefruits

2 cups water

$2^{1}/2$ cups sugar

METHOD

Peel the grapefruits and cut the peel into long $1/4$-inch wide julienne.

Place the peels in a medium saucepan and add cold water to cover.

Boil for 10 minutes and drain.

Repeat this process 2 times more with fresh water.

In the saucepan, mix 2 cups water with $1^{1}/2$ cups of sugar.

Add the grapefruit peels and bring to a boil.

Simmer until peels become translucent and the liquid becomes a thick syrup, approximately 45 minutes.

With a slotted spoon, transfer the peels to a sheet of waxed paper.

Allow to set for 7 minutes.

Transfer the peels to another sheet of waxed paper and sprinkle with the remaining cup of sugar.

Roll the peels in the sugar and let stand for 2 hours to dry.

Store in an airtight container until ready to serve.

Serve 2 to 3 strips of peel per person.

Makes about 3 cups

Crab Soup Lunch

SHE-CRAB SOUP ○ COUNTRY HAM BISCUITS ○ SALAD ○ LIME CURD TARTLETS ○
Elk Run Cold Friday Rosé, MD or Palmetto Pale Ale, SC

She-crab soup is a delicacy of Charleston. The roe-filled sooks make the dish authentic, but a valid interpretation can be made with freshly pasteurized crab. A lighter version of the beaten biscuit, with flecks of salt-cured ham, should come to the table so piping hot that the butter will be absorbed immediately. Lime curd, a twist on English lemon curd, is served in tart shells.

SHE-CRAB SOUP

INGREDIENTS

4 cups heavy cream
4 tablespoons butter
1/4 cup shallots, finely chopped
1 pound fresh lump crabmeat with roe
Freshly grated nutmeg to taste
1/8 teaspoon cayenne pepper
Grated zest of 1/2 lemon
Salt
1 tablespoon fresh parsley, finely chopped
Dry sherry (optional)

METHOD

In a small saucepan, reduce the cream over
   moderate heat by 1/3.
In a large saucepan, melt the butter. Add the
   shallots and sauté until wilted.
Add the crabmeat and cook gently, tossing
   for 2 minutes.
Pour in the reduced heavy cream and simmer for
   5 minutes.
Season with the nutmeg, cayenne pepper,
   and lemon zest.
Check the seasonings and add salt to taste.
Divide the crabmeat among the warm soup plates
   and ladle in the soup.
Sprinkle with parsley and serve.
If desired, serve the sherry at the table, adding a
   spoonful to each portion.

Serves 4 to 6

COUNTRY HAM BISCUITS

INGREDIENTS

2 cups all-purpose flour
2 tablespoons baking powder
1/8 teaspoon sugar
5 tablespoons shortening
1 cup milk
1 cup finely diced leftover prepared salt-cured
   ham or sweet-cured ham

METHOD

Preheat the oven to 450° F.
In a mixing bowl, sift together the dry ingredients.
Using your fingers, cut the shortening until the
   mixture is coarse and crumbly. Add the milk and
   mix slightly.
Fold in the ham.
On a floured surface, roll or pat out the dough
   about 1/2-inch thick.
Cut out biscuits with a cookie cutter and bake on
   an ungreased baking sheet for approximately
   12 minutes, or until the tops are brown.

Makes 2 dozen small or 1 dozen large biscuits

LIME CURD TARTLETS

INGREDIENTS

1 recipe pie dough, made with butter
   (see Basics, page 335)
$1/2$ cup fresh lime juice
$1 1/2$ cup water
$1/2$ cup sugar
1 tablespoon cornstarch
8 egg yolks, at room temperature
2 tablespoons unsalted butter
6 sprigs of mint

SPECIAL TOOLS

Six $3 1/2$-inch shallow tartlet molds

METHOD

Use the pie dough to make 6 pastry shells.

Bake thoroughly and set aside to cool.
Place the lime juice, 1 cup of water, and the sugar
   in a saucepan and bring to a boil over high heat.
Meanwhile, in a mixing bowl, dissolve the
   cornstarch in $1/2$ cup water. Whisk in the
   egg yolks.
Slowly pour 1 cup of the boiling lime syrup into the
   yolk mixture and blend it thoroughly.
Pour the mixture back into the saucepan and
   bring to a boil, stirring constantly.
Remove from the heat, add the butter, and mix.
Pour into the prebaked tart shells and let set for
   approximately 30 minutes.
Garnish with fresh mint and serve.

Serves 6

Southern Picnic

STRAWBERRY AND CREAM CHEESE SANDWICHES ○ DEVILED EGGS ○ FRIED CHICKEN ○ POTATO SALAD ○ COLESLAW ○ PICKLES ○ BISCUITS ○ COCONUT CAKE ○ Westbend Vineyards Yadkin Fumé, NC or Old Dominion Hop Pocket Ale, VA

Picnics were very much a custom in spring. Families and friends went off into the woods and set out elegant spreads. Dainty strawberry sandwiches and stuffed eggs were served with white wine and champagne, and the meal immediately took up its Southern roll. The key to good fried chicken is in the turn of the fork, and if you were not lucky enough to learn from a true Southern cook, the secret may elude you forever. Chicken can be fried in vegetable oil or in shortening but never, ever in butter.

STRAWBERRY AND CREAM CHEESE SANDWICHES

INGREDIENTS

1 8-ounce package of cream cheese, preferably without gum additives, at room temperature
1 tablespoon unsalted butter, at room temperature
1/8 teaspoon ground cinnamon
16 very thin slices of white bread
1 cup firm, ripe strawberries
Granulated sugar

METHOD

In a bowl, cream together the cream cheese and butter with the cinnamon until soft and smooth.
Lightly spread the mixture on all of the bread slices.
Hull the strawberries and thinly slice.
Arrange the strawberries on 8 slices of the bread, covering the entire surface.
Lightly sprinkle the berries with granulated sugar and top each sandwich with a remaining slice of bread.
Trim off the crusts and cut the sandwiches into 4 triangles.
Place the sandwiches in a pan lined with a damp paper towel.

Cover with another damp paper towel and keep wrapped in plastic wrap until ready to serve.

Makes 32 tea sandwiches

DEVILED EGGS

INGREDIENTS

1 dozen eggs
1/4 cup homemade mayonnaise (see Basics, page 334) or Hellman's
1 tablespoon Dijon-style mustard
1/2 teaspoon fresh tarragon, finely minced
1 tablespoon butter, softened
Salt and freshly milled pepper

SPECIAL TOOLS

Pastry bag fitted with star tip

METHOD

Place the eggs in a large pot of cold water.
Bring to a boil and cook for 12 minutes.
Set in the sink under cold running water.
Crack the shells and remove them while under the running water.
Refrigerate until chilled.

Cut the eggs lengthwise in half.

Remove the yolks to a separate bowl and mix in remaining ingredients. Beat the yolk mixture with a wooden spoon until smooth.

Discard 4 egg white halves or reserve for another use.

Fill a pastry bag with the yolk mixture and pipe it into the remaining 20 egg white halves.

Cover and chill until ready to serve.

Makes 20 deviled eggs

FRIED CHICKEN

INGREDIENTS

3 chickens (each approximately $3^1/2$ pounds), cut into small serving pieces

Vegetable oil, for frying

2 cups all-purpose flour

1 tablespoon salt

$1/2$ teaspoon fresh milled white pepper

METHOD

Preheat oven to 275° F.

Wash the chicken pieces and pat dry with paper towels.

Pour $1/2$ inch of vegetable oil into a heavy skillet and place over high heat.

When the oil is hot, reduce the heat to moderate.

Mix the flour with the salt and white pepper and dredge the chicken pieces. Shake off any excess flour.

Working in batches, fry the chicken slowly until cooked through and deep golden brown and drain on a paper towel.

Keep the chicken warm until serving.

Serves 8

POTATO SALAD

INGREDIENTS

12 to 14 medium waxy potatoes, cooked, peeled, and sliced

$3/4$ cup vinaigrette (see Basics, page 334)

2 cups homemade mayonnaise (see Basics, page 334) or Hellman's

3 tablespoons Dijon-style mustard

1 dill pickle, cut in strips and chopped

2 to 3 tablespoons pickle juice

3 ribs celery, trimmed, cut in strips, and diced

4 scallions, including some of the green, chopped

$1/4$ cup parsley, chopped

3 hard-boiled eggs, diced into $1/4$-inch pieces

Salt and freshly milled pepper

METHOD

In a large mixing bowl, combine the potatoes with the vinaigrette.

In another bowl, combine the remaining ingredients, then fold into the potatoes.

Season with salt and pepper to taste.

Cover and refrigerate for at least 4 hours.

Serves 10 to 12

COLESLAW

INGREDIENTS

1 medium head white cabbage

Salt and freshly milled black pepper

1 cup homemade mayonnaise (see Basics, page 334) or Hellman's

2 tablespoons white or cider vinegar

$1/4$ teaspoon sugar

1 red or green bell pepper, cored, seeded, and diced

METHOD

Trim the cabbage of its outer leaves and cut in half.

Core and, beginning at the cored end, slice thinly.

Place the sliced cabbage in a large mixing bowl.

Toss with 2 tablespoons salt and add cold water to cover.

Let stand for 1 hour.

Drain and dry thoroughly in a salad spinner.

In a large bowl, combine the mayonnaise with the vinegar and sugar.

Add the cabbage and bell pepper and toss with

the mayonnaise dressing. Season to taste with salt and pepper.

Refrigerate and remove 20 minutes before serving. Best made a day ahead.

Serves 8

COCONUT CAKE

INGREDIENTS

Cake:

1/4 pound unsalted butter plus 2 tablespoons for the pans

1 cup sugar

4 eggs, separated

2 cups all-purpose flour

1 tablespoon plus 1 teaspoon baking powder

1/2 teaspoon salt

1/3 cup fresh or canned coconut milk

Grated zest of 1 lemon

Lemon Filling:

1/3 cup fresh lemon juice

1/2 cup sugar

1 1/3 cups water

1 1/2 tablespoons cornstarch

8 egg yolks, at room temperature

2 tablespoons butter, cut into 4 pieces

Seven-Minute Icing:

1 1/2 cups sugar

2 egg whites, at room temperature

2 teaspoons light corn syrup

1/3 cup cold water

Dash of salt

1 teaspoon vanilla

1 to 1 1/2 cups freshly shredded unsweetened coconut, for covering the cake

METHOD

Prepare the cake:

Butter and lightly flour two 8-inch cake pans.

Preheat the oven to 350° F.

In a large bowl, cream together the butter and sugar using an electric mixer.

Add the egg yolks one at a time and mix until blended.

Sift together the flour, baking powder, and salt, and add alternately with the coconut milk.

Stir in the lemon zest.

In another bowl, beat the egg whites until stiff but not dry.

Fold the whites into the batter with a rubber spatula.

Divide the batter equally between the cake pans and bake for 40 minutes, or until the cake pulls away from the sides of the pan.

Remove the cakes from the oven. Let cool for 10 minutes, then remove from the pans and put on a wire rack to cool thoroughly.

Prepare the lemon filling:

In a medium saucepan, bring the lemon juice, sugar, and 1 cup water to a boil.

In a bowl, dissolve the cornstarch in 1/3 cup water and mix in the yolks.

When the lemon syrup boils, remove from the heat and gradually whisk it into the yolk mixture.

Return to the saucepan and bring to a boil.

Remove from the heat and whisk in the butter.

Place a sheet of plastic wrap directly on the surface of the filling and refrigerate.

Prepare the seven-minute icing:

In a large, clean heatproof mixing bowl, combine all of the ingredients except the vanilla and coconut and beat with an electric mixer for 1 minute to blend.

Set the bowl over a pot of simmering water and beat with an electric mixer for approximately 7 minutes, until white peaks form.

Remove from the heat and beat in the vanilla until the icing stiffens and becomes spreadable, approximately 2 minutes.

Final assembly:

Trim the tops and bottoms of each cake with a long serrated knife.

Cut the cakes horizontally in half.

One at a time, spread each layer with the lemon filling, stacking evenly.

Ice the cake with seven-minute frosting.

Cover the tops and sides of the cake with the shredded coconut.

Serves 10

Beaufort Soused Corn and Shrimp Lunch

CURRIED BUTTERMILK VICHYSSOISE ○ BEAUFORT SOUSED CORN AND SHRIMP ○ FRIED GREEN TOMATOES ○ CORN BREAD ○ PEACH COBBLER ○ Keswick Vineyards Viognier, VA

Vichyssoise is one of the most refreshing soups in warm weather, and it's certainly substantial. This soup, first served at the Ritz Hotel in Boston, is really no different from potato soup, but seems more elegant because it's been pureed and doused with cream. Waters off the Carolina coast yielded some of the best shrimp available, and Beaufort is a small port that once was crowded with fishing boats. The shrimp industry has dwindled to a handful of boats, but shrimp dishes and pies are still very popular in that area. I took the shrimp and the corn out of the pie shell, and soused them with a vinaigrette; it's lighter than a doughy pie. Cobbler is usually blanketed with biscuit dough; here a rich buttery crust is rolled out to fit the skillet, all baked into a lighter version of traditional cobbler.

CURRIED BUTTERMILK VICHYSSOISE

INGREDIENTS
4 medium leeks
4 medium potatoes
4 tablespoons butter
1 tablespoon curry powder
1 quart chicken stock (see Basics, page 332)
   or canned low-sodium chicken broth
Salt and freshly milled pepper
1 quart buttermilk
2 tablespoons snipped fresh chives

METHOD
Discard the green tops of the leeks and split the leeks lengthwise.
Wash in cold running water to remove all sand.
Drain and finely chop.
Peel and slice the potatoes.
Melt the butter in a large pot.

Add the leeks and sauté over moderate heat, until wilted.
Add the curry powder and cook for 1 minute.
Add the chicken stock and potatoes.
Bring to a boil, reduce the heat to low, and simmer for 45 minutes to 1 hour, until the potatoes are tender.
Puree the mixture in a food processor or pass through a food mill. Cover and refrigerate until cold.
When ready to serve, whisk in the buttermilk.
Check the seasonings.
Serve in chilled bowls, with a sprinkling of the snipped chives and a grind of black pepper.

Note: The soup can be made a day ahead.

Serves 8 to 10

BEAUFORT SOUSED CORN AND SHRIMP

INGREDIENTS
5 pounds medium shrimp, peeled with tails intact
1 bay leaf
1 teaspoon crushed peppercorns
1 lemon, halved
12 ears sweet corn, cut from the cob
1 cup scallions, thinly sliced
1 lemon, thinly sliced
Salt

Vinaigrette:
1/3 cup fresh lemon juice
1/2 cup olive oil
Salt and freshly milled black pepper

METHOD
In a large saucepan, place the shrimp in 2 quarts
   of cold water.
Add the bay leaf, peppercorns, and the halved
   and squeezed lemon.
Bring to a boil over moderately high heat.
Add the corn and remove from the heat. Drain
   and turn into a serving bowl.
Remove and discard the halved lemon and
   bay leaf.
Fold in the scallions and lemon slices.
Make the vinaigrette and pour over the corn and
   shrimp, tossing to coat.
Let stand for 15 minutes.
Season to taste with salt and serve warm.

Note: To serve with Corn Bread, follow the recipe
on page 234, omitting the vegetables. This dish
may also be served at room temperature.

Serves 8

FRIED GREEN TOMATOES

INGREDIENTS
4 green tomatoes
1/4 cup rendered ham or bacon fat
1 cup all-purpose flour, seasoned with salt
   and pepper

METHOD
Slice the tomatoes 1/4-inch thick.
In a large heavy cast-iron skillet, melt the fat.
Lightly dredge the tomatoes with flour, shaking
   off any excess.
Fry the tomatoes until lightly golden on each side.

Serves 4

PEACH COBBLER

INGREDIENTS

Cobbler Dough:

2 cups all-purpose flour

1 tablespoon sugar

$1/4$ teaspoon salt

$1/2$ pound unsalted butter, cut into chips
  and chilled

3 tablespoons ice water

Filling:

12 large, ripe peaches

Juice of 1 lemon

$1/4$ cup sugar

1 tablespoon sugar, for the top of the crust

Heavy cream or vanilla ice cream, for serving

METHOD

Prepare the dough:

In a bowl, sift together the dry ingredients and work
  in the butter with a fork, your fingertips, or a pastry
blender, until the mixture has a mealy consistency.

A little at a time, toss the ice water with the flour
  mixture until the dough sticks together. Do not
  overmix.

Shape into a ball, wrap in waxed paper, and
  refrigerate for 15 minutes.

Preheat the oven to 425° F.

Prepare the filling:

Peel and slice the peaches and toss with the
  lemon juice and sugar.

Place the peaches in an ovenproof skillet or
  shallow baking pan.

On a floured surface, roll or pat out the dough to
  fit the pan.

Place the dough over the peaches.

Dust with sugar.

Bake for 45 minutes or until golden brown.

Serve warm, with heavy cream or vanilla
  ice cream.

Serves 4 to 6

Hopping John Dinner

GRILLED OYSTERS ○ GLAZED COUNTRY-CURED HAM ○ ONION VINAIGRETTE ○ HOPPING JOHN ○ GLAZED SWEET POTATOES ○ COLLARD GREENS ○ HOT CURRIED FRUIT ○ POUND CAKE ○ Michael Shaps Cabernet Franc, VA

The oyster roasts of the colonial South developed into huge feasts at election time, the various candidates holding elaborate get-togethers. Who would win popular favor more or less depended on the food and drink served, both the amount and the selection. It is a subtle, hidden, but important, fact of postcolonial life that the American politician got to the voter through his stomach. Hopping John is always served on New Year's Day. A coin was thrown into the pot, and whoever found it was assured of good luck. A locally cured ham presided over the Hopping John and a variety of vegetables and sweet potatoes in one form or another. Spiced fresh fruits were a luxury. Rich cake, measured out in a pound each of sugar, eggs, butter, and flour, was beaten by the sturdy family cook.

GRILLED OYSTERS

INGREDIENTS
10 to 12 oysters per person

METHOD
Wash and clean the oyster shells thoroughly. Keep the oysters on ice until ready to cook.
Prepare a hardwood charcoal fire.

Set a large rack over the fire.
When the coals have a red glow, place the oysters on the rack and cook.
As the oysters open, remove with long tongs.
Pry open with a knife and eat immediately.
The oysters will have a pungent, smoky flavor.

GLAZED COUNTRY-CURED HAM

INGREDIENTS
1 Virginia ham (Smithfield type, 12 to 14 pounds)

METHOD
Scrub off any mold that has developed on the skin of the ham.

Place the ham in a pot with water to cover and allow to sit for at least 8 hours or overnight.

Drain and place in a pot with enough fresh cold water to cover the ham.

Bring to a simmer and reduce the heat to just a slight bubble.

Cook for 6 hours, replacing any evaporated water with boiled hot water to cover.

Check the meat by piercing it with a metal skewer. If firm, continue cooking for an additional 2 hours.

When cooked, drain off the water and cool the ham.

Preheat the oven to 425° F.

Peel back the skin 2 inches below the hock and reserve the skin for the Hopping John or collard greens.

Place the ham on a roasting pan.

Remove the excess fat, leaving a $1/2$-inch covering over the meat. Reserve the fat.

Score the ham and cover with ham glaze.

Bake for 20 to 30 minutes, until heated through and browned.

Slice very thinly.

Serves 15 or more

HAM GLAZE

INGREDIENTS
1 cup dark brown sugar
1 tablespoon dry mustard
$1/3$ cup bourbon or corn whiskey
$1/4$ cup blackstrap molasses

METHOD
In a bowl, combine the brown sugar with the dry mustard and bourbon. Stir in the molasses.

Coat the ham.

Baste twice while the ham bakes.

Makes approximately $1 1/4$ cups

ONION VINAIGRETTE

INGREDIENTS
12 medium white onions
1 cup pearl onions
1 cup shelled fresh green peas
Vinaigrette (see Basics, page 334)

METHOD
Slice off the top $1/3$ of each white onion and cut and "X" at the base.

Place the onions in a steamer and cook for 10 to 15 minutes, or until tender and set aside.

Meanwhile, cut an "X" on the bottom of each pearl onion and poach in boiling, salted water for 5 minutes.

Drain and peel.

Blanch the peas in salted boiling water for 4 minutes.

Drain and mix with the pearl onions.

Peel off the outer skin and scoop out the heart of the larger onions to make onion shells.

Coat the pearl onions and peas with vinaigrette and spoon into the hollowed onions.

Serve at room temperature.

Serves 12

HOPPING JOHN

INGREDIENTS
1 pound dried black-eyed peas
Ham hock or country-cured ham skin and fat trimmings
1 medium onion, finely chopped
1 bay leaf
3/4 cup long-grain rice
Salt and freshly milled pepper

METHOD
Soak the peas overnight in several quarts of water.

Dice the ham fat and render it in a large pot over moderate heat.

Add the onions and cook until wilted.

Drain the peas and add them to the onions, along with the bay leaf and enough cold water to cover.

Add the ham hock or a large piece of ham skin.

Bring to a boil and reduce the heat to a simmer.

Cover and cook for 45 minutes, or until the peas are almost tender.

Add the rice, cover, and cook for 20 minutes, adding more water if necessary, until the rice is tender.

Season to taste with salt and pepper and serve.

Serves 8 to 10

GLAZED SWEET POTATOES

INGREDIENTS
6 sweet potatoes
1 cup packed brown sugar
1/4 cup bourbon
4 tablespoons butter, melted
Grated zest of 1 lemon

METHOD
Boil the potatoes until almost tender.

Preheat the oven to 350° F. Butter a shallow ovenproof baking dish.

When cool enough to handle, peel the potatoes and cut into 1/2-inch thick slices.

Place in the prepared baking dish.

In a small saucepan, dissolve the brown sugar in the bourbon over moderate heat.

Add the melted butter and lemon zest.

Pour the glaze over the potatoes and bake for 15 to 20 minutes, until glazed and heated through.

Serves 8 to 10

COLLARD GREENS

INGREDIENTS
3 pounds collard greens, washed, with stalks removed
Reserved ham skin or a ham hock
1 tablespoon sugar
Salt and freshly milled pepper

METHOD
Wash, drain, and chop the greens. Set aside.

Place the ham hock and skin in a large kettle, and add approximately 3 quarts of cold water to cover.

Bring to a boil over high heat.

Simmer over moderate heat for 30 minutes.

Add the greens and sugar and simmer for 2 hours.

Drain the "pot licker" and serve it with the greens and spooned over cornbread.

Serves 8 to 10

HOT CURRIED FRUIT

INGREDIENTS

12 firm ripe pears

Approximately 3 1/2 cups sugar (depending on the sweetness of the fruit)

1 small cinnamon stick

5 whole cloves

Juice of 2 lemons

12 oranges

1 winter melon (optional)

1 bunch red grapes, preferably seedless, cut into small clusters

1 lemon, sliced

1 tablespoon curry powder

1/2 cup crystallized ginger, cut into julienne

METHOD

Peel the pears, leaving the stems intact.

Place them in a large pot with enough water to cover.

Add the sugar, spices, and lemon juice.

Cover the pears with a round of waxed paper cut to fit the interior of the pot.

Bring to a boil, reduce to a simmer, and cook until the pears can be easily pierced with a knife.

Meanwhile, slice away the skin and pith from the oranges.

Move the pears to a serving bowl and add enough syrup to cover.

Place the oranges in the cooking liquid and simmer for 15 minutes or until tender.

Peel and seed the melon. Cut into long 1-inch-wide strips.

Add the melon strips to the poaching oranges and simmer for 5 minutes.

Remove from pot and place in the serving bowl.

Add the grapes and lemon slices to the poaching liquid and simmer for approximately 3 minutes.

Transfer the fruit to the bowl.

In a small bowl, whisk the curry powder in a 1/2 cup of the poaching liquid and return the mixture to the pot.

Cook the liquid until it is reduced by half. Strain through a double thickness of dampened cheesecloth.

Drain away any juices that have collected in the serving bowl and pour the syrup over the fruits.

Serve the fruit with a little of the crystallized ginger julienne spooned over each portion.

Serves 8 to 12

POUND CAKE

INGREDIENTS

1/2 pound unsalted butter, plus 3 tablespoons for greasing the loaf pans

1 cup sugar

5 eggs

2 1/4 cups cake flour

1 teaspoon baking powder

1/2 teaspoon salt

1/2 cup sour cream

Confectioners' sugar

METHOD

Generously butter 2 medium loaf pans.

Preheat the oven to 350° F.

In a mixing bowl, cream together the butter and sugar.

One at a time, add the eggs, mixing thoroughly.

Sift together the flour, baking powder, and salt.

Add the dry ingredients alternately with the sour cream.

Divide the batter between the loaf pans.

Bake for 40 minutes, or until the loaves pull away from the sides of the pan.

Allow the cakes to rest for 10 minutes, remove from the tins, and cool on a rack.

Dust with confectioners' sugar.

Makes two 1-pound loaves

Street Food

Crab Cakes

Crab cakes make a very pleasant meal. They join the common ranks of lobster salad and fried oysters just slapped on a hamburger bun. The perpetual accompaniment is little paper cups of creamy coleslaw and tartar sauce.

CRAB CAKES

INGREDIENTS

1 pound (approximately 2 1/2 cups) flaked crab meat, picked over
2 scallions, trimmed and minced
1 tablespoon parsley, chopped
1/4 teaspoon Old Bay seasoning
1/4 cup cracker meal
1/4 cup homemade mayonnaise (see Basics, page 334) or Hellman's
1/2 teaspoon Dijon mustard
A few drops Tabasco sauce
1 egg, beaten
For Frying:
Cracker crumbs, for dredging
1/2 cup of clarified butter (see Basics, page 333)
1 tablespoon vegetable oil

METHOD

In a bowl, combine all of the ingredients for the crab cakes.
Cover and refrigerate for at least one hour.
Shape the crab mixture into 4 to 6 cakes.
Coat each one generously with cracker crumbs and place on a plate.
Cover lightly with waxed paper and refrigerate another hour or more.
In a heavy skillet, heat the clarified butter and the vegetable oil over moderate heat.
Fry the cakes on both sides until golden brown.
Serve with Tartar sauce (see Basics, page 334).

Makes 4 large or 6 small crab cakes

Mint Julep

How to make a julep: crush the mint or bruise the mint; freeze the glass or freeze the silver chalice; make it with rye or make it with bourbon. These are the disputes. I offer my julep recipe—I make it with scotch.

MINT JULEP

INGREDIENTS

1/2 cup packed fresh mint sprigs
1/4 cup simple syrup (see Basics, page 337)
2 to 2 1/2 cups shaved ice
6 ounces scotch

SPECIAL TOOLS

Blender
Two julep cups
Glass straws

METHOD

In a blender, combine the mint and simple syrup, mixing until pureed thoroughly.
Place 1/2 of the mint mixture and 1 straw in each julep cup.
Pack the ice around the straw and fill the cup almost to the top with shaved ice.
Set the cups in the freezer for at least 30 minutes.
Touching the outside as little as possible, remove the cups from the freezer and pour scotch over the shaved ice.
Decorate with mint sprigs and sip in the shade.

Make two 12-ounce drinks

DEEP SOUTH

DEEP SOUTH

The extraordinary yield of Southern rice fields was the result of backbreaking labor. Rice tending is a year-round vigil, from clearing the irrigation ditches of clogging grasses (60 miles of ditch for every 500 acres of field) to a long winter's work of threshing in the mills. The great rice industry in the South had sprung from one small bag of Madagascar rice carried by an English sea captain. For nearly 200 years, harvests flourished before falling away to a single, stately plantation. Beyond the swamps and up the grand oak-lined drives that lead to once-proud mansions, it is hard to imagine that there was once a way of life modeled on that of England's feudal lords.

The Civil War marked the decline of the plantation. Slaves were freed and the countryside ravaged, and only a handful of plantations were restored to their former glory during the Reconstruction. Most African Americans, newly homeless, looked for work far from the plantation, taking with them their skill at operating the trunks, ditches, canals, and levees. Deprived of their usual help, field foreman hired immigrant workers, mostly Irish and Italians from the brickyards on the Hudson River, but the labor was neither cheap nor satisfactory. Rice culture declined rapidly at the beginning of this century, and by 1920 there were no more than 500 acres of cultivated land along the rivers.

Today, rice fields thrive in the small towns of southern Louisiana, on Bayou Teche, and down the intercoastal water route. No longer the domain of the gentleman farmer but the realm of the working land farmer, Louisiana remains one of this country's great rice producers. Although Louisiana shares the export market with other states, her people consume as much rice at their tables as do most Asians. Rice and hominy are the staples of the low country and on through the Deep South. Hominy is prepared for breakfast and used as a foundation for breads and batter. Rice is for dinner, passed at the table hot and fluffy with gumbos, jambalayas, okra soups, and stews, the backbone of vegetable and meat pilafs. (Servants once saved the starchy rice water for pressing household linen and cotton, just as the frugal New England housewife reserved the water in which she'd soaked beans to clean her kerosene lamps.) Rice is the cornerstone of any southern kitchen, the basis of elegant dishes and humble ones alike.

Flooded fields make perfect crawfish farms. Louisiana produces more than 100 million pounds annually, keeping three-quarters of the catch for herself. The rest is shipped throughout the country. (Crawfish, followed by catfish, has become as standard as production-line chicken.) During the crawfish season, flat-bottomed pirogues, some still made from hollowed cypress logs, are poled through the swampy bayou, the navigator emptying wire traps until he is boot deep with crawling, tiny-clawed critters. Cranes, herons, and egrets nest in the trees above, while alligators and turtles wait below in the hope that an egg or chick will fall their way. Crawfish, or "mud-bugs" (so-called because they burrow into the mud when their watery environment goes dry), like soft-shell crabs, must be shipped live. Cooked crawfish will keep only a short while, and the meat spoils quickly when frozen with its own fat. On Good Friday, picnickers take to the levees and boil up hundreds of pounds of crawfish in sawed-off oil drums, generously figuring about seven pounds for every man, five for every woman. Southerners are very practical when it comes to this type of cooking, and keep it out-of-doors because of smoke and smell.

The Cajuns left their Atlantic coast of France in the 1600s, settling in Acadia in Nova Scotia, near the St. Lawrence River. Cajun (slurred from the word Acadian) is a language closer to French than any other, although removed by 300 years and further spiked with Spanish, English, and American Indian languages. The Cajuns

concerned themselves with fishing, trapping, and farming, and adamantly refused to swear British allegiance. When banished from this territory in 1755, the Cajuns crept down the St. Lawrence to the Great Lakes, across the plains and down the Mississippi, settling between 1760 and 1785 in the waterlogged parishes of southern and western Louisiana. As a society they have kept their customs, trades, and language, although the language is now in danger of extinction. Slapdash and impulsive, Cajun cooks use more spices, herbs, and hot peppers than their Creole brothers and sisters in the city. Filé (pronounced fee-lay) is very much a part of Cajun cooking, and was long known to the Choctaw Indians who would dry the young sassafras leaves and grind them to a powder. A small amount seasons jambalaya, etouffé, and gumbo. Roux and okra also are used to thicken gumbos and soups. (Okra and filé must not be used together or the intended soup would turn to sludge. Filé is added off the heat, because it turns stringy if boiled.)

This area has a reputation for hot and spicy food. There are more peppers grown and used in Louisiana than in any other region, including the Southwest. Anaheim chiles, Louisiana sports, serranos, torridos, jalapeños, Bahamian reds, powdered peppers for cayenne, crushed red pepper flakes and seeds, red and green Tabasco (combined in a secret formula for the bottled sauce of that name), as well as countless other types of peppers are grown in the parishes of Vermillion, Lafayette, New Iberia, and St. Mary. Hot sauce in one form or another is in every home, bar, and restaurant across the region. Louisiana exports paprika even to Hungary. Natives refer to black pepper as "aromatic," white as "bright," and red as a "burn." Pepper sauces range from "hot," to "hot hot," to the colloquial "hot damn!," and an evening in a local barroom will more likely end in a hot pepper–eating contest than in a brawl. There are as many gumbos as there are peppers and cooks: chicken, ham, Andouille sausage, tomato, shrimp, and "tasso," a peppery ham similar to Texas jerky, are all rich with peppers and a myriad of spices. Gumbo always begins with a roux, not in the classic manner of blending flour and butter, but using pork or bacon fat instead of butter, and cooking it until nearly burned. A devoted Cajun may "carry" her roux for close to an hour, to make it rich and dark, just shy of scorched. This roux has a pronounced flavor, preferred to the lighter golden roux of the city. Cajuns rarely cook with wine; with such flavor, why would they want to?

Unlike jazz, which can sustain itself with but a few players, Cajun gumbo offers a full orchestra of ingredients. The recipes which follow tend to complement a featured ingredient, embellishing it and weaving supporting themes. This isn't necessarily typical of all gumbos made locally, served alongside heaping plates of sweets and sours. And just as local cooking neatly suits local taste, local technique is the cook's own version of inherited tradition. Efforts to coax from a Louisianian just how he or she works out a dish may be rewarded with vague logic:

"How long do you cook the okra?"
"I put it on when I do the rice."
"How long do you steam the rice?"
"Till dinner's ready."

It is somehow mystifying to observe the nonchalance of a Savannah cook who can rest one hand on hip, trading tales and laughing a

mile a minute, while simultaneously turning chicken and gesturing with a dripping two-pronged fork, casually bringing forth a mouthwatering masterpiece.

Eighteenth-century Louisiana acquired a diverse and unusual populace, and yet somehow managed to assimilate them all. At that time, Paris was clearing out her prisons and houses of correction, and many of these inmates flocked to the territory claimed by LaSalle for France in the seventeenth century. It was a dubious group who furthered settlement of this malaria-ridden backwash. By 1721, a German contingent had established itself on the west side of the river. Later aristocrats fleeing from the French Revolution sought refuge here (as did some footloose Parisian chefs, having seen their less fortunate employers carted off to the guillotine). New Orleans' *Vieux Carre* architecturally flaunts her Spanish ancestry (reflecting the change of hands when the French ceded their colony) with extravagant wrought-iron balconies from one end of the old city to the other. And with the Spanish came the spices and hot peppers of

South America. By the mid-eighteenth century, these various contributions were spawning yet another style, Creole, which emerged with the addition of Haitians to Louisiana society. By 1810, there were more than 100,000 French-speaking *gens de couleur*, and today the French language is taught throughout the Bayou, in part subsidized by the French government.

If Cajun is country food, then Creole is city food. Creole society blossomed until the Civil War, and southern fortunes were made and lost in cotton, sugar, and rice. Elegant townhouses were fully staffed and stood ready for the merchant's visits to town, but the flavor of this era has been brought to the 21st century more by the legacy of restaurants than of homes. Creole food is very sensual in comparison to the comforting, homey dishes typical of most of this country, and New Orleans jazz halls and turn-of-the-century restaurants are lingering reminders of the lush life.

New Orleans's old market runs parallel to Decatur Street and the River, and supplies many of the vendors and restaurants in the Quarter. Farmers arrive at dawn, having driven from as far

as 150 miles away. The array of their produce stalls reads like a recipe for gumbo: big red and green bell peppers, little baskets of yellow onions, strings of garlic, tin tubs of fresh herbs mingling the pungent fragrances of thyme, rosemary, mint, basil, cilantro, fennel, tarragon, and even cardoons (a member of the artichoke family, once rarely seen in our markets). The Creole tomatoes are vine-ripened and bursting with juice. One plunge in hot water and these large, sweet-acid tomatoes slip obligingly out of their skins.

Fresh fish and shellfish are the province of New Orleans dining. Descendants of Croatian immigrants continue to fish these coastal waters, where the oysters, culled from the beds of Lac Bare and Barataria Bay, were as famous as the Chincoteagues of the Chesapeake and the Wellfleets of Cape Cod. It is tragic that many of the local beds have been lost, not to overfishing, but to pollution, so that oysters are now farmed down on the lower Mississippi and shipped from Houma and Morgan City. Many of the oysters are farmed in the salt marshes and brackish waters of the Bayou, and when the spats reach maturity they may be moved four or five times to waters nearer to the Gulf, in order to take on the distinctive saline taste associated with good oyster flavor. New Orleans offers oysters year round, but it is in spring that the coast's oyster shacks and the city's oyster bars boast the most utterly luscious oysters; the females are plump with millions of eggs and the wobbly flesh just bursts on the tongue. (One must be wary, however, for not all oyster bars offer local bivalves, but rather serve up an Eastern imposter.) Quick to follow the oyster in season are the celebrated lake and river shrimp that get added into gumbos and jambalayas, grilled in hot sauces, barbecued in unthinkable amounts of crushed black pepper and oceans of butter, stuffed into artichokes, dipped into remoulades, coupled with merlitons in salads, or rolled into filleted catfish with capers and pecans, or with rockfish *en papillote*.

The fish markets are a feast of pompano, Spanish mackerel, grouper, redfish, speckled trout, freshwater green trout, dainty croakers, soft-shell and blue crabs, and sweet, ugly catfish. Frog's legs are conspicuous, often as heavy with meat as chicken legs.

Florida doesn't really feel like part of the Deep South. The interior is a green maze of swamps and rivers, miles of cattle ranches, citrus groves, and farm communities that supply much of this country with salad greens from November to June. The northern part of Florida smacks of southern cooking, with its biscuits, cornbreads, muffins, and pies. The Gulf shore cooking, though, has a Caribbean feel to it—paellas, conch stews and chowders, coquina soups swimming with tiny shellfish no bigger than a fingernail, thick bean soups, and chorizo sausages. And, naturally, rum was drunk here before it reached New England. Cuba's strong influence is reflected in the food throughout southern Florida. The yard-long, pale and crusty loaves of Cuban bread with their fluffy interiors set a high standard. Because the dampness encourages mold, particularly in yeast breads, the Cuban custom of flour, salt, and water as a bread base is still the tradition. Gulf Coast

meals harken back to the Spanish-Cuban influence with such romantically named dishes as *Morros y Christianos*, "Moors and Christians," which are made from black beans and white rice. Their fruit salads, composed of guava, mango, loquat, mammee-sapota, coconut, papaya, and cabbage palmetto are served not as dessert, but as part of the meal. The favorite dessert remains the flan, many preferring a short-cut version produced by boiling an unopened can of condensed milk (which some of us fondly remember as a nursery treat). Another equally delicious dessert of the region is the marvelous key lime pie. The joy of this pie is the key lime itself. The explosively flavored zest and astringent juice combine to punch right through the sweetened cream. A facsimile of the key lime pie can of course be tried with ordinary limes, but the resulting flavor will be only a ghost of the original. And the true pie has always been made with condensed milk.

Breakfast

CALAS ○ CAFÉ AU LAIT

Calas were an early morning New Orleans snack, a hot, sweet-spiced rice cake fried crispy and served with the morning's café noir or café au lait (that wonderful combination of half rich coffee and half hot milk). As New Orleans was going through her growing pains, this great breakfast drink was not only thought to be good for the health, but also a preventative for such infectious diseases as malaria. These Creole fritters were sold at the marketplace and at the trolley platform by ladies in gingham dresses with starched white aprons who carried them in baskets, singing their vending song, "Belle Calas!"

CALAS

INGREDIENTS
1/2 cup long-grain rice
Salt
1/2 ounce fresh cake yeast or 1 package
    active dry yeast
3 tablespoons lukewarm water
2 eggs, separated
4 tablespoons sugar
1/8 teaspoon freshly grated nutmeg
1/8 teaspoon ground allspice
1/8 teaspoon cinnamon
A pinch of salt
1/2 cup all-purpose flour, sifted
Vegetable oil, for deep frying
Confectioners' sugar, for dusting

SPECIAL TOOLS
Deep-fat frying thermometer

METHOD
Boil the rice in salted water until soft and mushy.
Drain thoroughly and mash the rice until soft
    and creamy.
Dissolve the yeast in the lukewarm water and add
    to the rice.
Cover with a clean cloth and allow to sit overnight.
In a mixing bowl, beat the egg yolks until thick and
creamy, gradually adding 2 tablespoons of
    the sugar.

Fold in the spices.
In another bowl, beat the egg whites with
    the remaining 2 tablespoons sugar until stiff
    and glossy.
Combine the egg yolks with the rice.
Sift the flour into the mixture and mix well.
Fold in the egg whites and mix just until no
    streaks show.
In a large, deep heavy skillet, bring 1 inch of oil to
    about 365° F. One at a time, drop the mixture by
    teaspoonfuls into the hot oil and fry until golden,
    5 to 7 minutes.
Drain on paper towels.
Dust the calas with confectioners' sugar and serve
    in batches.

Makes 5 dozen calas

Ghost Mansion Picnic

CHILLED CRAWFISH BISQUE ○ ROAST CHICKEN WITH CORN BREAD AND OYSTER STUFFING ○ BOILED RICE ○ PECAN PIE ○ Far Niente Chardonnay or Villa Mt. Eden Chardonnay, Grand Reserve Bien Nacido Vineyard

This is not at all a traditional crawfish bisque. Usually the crawfish heads are stuffed with a mixture of spicy bread crumbs and crawfish fat and set adrift in the soup, but this is a nit-picking preparation that adds little to the essence of the dish. Crushed crawfish shells infuse the bisque with flavor, and the tail meat, fat, and tomalley enrich this cool, elegant soup. The ghost chicken (unphotographed) invisibly follows the bisque; it's really not a figment of the readers' imagination, and, indeed, a recipe follows. It is stuffed with seasoned corn bread, moistened with enough oyster liquor to keep the oysters plump. Pecan pie is the quintessential end to this Southern meal. Try to time the baking of the pie shell so that it is still hot when you pour in the filling to bake.

CHILLED CRAWFISH BISQUE

INGREDIENTS

7 pounds live crawfish, cooked (see page 152)
1/4 pound unsalted butter
1 medium yellow onion, finely chopped
1 celery heart, finely chopped
1/4 teaspoon cayenne pepper
2 quarts heavy cream
Salt

METHOD

Break the cooked crawfish in half and remove the tail meat and fat.

Set aside the shells and meat separately.

In a stockpot, melt the butter and sauté the onion and celery until wilted.

Add the cayenne, heavy cream, and reserved crawfish shells, heads, and fat.

Simmer over low heat for 45 minutes.

In a food processor, blend the shells with the cream in small batches.

Pass the soup through a fine sieve and discard the solids.

Add the reserved tail meat and chill until ready to serve.

Note: The bisque may also be served hot.

Serves 6

ROAST CHICKEN WITH CORN BREAD-AND-OYSTER STUFFING

INGREDIENTS

Stuffing:

1/4 pound unsalted butter

1 small yellow onion, finely chopped

2 celery ribs, finely chopped

2 cups crumbled corn bread (see recipe, omitting the vegetables, page 246)

1 teaspoon fresh sage, finely chopped

1/2 teaspoon fresh thyme, chopped

1/2 teaspoon fresh rosemary, chopped

1/4 cup heavy cream

1 dozen oysters, shucked and drained with approximately 1/2 cup oyster liquor reserved

1 egg

Salt and freshly milled black pepper

2 whole chickens (each approximately 3 1/2 pounds)

METHOD

Preheat the oven to 450° F.

In a medium skillet, melt the butter and sauté the onions and celery until wilted.

Turn into a bowl and toss them with the remaining stuffing ingredients.

Stuff and truss the chickens and set them on a rack in a large roasting pan.

Roast for approximately 45 minutes, or until the thigh juices run clear.

Allow to rest for 10 minutes before serving.

Serves 6

PECAN PIE

INGREDIENTS

2 cups shelled pecans

6 tablespoons unsalted butter, cut into pieces

1 cup dark brown or muscovado sugar

1/2 teaspoon salt

3 large eggs

3/4 cup light corn syrup

1 tablespoon pure vanilla extract

1 hot, prebaked 9-inch pie crust (see Basics, page 335)

Whipped cream

METHOD

Preheat the oven to 300° F.

Toast pecans (see Basics, page 337) and chop roughly with a knife.

Melt butter in the double boiler.

Stir in sugar and salt.

Using a whisk, beat in the eggs, one at a time, along with the corn syrup and vanilla.

Cook, while whisking, over the gently simmering water until the mixture is warm to the touch and the sugar is dissolved.

Stir in the pecans, pour the mixture into the prebaked crust, and place in the preheated oven to bake until the center is set but still soft, about 40 minutes. (If the crust looks like it will get too brown during this second baking, wrap the edge in foil to protect it from the heat.)

Let the pie cool completely before serving, a minimum of 4 hours.

Serve at room temperature with whipped cream.

Serves 6 to 8

A Red Dinner

BOILED CRAWFISH ○ SHRIMP BOIL ○ CAJUN REMOULADE SAUCE ○ HOT PICKLED RED PEPPERS ○ CREAMERS ○ STRAWBERRIES WITH BOURBON AND WHIPPED CREAM ○ Lagniappe Beer, LA

Louisiana's lust for the spice and heat of pepper culminates in this red hell of a dinner. Natives are willing to eat river and lake shrimp and crawfish for breakfast, lunch, and dinner. Boiled up in hot peppery shrimp and crawfish boil, they are served with this Cajun remoulade, fiery red peppers, and creamers spiced with the same pungent boil—all washed down with beer, the only beverage that will quench the heat of all these spices. Local strawberries—their season lasts but a few weeks—are the most fragrant and taste the way a strawberry ought to.

BOILED CRAWFISH

INGREDIENTS
4 cloves garlic, unpeeled
3 lemons, thinly sliced
1 cup celery leaves, chopped
4 sprigs fresh parsley
3 medium yellow onions, sliced
1 package (3 ounces) shrimp or crab boil seasoning
7 pounds live crawfish

METHOD
Fill a large stockpot 1/3 full of cold water.
Add all of the ingredients except the crawfish and boil for 20 minutes.
Meanwhile, soak the crawfish in salted cold water for about 15 minutes; rinse.
Strain the stock and discard the vegetables.
Place the crawfish in the stock and add more water to cover, if necessary.
Bring to a rolling boil, reduce the heat and simmer for 15 minutes.
Drain and serve.

Note: The crawfish will become spicier the longer they sit in the liquid. To make Boiled Shrimp, use 5 pounds shrimp instead of the crawfish and remove the shrimp as soon as they come to a boil. Creamers (baby new potatoes) are the usual accompaniment, cooked in the same crawfish liquor.

Serves 5

CAJUN RED REMOULADE SAUCE

INGREDIENTS
1/2 of a sweet red bell pepper, roasted and
   peeled (see Basics, page 338)
1 cup homemade mayonnaise
   (see Basics, page 334) or Hellman's
1 scallion, including some of the green, minced
   (approximately 2 tablespoons)
1 tablespoon lemon zest, minced
1/4 cup dill pickle, minced
2 tablespoons fresh or pickled hot peppers (such
   as serrano, tabasco, or cayenne), chopped
1 tablespoon freshly grated horseradish
1 tablespoon capers, washed of brine, dried,
   and chopped
1/4 cup fresh parsley, chopped

METHOD
Puree the roasted pepper with the mayonnaise in
   a food processor.
Add the remaining ingredients and puree
   until smooth.
Do not overprocess.
Chill for 30 minutes before serving.

Makes about 2 cups

STRAWBERRIES WITH BOURBON AND WHIPPED CREAM

INGREDIENTS
2 quarts ripe strawberries, with stems
1/2 cup bourbon
1/2 cup confectioners' sugar
1 cup heavy cream, whipped

METHOD
Wash the strawberries and leave the stems
   attached and drain.

Place the berries, bourbon, and confectioners'
   sugar in separate bowls.
Dip the berries in the bourbon and then in
   the sugar.
Serve, accompanied with the whipped cream.

Serves 5 to 6

Creole Dinner

CREOLE OYSTERS WITH CARDOONS ○ SAUTÉED FROG'S LEGS ○ MUSTARD GREENS AND CREAMERS ○ BREAD PUDDING SOUFFLÉ WITH WHISKEY SAUCE ○ Au Bon Climat Chardonnay, CA

This simple stew is nothing more than a reduction of cream and oyster liquor, with the addition of cayenne pepper to give it a Southern jolt. Cardoons are a Mediterranean vegetable that are popping up at farmer's markets throughout the country. "Creole Oysters" is a dish inspired by the unexpected appearance of this vegetable in a New Orleans market. Jumbo frog's legs are as tender as butter and are accompanied with peppery mustard greens, blanched and sautéed in butter. Creamers—baby potatoes that, like the culls of New England— are usually served with sour cream (which is how they came to be called "creamers"). Bread pudding is one of the favorite desserts of the Deep South, always served hot with a whiskey sauce or vanilla cream. In soufflé form it is light and airy.

CREOLE OYSTERS WITH CARDOONS

INGREDIENTS
10 stalks cardoons
Juice of 1 lemon
6 cups heavy cream
4 dozen oysters, shucked with 1 cup of their
    liquor reserved
1/2 teaspoon cayenne pepper
2 teaspoons filé gumbo powder

METHOD
Peel and clean the cardoons. Cut into
    2-inch julienne.
Set aside in cold water to cover with the
    lemon juice.
In a heavy saucepan, reduce the cream by 1/2
    over moderate heat.
While the cream reduces, cook the cardoons in
    salted boiling water until tender.
Drain and keep warm.
Strain the oyster liquor into the reduced cream
    and reduce the mixture by 1/3 to approximately
    2 1/2 cups.
Add the cayenne pepper.

Poach the oysters in the cream for 3 minutes.
Off the heat, stir in the filé gumbo powder or add
    a pinch to each serving at the table.
Drain the cardoons thoroughly and arrange them
    on a heated deep platter.
Pour the oysters and cream over the cardoons.
Serve in heated soup plates.

Serves 8

SAUTÉED FROG'S LEGS

INGREDIENTS
1/2 pound unsalted butter
Salt and cayenne pepper
1 cup all-purpose flour
16 frog's legs (each about 4 ounces)
2 tablespoons fresh rosemary, chopped
1 cup dry white wine

METHOD
Preheat the oven to 250° F.
Melt 1/4 pound of butter in a large heavy skillet.

Lightly salt half of the frog's legs and sprinkle with cayenne pepper.

Dredge lightly in the flour.

Sauté the floured frog's legs over moderately high heat until golden.

Sprinkle with half of the rosemary.

Keep warm in the oven.

Repeat the process with the remaining frog's legs and keep warm.

To deglaze the pan, add the wine and cook over high heat, scraping up the brown bits that cling to the bottom of the pan until the liquid is reduced by half.

Strain the sauce over the frog's legs and serve.

Serves 8

BREAD PUDDING SOUFFLÉ WITH WHISKEY SAUCE

INGREDIENTS

Soufflé:

Butter and sugar for the mold

4 eggs, separated and at room temperature

1 cup sugar

1 teaspoon vanilla extract

1/4 teaspoon cinnamon

1/4 teaspoon freshly grated nutmeg

4 cups milk

Pinch of salt

1/2 cup sultanas, soaked in enough dark rum to cover

1/2 cup pecans, chopped

5 cups day-old French bread (from a large loaf, not a baguette), cut into 1-inch cubes

Whiskey Sauce:

1 cup heavy cream

2 egg yolks, at room temperature

2 tablespoons sugar

1/4 cup bourbon

METHOD

Prepare the soufflé:

Preheat the oven to 350° F.

Coat a large, deep baking dish with butter and sugar.

In a mixing bowl, beat the egg yolks with 3/4 cup of the sugar, the vanilla, and spices until thick, creamy, and lemony in color.

Mix in the milk.

Place the cubed bread in a large bowl and pour the yolk-milk mixture over the bread.

Set aside for 45 minutes.

In a bowl, beat the egg whites with the salt and the remaining 1/4 cup sugar until stiff, glossy peaks form.

Stir the sultanas and pecans into the soaked bread and fold in the meringue.

Turn the mixture into the prepared mold and bake for 35 to 40 minutes, until puffed and golden.

Prepare the whiskey sauce:

Heat the cream over simmering water in a double boiler.

In a bowl, whisk the egg yolks with the sugar until thick.

Off the heat, whisk the yolks into the heated cream.

Return the mixture to the double boiler and cook over simmering water, stirring constantly, until thickened enough to coat the back of a spoon.

Slowly add the bourbon and continue to cook until lightly thickened and smooth. Serve warm with the soufflé.

Serves 8

Oyster Lunch

OYSTERS ROCKEFELLER ○ Domaine Carneros Brut Cuvee Sparkling Wine, CA

The less you cook oysters, the more delicious they will be. Blanketing them with crumbs or cream results in smothered oysters. Of the many ways to serve them in the South, Oysters Rockefeller remains the most famous. It was invented around 1900 by Jules Alciatore, son of the founder of Antoine's Restaurant.

OYSTERS ROCKEFELLER

INGREDIENTS
Filling:

1 pound spinach, thoroughly washed, drained, and stemmed
4 tablespoons unsalted butter
3 scallions, chopped
2 large shallots, minced
1 clove garlic, minced
1 cup fresh parsley, chopped
2 tablespoons dry vermouth
1 tablespoon heavy cream
1 tablespoon fresh lemon juice
1 tablespoon Herbsaint or Pernod
Few dashes of hot sauce
1/4 cup fresh bread crumbs

Rock salt or kosher salt, for the oyster pans
2 dozen oysters, shucked and left in the half shell

METHOD

Preheat the oven to 400° F.
Bring a large pot of lightly salted water to a boil.
Submerge the spinach in the water and drain immediately.
Melt the butter in a large skillet and sauté the scallions, shallots, and garlic over moderate heat until wilted.
Press any excess liquid from the spinach and add it to the pan.
Fold in the parsley and the remaining filling ingredients.
Put the spinach mixture on a cutting board. Using a large chef's knife, chop the mixture to a fine consistency (or puree the mixture in a food processor).

To assemble:

Put 1/2 inch of rock salt into the bottom of an ovenproof pan large enough to hold all of the oysters, or divide them between two pans.
Nestle the oysters (in their shells) into the salt; it will keep them level and retain the heat.
Spread 1 tablespoon of the spinach mixture over each oyster and sprinkle with breadcrumbs.
Bake for 10 minutes, or until the edges of the oysters begin to curl.
Serve immediately.

Note: Do not wash the oysters after shucking in order to keep the saline flavor.

Serves 2 to 3

Mackerel Dinner

BLACK BEAN SOUP ○ CORN STICKS ○ BAKED SPANISH MACKEREL ○ BURNT ALMOND-
AND-APRICOT ICE CREAM ○ Babcock Sauvignon Blanc, CA or Darioush Signature
Merlot, CA or Sweet Georgia Brown Ale, Sweetwater Brewery, GA

*Black bean soup and hot buttered corn sticks are a rich beginning to a meal. The Southern
penchant for using sherry to flavor soups is their little signature of elegance. Sherry in soup is not
everyone's preference, however, so use it with a light hand or serve it on the side. Spanish mackerel,
a Gulf fish, is available in profusion. When sparklingly fresh, it is very tasty.*

BLACK BEAN SOUP

INGREDIENTS

1 pound dried black beans

6 ounces smoked bacon, diced

2 medium yellow onions, finely chopped

3 quarts chicken stock (see Basics, page 332) or
   canned low-sodium chicken broth

1/8 teaspoon ground cloves

1/4 teaspoon cayenne pepper

1 cup mustard greens, washed, chopped,
   and packed

1 lemon, thinly sliced

Dry sherry

METHOD

Wash the beans thoroughly in cold water.

In a large pot, render the bacon until golden.

Drain bacon on paper towels.

Add the onions to the fat and cook until wilted.

Add the stock and beans, bring to a boil, and
   reduce the heat to a simmer.

Add the spices and simmer for 2 to 2 1/2 hours, until
   the beans are soft.

Add the mustard greens and cook for 1 hour more.

Serve in warmed soup bowls with a thin slice
   of lemon.

Top with of spoonful of dry sherry at the table.

Serves 6 to 8

CORN STICKS

INGREDIENTS

1 cup all-purpose flour

1 cup yellow cornmeal

1 tablespoon baking powder

1 1/2 teaspoons salt

1 1/2 teaspoons sugar

1 cup buttermilk or milk

2 tablespoons butter, melted

2 eggs, lightly beaten

Bacon fat

SPECIAL TOOLS

Cast-iron corn-stick mold

METHOD

Preheat the oven to 400° F.

In a large bowl, mix together the dry ingredients.

Stir in the buttermilk, butter, and eggs.

Generously grease the corn-stick mold with
   bacon fat and place in the oven for 5 minutes,
   or until smoking.

Remove the mold from the oven and spoon batter
   into each mold until 1/3 full and quickly
   return the mold to the oven and bake for 12 to
   15 minutes, or until golden.

Remove the cornsticks, regrease the mold with
   bacon fat and repeat until all of the batter is used.

Makes 1 1/2 dozen corn sticks

BAKED SPANISH MACKEREL

INGREDIENTS

3 to 4 tablespoons melted butter

One 4-pound or two 2 1/2-pound Spanish mackerels,
    cleaned, gutted with head and tail intact

4 strips lemon zest

4 strips orange zest

1 sprig rosemary

1 tablespoon fresh rosemary, chopped

2 ripe tomatoes, peeled, seeded, and thinly sliced

2 dozen green and black Italian or Greek olives

Freshly milled black pepper

4 large scallions, thinly sliced

Two 2-ounce cans anchovy fillets, drained of oil
    and patted dry

SPECIAL TOOLS

Parchment paper

METHOD

Preheat the oven to 375° F.

Place a piece of aluminum foil large enough to
    envelop the fish on a baking sheet.

Line the foil with a large sheet of
    parchment paper.

Brush the bottom of the parchment with melted
    butter and place the fish on top.

Stuff the cavity with the citrus zest and sprig
    of rosemary.

Scatter all of the remaining ingredients except the
    anchovies on and around the fish.

Arrange the anchovies on top of the fish in
    herringbone fashion.

Tightly wrap the fish in the parchment and foil and
    bake for 10 minutes for every inch of thickness.

Place on a platter and serve.

Note: If you have two fish, place them side by side
and cook together, in one package.

Serves 4

BURNT ALMOND-AND-APRICOT ICE CREAM

INGREDIENTS

1 quart English Cream (made with 1/3 cup sugar;
    see Basics, page 337)

2 cups dried apricots

1/3 cup bourbon

1/2 cup sugar

1 cup slivered blanched almonds

SPECIAL TOOLS

Ice cream machine

METHOD

Chill the English Cream.

Place the apricots in a small saucepan.

Cover with the bourbon and enough cold water
    to cover.

Simmer over moderate heat until the apricots
    plump up and soften.

Remove from heat and cool.

Place the sugar in a small heavy skillet and melt
    over moderate heat, stirring with a wooden
    spoon just until it starts to caramelize.

Immediately remove from heat.

Fold in the almonds and pour onto a sheet of
    waxed paper.

Place the apricots in a food processor with 1/2 cup
    of the bourbon liquid and pulse on and off 5
    or 6 times.

The apricots should be chunky.

Place a sheet of waxed paper over the almonds
    and lightly crush with a rolling pin.

Stir the apricots and almonds into the English
Cream and place the mixture in an ice
    cream machine.

Freeze according to the manufacturer's directions.

Makes 1 1/2 quarts

Jambalaya

SHRIMP JAMBALAYA ○ ORANGE AMBROSIA AND PRALINES ○ Abita Amber Beer, LA

Jambalaya is as famous a Creole-Cajun dish as gumbo. Howard Mitcham, who wrote a wonderful entertaining book entitled Creole Gumbo and All That Jazz, *suggests that the word "jambalaya is probably derived from 'jambon,' which means ham in both Spanish and French. The 'a-la-ya' is probably an African expletive, which can be interpreted as either acclaim or derision." Though the tendency is to include a mess of spices, sausages, ham, and tasso, as well as okra, I prefer this simple version which plays up the shrimp. Rice is traditionally incorporated and cooked into the jambalaya. I like it served on the side.*

SHRIMP JAMBALAYA

INGREDIENTS
1/4 pound unsalted butter
1 medium yellow onion, minced
4 medium cloves garlic, minced
1 cup celery, very thinly sliced
3 green or red bell peppers, seeded, deveined,
    and cut into long julienne
4 to 5 semi-hot frying peppers, seeded, deveined,
    and cut into long julienne
3 medium tomatoes, peeled, seeded,
    and chopped
2 pounds medium shrimp, peeled with tails intact
1 cup Fish Stock (see Basics, page 333),
    or shrimp stock
Salt and cayenne pepper

METHOD
In a large skillet, melt the butter over
    moderate heat.
Wilt the onions in the butter.
Add the garlic and all of the vegetables and
    simmer over low heat.
When the vegetables are still slightly crisp, add the
    shrimp and the stock.

Bring to a simmer, season to taste, cover, and cook
    for approximately 5 minutes, until the shrimp are
    just cooked through.
Do not overcook the shrimp.
Serve with boiled white rice.

Serves 6

ORANGE AMBROSIA

INGREDIENTS
6 navel oranges
1/2 cup Grand Marnier
1 cup fresh, shaved coconut

METHOD
Slice the ends off each orange, and remove all
  the peel and pith.
Slice each orange 1/4-inch thick and arrange
  on a platter.
Sprinkle with Grand Marnier.
Cover tightly with plastic wrap and refrigerate for
  at least 1 hour.
Remove 15 to 20 minutes before serving.
Uncover and sprinkle with the coconut.

Serves 6

PRALINES

INGREDIENTS
2 cups sugar
1/2 cup heavy cream
1 cup pecan pieces, toasted (see Basics, page 337)

SPECIAL TOOLS
Candy thermometer

METHOD
In a heavy saucepan, combine 1 1/2 cups of the
  sugar and the cream over moderately high heat.
Stir the mixture until the sugar begins to melt.
Place the thermometer in the mixture and cook
  until it registers 220° F or the soft-ball stage.
Meanwhile, place the remaining 1/2 cup sugar in a
  heavy saucepan and stir constantly over
  moderately high heat until the sugar melts and
  begins to turn a golden caramel color.
Pour the hot cream mixture into the caramelized
  sugar and stir in the pecans.
With a large soup or dessert spoon, immediately
  spoon out the mixture onto a cool marble
  surface or into a sheet of parchment paper.
Allow to cool.

Note: Pralines will keep for a week in an airtight
container. They are best served when fresh.

Makes 2 to 2 1/2 dozen

Soul Food

CATFISH WITH SESAME SEEDS ○ WHITE REMOULADE ○ HUSH PUPPIES ○ WATERMELON ○
Grgich Hills Fume Blanc, CA or Terrapin Rye Pale Ale, GA

In Plantation times, slaves ate differently from everybody else. From the "largesse" of their owners, and with the wild greens and roots they scavenged, they defied the meagerness of these offerings and created a cooking of their own, calling it "soul food." The best catfish are the firm, sweet bullheaded ones from the channels of Louisiana. It's an ugly fish, but it fillets well and is close to flounder in texture. Catfish has caught the fancy of the American public, and catfish farms from Texas to Arkansas are flourishing. Hush puppies are yet another cornbread invention of African American cooks, a bread so rustic that it didn't make it into the formal lexicon of plantation recipes.

1 tablespoon capers, washed, drained,
  and chopped
1/4 cup sour gherkin pickles, finely chopped
1/2 teaspoon Worcestershire sauce
1/4 teaspoon cayenne pepper
1/4 cup fresh parsley, finely chopped
3 anchovy fillets, mashed
Juice of 1/2 lemon

METHOD
In a bowl, whisk together all of the ingredients and
  chill for 1 hour before serving.

Makes approximately 2 1/2 cups

HUSH PUPPIES

INGREDIENTS
1/2 cup white or yellow cornmeal
1/2 cup all-purpose flour
1/2 teaspoon salt
1 teaspoon baking powder
1/2 teaspoon sugar
1 egg beaten
Approximately 1/4 cup milk
1 jalapeño pepper, finely chopped
4 scallions, including some of the green,
  finely chopped
1/8 teaspoon cayenne pepper
Vegetable oil, for frying

METHOD
Sift the dry ingredients into a mixing bowl.
Add the beaten egg and enough of the milk to
  make a light paste.
Add the jalapeño pepper, scallions, and cayenne
  pepper and blend thoroughly.
In a large heavy deep pot, heat at least 2 inches
  of the oil until it just begins to smoke.
Drop the batter by the tablespoonfuls into the hot
  fat and fry until golden.

Makes approximately 1 dozen

CATFISH WITH SESAME SEEDS

INGREDIENTS
1 pound catfish fillets
1/2 cup yellow cornmeal
1/2 cup all-purpose flour
Salt and freshly milled black pepper
1/4 pound lard or unsalted butter
1/4 cup sesame seeds, toasted in a dry skillet

METHOD
Wash and pat the fish with dry paper towels.
Cut the catfish diagonally into 1-inch strips.
In a shallow pan, combine the cornmeal, flour, salt
  and pepper to taste.
Lightly dredge the fish in the cornmeal mixture.
Melt the lard or butter in a large skillet and pan-fry
  the catfish until golden brown.
Drain on paper towels.
Sprinkle the fish with the toasted sesame seeds and
  serve with White Remoulade.

Serves 2 to 3

WHITE REMOULADE

INGREDIENTS
2 cups homemade mayonnaise
  (see Basics, page 334) or Hellman's
1 clove garlic, finely chopped
4 scallions, including some of the green,
  finely chopped

Stone Crab Lunch

STONE CRAB CLAWS ○ MUSTARD MAYONNAISE ○ CHOPPED SALAD (See page 180) ○ CUBAN BREAD ○ KEY LIME PIE ○ Clos du Val Chardonnay, CA or Chateau Montelena Winery Chardonnay, CA or Dunedin Piper's Pale Ale, FL

Winter stone crabs, looking like bright red parrot heads with jet-black beaks, are bought fully cooked because they are steamed and refrigerated aboard ship as soon as they are caught. Only the claw of the crab is kept, and this crustacean is thrown back into the sea to grow another. There is some debate about which crust is the best with key lime pie: the graham cracker version or a flaky butter crust? Here, we use the latter.

MUSTARD MAYONNAISE

INGREDIENTS

4 egg yolks, at room temperature

Salt and freshly milled pepper

1 teaspoon Dijon-style mustard

1 tablespoon dry mustard

1/4 teaspoon cayenne pepper

3/4 cup olive oil

3/4 cup vegetable oil

2 tablespoons fresh lemon juice

1 tablespoon boiling water

METHOD

Place the yolks, salt, pepper, mustard, dry mustard, and cayenne pepper in the bowl of an electric mixer or food processor and beat at high speed for 2 minutes, or until the mixture is creamy.

In a thin stream, gradually add the oils, beating all the while until thickened.

Add the lemon juice and adjust the seasonings to taste.

Add the boiling water and mix for 2 to 3 seconds, just until incorporated.

Refrigerate the mayonnaise in a covered container.

Serve the mayonnaise with very well-chilled stone crabs.

Makes about 1 1/2 cups

KEY LIME PIE

INGREDIENTS

4 egg yolks

1 14-ounce can sweetened condensed milk

1/2 cup of freshly squeezed lime juice, preferably from key limes

1 teaspoon finely grated lime zest (scrub the lime if it is not organic)

6 egg whites

1/4 teaspoon cream of tartar

3/4 cup of sugar

1 prebaked single 9-inch pie crust, cooled to room temperature (see Basics, page 335)

METHOD

Preheat oven to 325° F.

To make the filling:

In a medium-sized bowl, beat the egg yolks until lemon colored.

Blend in the sweetened condensed milk slowly, then add the lime juice and zest and mix well.

Set aside.

To make the meringue:

Put the egg whites into a grease-free, medium-sized bowl, along with the cream of tartar.

Beat the egg whites until they are very soft and foamy, then add the sugar in a a slow, continuous stream until stiff, glossy peaks form.

Fold 6 tablespoons of the meringue into the filling mixture and pour into the pie crust.

Mound the remaining meringue on top of the pie, spreading it gently until it touches the edges of the pie crust. Swirl decorative peaks into the surface.

Bake in a slow oven until golden brown.

Remove from oven, cool to room temperature, then refrigerate for at least 4 hours before serving.

Serves 6 to 8

Street Food

The Oyster Bar

There was a time when oyster bars offered up a platter of these succulent bivalves for the price of a five-cent beer. Times have changed, but the good oyster bars, scattered throughout the old quarter of town, serve forth these plump refreshers on shells still coated with the salty mud from the oysters beds. From morning until night you can step up to the counter and indulge in these luscious oysters, saucing them to suit your taste. Ketchup, horseradish, hot sauces, and lemons are set out on the bar to allow the patrons to stir up their own concoctions.

Mandiche's Po' Boy

The po' boy was known as the peacemaker. After a night of hooch and jazz, the typical wayward husband brought home this toasted loaf of French bread filled with succulent fried oysters as an early Sunday morning peace offering to his wife.

MANDICHE'S PO' BOY

INGREDIENTS
Sauce:

1 cup olive oil

1 head of garlic, peeled and finely chopped

3 scallions, including some of the green, chopped

1 teaspoon salt

1/4 teaspoon freshly milled pepper

1 1/2 teaspoons cold water

2 tablespoons dry sherry

Sandwich:

1/2 loaf of French bread, halved lengthwise

3 tablespoons unsalted melted butter

1 quart vegetable oil, for deep-frying

1 dozen oysters, shucked

2 eggs, beaten

1 cup all-purpose flour

1 tablespoon fresh parsley, chopped

SPECIAL TOOLS
Deep-fat frying thermometer

METHOD
Prepare the sauce:

Combine all of the ingredients except the sherry in a medium saucepan and bring to a boil.

Reduce the heat and simmer until the garlic is soft.

Remove from heat and stir in the sherry. Set aside.

Prepare the sandwich:

Preheat the oven to 400° F.

Generously brush the French bread with melted butter and place it on a baking on a sheet.

Bake for 10 minutes, or until the edges are brown.

In a deep pot, heat the oil to 365° F.

Dip the oysters in the beaten eggs and dust them lightly in flour.

Deep-fry until golden and crisp.

Drain on paper towels.

Quickly dip the oysters into the sauce and place on the bottom half of the French bread.

Sprinkle with the parsley and serve hot.

Serves 1

Sazerac

Of all the drinks to come out of the watering holes of the Delta and the Quarter—the fizzes, punches, café brulots, and café diablos—the Sazerac is without doubt one of the world's great mixtures, on par with the Negroni for taste and the Martini for the skill required to make it right. Originally the recipe called for the Sazerac glass to be lightly coated with absinthe (which is, of course, no longer available) and Peychaud bitters, a Creole creation of Antoine Amedea Peychaud who brought his recipe from Haiti. The Sazerac cocktail was invented at the Sazerac Bar in New Orleans.

SAZERAC

INGREDIENTS
4 drops Herbsaint or Pernod
Ice cubes
3 ounces rye or bourbon
1/2 to 1 ounce Simple Syrup (see Basics, page 337)
4 to 5 dashes Angostura or Peychaud bitters
Small strip of lemon zest

SPECIAL TOOLS
Cocktail pitcher and stirrer
1 double old fashioned glass

METHOD
Swirl the Herbsaint around the glass and discard any excess.
Place 6 to 8 ice cubes in a pitcher and pour in the rye, simple syrup, and bitters.
Stir briskly and strain into the glass.
Add 1 ice cube.
Twist the lemon zest over the top of the liquor.

Serves 1

Pecans

The ubiquitous Southern pecan is served in many guises. Here the pecans are warmed, coated with a little butter and salt. It's the perfect predinner nibble and pairs perfectly with the Sazerac.

TOASTED PECANS

INGREDIENTS
1 pound shelled pecan halves
6 tablespoons butter, melted
1 tablespoon kosher salt

METHOD
Preheat the oven to 325° F.
Toss the pecans with the melted butter and spread out on a baking sheet.
Toast, stirring, for about 10 minutes, or until the nuts begin to turn lightly golden.
Remove and place in a paper bag.
Add the salt and shake.
Serve warm.

Makes 1 pound

MIDWEST

MIDWEST

America is often thought of as a nation overrun with cattle and gorged on wheat. Our anthem invokes "amber waves of grain," but the early years of the Midwest saw neither wheat nor beef. Instead there were patches of Indian maize, and waves of buffalo blackened the plains. Wheat only drifted into this region from the Atlantic coast in the early 1780s, immediately taking hold and flourishing. By the mid-nineteenth century, the prairies of Illinois, Indiana, and Wisconsin had become the great wheat producers; by 1870 the hard, matted grass of Kansas and Nebraska had turned to gold.

Man can in fact live almost by bread alone (although butter and wine do much to help). Entire nations depend on bread, and this country's Plains states remain, as they have been for more than a century, the "bread basket of the world." Many civilized cultures consider bread not a mere supplement to a meal, but the meal itself. Wheat has always been the premier grain for bread baking here, because it contains gluten, which in combination with the action of yeast makes a light, leavened bread. (Commercial wheat is grown principally to make different types of flour: common or "bread" flour, cake flour for pastries, and durum for noodles.) Wheat keeps and travels well, and was carried whenever possible by settlers bound for wheat-barren lands. This grain was something the Puritans had missed, and was a prestigious addition the Southern gentry insisted upon. Pioneer wagons rolling over the grazing fields of the buffalo carried as much as 200 pounds of flour per family for their journey. The simple meal settlers ate when they paused along the trail was "journeycake" or "johnnycake." An "X" was cut into a sack of flour, and water poured in; the flour which absorbed the water was used immediately, baked on boards set next to an open fire or in hastily assembled Dutch ovens (cast-iron pots with fitted lids, set right among the coals, like makeshift ovens).

Wheat is our luxury grain, and we have refined it more than any other. Huge quantities of the other cereal grains, such as corn, soybeans, oats, and barley, nourish us less directly as fodder for the animals on which we feed. About one-quarter of the millions of bushels of barley grown every year is used to produce alcoholic beverages, such as beer and whiskey.

For the nineteenth-century American, the Western horizon seemed endless. The population of the East grew dramatically, the slave controversy in the South escalated, and families of modest means were lured west in search of land and better lives. The Kansas-Nebraska Act of 1854 caused a homesteading fever that swept through the country from every New England town to every Southern city. Wagons were loaded with carpetbags and trunks, supplied with tins of crackers, dried apples, pounds of flour, cornmeal, sugar, rice, and salt pork, and drawn by ox or mule. No corner of the wagon was left empty, and some pioneers used wooden washtubs to plant little fruit trees for tending along the way. Some live chickens and perhaps a cow were indispensable for a family with children. Babies were lulled to sleep by the bumping up and down of the wagon, and women often walked the entire journey, boarding only now and again to churn butter to the heaving rhythm of the cart. As perilous as the journey itself was, the calamities in store for homesteaders when they reached their destination were even more daunting: American Indian raids, droughts, fires, hail storms, cyclones, rattlesnakes, wolves, outlaws, and plagues of locusts. Farmers have always had to contend with disaster.

Kansas became a focal point in the slave debate: the North wanted it to remain free while the South hoped to claim it as a slave state. After the Civil War, the pioneers were joined by the destitute, by freed slaves, and by widows with money to invest in land—all of them eager to start life anew. Alexis de Tocqueville wrote on October 2, 1831, "Sparks said to me today, 'Landed estates in Massachusetts are no longer being divided up. The eldest always inherits the whole of the land.' 'And what happens to the other children?' I asked. 'They emigrate to the West.'"

Many of the pioneer women transplanted from the cities to the plains found a very different life awaiting them. "Women's work" included seeding fields, herding cattle, tending animals, and washing, nursing, and feeding their young. The prairie woman became an expert marksman, not only to hunt for food, but to protect her brood as well. If married, her life was a partnership in which she shouldered the fearsome burdens of prairie survival equally with her husband. If on her own, she shouldered it all.

The early Midwest diet was high in salt pork, fried beef, eggs, milk, butter, buckwheat cakes, potato cakes, johnnycakes, and sometimes a good dose of mercury from wells dug in the developing mining areas. Here again, corn was king, and every pioneer table used corn flour for bread, mush, grits, or pudding (white flour was so hard to come by that when available, its price was gold). Sorghum, the "sugar of the plains," was a sweetener, sometimes boiled down to syrup. In the mid-nineteenth century this cereal grain ranked fourth after wheat, rice, and maize, and in time was used to fatten cattle before they were driven from the Texas Panhandle to Kansas.

In 1874, 34 Russian Mennonites were given free transportation by the Santa Fe Railroad to Kansas, where the government had set aside an 8,000 acre tract for them to farm. Among their few belongings was a jar of drought-resistant winter wheat called Turkey Red, later to become one of the most valuable strains of wheat farmed in this country. Other European immigrants would settle the Plains states: Germans flocked to Ohio and into Missouri, the Dutch to Michigan, the Swiss to Wisconsin along with the Swedes and Norwegians, who also moved deeper into the northern regions.

For some, emigration to the Midwest was merely a stop on the long haul to the very western end of the continent. By the end of the nineteenth century, the United States was in an unprecedented state of flux. The railroads had opened the country, and with them came industrialization. With workers now going to factories instead of fields, the noonday lunch was now packed in a lunch box. The same railroad that brought kegs of salted mackerel and barrels of fresh oysters to the tables of the Midwestern well-to-do returned East with smoked buffalo tongues for restaurants or for export to Europe as novelty food. The dairymen of Iowa and Wisconsin had overstocked cheese sheds filled with cheddars, blues similar to those of Scandinavia, and wonderful imitations of Swiss, so cheese veined the country following the railroad lines. By the close of the century, refrigerator cars, modeled after home iceboxes, were swiftly transporting perishables in every direction.

This was a new age of advertising. Packaged cake mixes found a ready market, while at the same time, flour mills and baking powder and chocolate companies offered recipes appealing to the sweet tooth with every purchase. American cookbooks proliferated, and *Fannie Farmer* was the cooking bible until Rombauer and Becker and their *The Joy of Cooking* took its place in the 1930s.

The American housewife was much taken with desserts, and her repertoire included dozens of versions of rich devil's food cake, marble cake, tea cake, spice cake, angel food cake, and coconut and cream pies. There were taffies, puddings, and junket and gelatin salads (the *pièce montée* crowning the tables of a thriving middle class). The kitchen hearth was replaced by cast-iron, nickel-trimmed cookstoves. Visitors to the 1893 Chicago World's Fair were dazzled by the first electric kitchen and by a snack called Crackerjacks. German wurst makers from Wisconsin put forth the frankfurter on a roll with mustard, and the hamburger on a bun was introduced at the 1904 St. Louis Fair.

In rural areas, the main meal was still usually served at home at noontime. In the thriving cities (such as Chicago, the grain-receiving center and on its way to becoming the meatpacking metropolis of the country), the worker carried his lunch pail and the wealthy dined out. Chop houses, restaurants, oyster bars, and saloons had a booming lunch business. With a nickel beer or shot of whiskey, the customer was offered a free lunch and stuffed himself from a display of hams, ribs, roasts, sausages, herring, pickled eggs, pig's feet, stews, beans, and potato salad. From Boston to Denver, baronial luncheons were served from silver trays and tureens in oak-paneled halls resplendent with linen, china, crystal, and service to match. Equally plush were the dining cars featuring fresh delicacies from the regions the trains crossed: crab imperial, oysters, and bisques on the Boston-Ohio route, and terrapin stews and barons of beef served up with potatoes on the Kansas-Pacific Railroad.

By 1850, the Kansas-Pacific line offered daily excursions into buffalo country, including refreshments and a guaranteed kill. An efficient sporting party could kill 20 to 50 buffalo in a day, and with the development of a Smith and Wesson rifle . . . unfortunately, the rest is history. Buffalo were occasional nuisances to the railroads, which encouraged these excursions (sometimes trains had to wait three hours for a herd to pass over the tracks). But it was the buffalo that gave the American Indian independence. They were a source of food, clothing, bedding, saddlebags, tepees, shields,

utensils, and ornaments. American Indians used every bit of the animals: the marrow-filled bones were roasted, the tongues smoked, flesh "jerked" (cut into long strips and sun-dried for winter use), and pemmican made with the addition of berries and nuts (just as natives of the East and North made pemmican with venison, elk, and moose). Hunts ended with a feast of thankful celebration, honoring the beast that was God's gift to them.

When white hunters traveled to the plains, it was to hunt buffalo. Great herds once grazed as far north as Montana, down through Wyoming and Nebraska, to Colorado and Kansas, to the Texas panhandle. The U.S. Army encouraged white hunters with free ammunition. A large beast of small intelligence, the buffalo must have been a pathetically docile target. When threatened, the bulls would encircle their cows and calves, snorting and pounding the grass with their hooves. Facing their enemies, with heads bowed, they were an easy kill, dead center in the forehead. (Most of the buffalo skulls and horns that decorate homes of the Plains bear witness to this.) As each bull fell, his brethren would tighten their protective circle until all had been killed, leaving the defenseless cows for the final slaughter. The creature's hides were sold to tanners for lap throws, and buffalo steaks were more fashionable than the beef T-bone in the East. Taking only a haunch or two for their own provisions, the hunters left most of the carcass to the wolves and vultures. When the hunting season of 1883 came to a close, the northern buffalo was wiped out. The remaining herds perished soon after. Gradually cattle took their place in huge numbers, and land not used for grazing gave itself up to the farmer and his crops.

Breakfast

SOFT BOILED EGGS ○ BACON ○ JASON'S BLUEBERRY MUFFINS ○ MILK

This simple child's breakfast is reminiscent of trips to my grandmother's house, when she and I would go out to the hen house. We'd shoo the hens away and take the still-warm eggs from the straw straight to the kitchen to be boiled up for me. The memory of this creamy, rich, orange-yellow yolk is difficult to capture today except from the eggs of free-range chickens. Hot blueberry muffins accompanied with a glass of cold milk are a delight for children of all ages.

JASON'S BLUEBERRY MUFFINS

INGREDIENTS

2 tablespoons butter, for greasing the muffin tins

2 cups all-purpose flour

1 cup blueberries

1 tablespoon baking powder

1 teaspoon salt

1/2 cup sugar

2 tablespoons butter, melted

2 eggs, lightly beaten

1 cup buttermilk

1 teaspoon grated lemon peel

1 teaspoon vanilla extract

METHOD

Lightly butter a 12-cup muffin tin and set aside.

Preheat the oven to 400° F.

In a small bowl, toss 1/4 cup of the flour with the blueberries and set aside.

In a large mixing bowl, combine the remaining 1 3/4 cups flour, baking powder, salt, and sugar.

Blend in the melted butter, eggs, and buttermilk until just combind.

Add the grated lemon peel and the vanilla extract.

Fold in the blueberries and fill the muffin cups two-thirds full.

Bake for 20 minutes.

Allow the muffins to set for 2 to 3 minutes before removing from the tin.

Serve warm.

Makes 1 dozen

Steakhouse Meal

STEAK ○ CHOPPED SALAD ○ SARATOGA CHIPS ○ FRENCH FRIED ONIONS ○
CHEESECAKE ○ Silver Oak Cabernet Sauvignon, CA or Free State Copperhead
Pale Ale, KS

I am from a generation that grew up on meat and potatoes. By the beginning of the twentieth century, the Midwest had graduated from the frugal pork barrel to steak and potatoes, the most solid meal in the American repertoire and simple American cooking at its best. Generations of families sat down to an evening meal consisting of meat, potatoes, gravy, and a green vegetable. This was our standard up until the 1960s. Since then the reputation and preference for beef has fluctuated. For many of us meat will remain a part of our diets as well as our pleasure. We can be thankful for the cattlemen today who are raising hormone-free, organic, range-fed beef.

STEAK

METHOD

Pan-fried method:

Club steak, T-bone, porterhouse, shell, and sirloin steaks can be adequately pan-fried over high heat in cast-iron skillets with a little oil or butter.

The best method I have found for home cooking is to choose a well-marbled steak that is 2 to 2$^{1}/_{2}$ inches thick.

Remove the meat from the refrigerator at least 45 minutes before cooking.

Salt and pepper the steak.

Brush a cast iron skillet with a light film of oil and place over medium-high heat.

When the pan is hot, sear the meat for 3 minutes on each side, at which point a light brown crust should form.

Place in preheated 250° F oven for 7 to 10 minutes to cook rare or medium rare.

Remove from the oven.

Place on a carving board and let rest for 5 minutes before slicing.

Grilling method:

Prepare a hardwood charcoal fire.

When the coals reach a dusty red glow, lightly brush the grill with oil.

Salt and pepper the steaks and sear for 4 to 5 minutes on each side or until the cooked side is a rich, light crusty brown.

Do not allow to char or the meat will toughen.

Place the meat in an oven preheated to 325° F and cook for 5 to 10 minutes, or until done to your preference.

Experienced cooks can test for doneness by pressing their index finger into the center of the steak; for those less experienced, the best (but not most efficient) way is to cut into the center with a sharp paring knife.

CHOPPED SALAD

INGREDIENTS

1 head garden lettuce, such as buttercrunch,
   loose-leaf, or oak leaf
1 medium-sized red bell pepper, cored, seeded,
   deviened, and finely diced
2 ears fresh sweet corn, cooked and
   kernels removed
2 ripe tomatoes, peeled, seeded, and chopped
1 small cucumber, peeled, seeded, and chopped
1 celery heart, finely chopped
8 red radishes, chopped
1 tablespoon capers, washed, drained,
   and chopped
6 anchovies, drained and chopped
$1/4$ cup olive oil
3 tablespoons red wine vinegar
Salt and freshly milled black pepper

METHOD

Place the vegetables in separate bowls, cover,
   and refrigerate until ready to serve.
When ready to serve combine the vegetables in a
   large mixing bowl with the capers and
   anchovies and toss with the oil and vinegar.
Season to taste and serve.

Serves 4 to 6

SARATOGA CHIPS

INGREDIENTS
4 Idaho potatoes
1 quart vegetable oil
Salt

SPECIAL TOOLS
Mandoline
Deep fryer and basket

METHOD
Peel and wash the potatoes.
Using a mandoline, thinly slice the potatoes
   $1/8$-inch thick.
Place the slices in a bowl of ice water and set

aside for 30 minutes.
Drain and dry thoroughly with paper towels.
Pour the oil into a deep fryer and heat to 360° F.
Test one slice to judge how hot the oil is and how
   quickly the potato cooks.
Working in cup batches, place the potatoes
   into the oil and stir lightly, using a wooden spoon.
When the potatoes are crisp and golden, remove
   the basket from the oil, shake lightly, and drain
   the potatoes on paper towels.
Repeat the process with the remaining potatoes.
Sprinkle with salt and serve.

Serves 4

FRENCH FRIED ONIONS

INGREDIENTS
4 medium-sized Spanish, Vidalia or Walla Walla
   onions, sliced $1/4$-inch thick
$1/2$ cup all-purpose flour
1 quart vegetable oil
Salt

SPECIAL TOOLS
Deep fryer and basket

METHOD
In a large bowl, toss together the onions with
   the flour.
Pour the oil into the deep fryer and heat to 360° F.
Approximately 1 cup at a time, add the onions
   and fry until golden brown.
Drain the onions on paper towels and repeat the
   process with the remaining onions. Sprinkle
   with salt
Serve hot.

Serves 4

Street Food

Barbecued Ribs

Eating fast in the West is eating big and hearty. Even food-on-the-run is substantial. No dainty sandwiches appear here. Connoisseurs maintain that the best barbecued meat is served in Texas, but the best barbecued ribs are in Kansas. Coleslaw, beans, potato salad, and white bread fill up the plate, and hot pepper sauce is always on hand.

HANK COLEMAN'S BARBECUE SAUCE

INGREDIENTS
4 cups ketchup (see Basics, page 335) or bottled Heinz ketchup
Grated zest of 1 large lemon
Juice of 2 large lemons
1/4 cup Creole mustard
2 tablespoons Trappey's Louisiana Red Sauce or 1 1/2 tablespoons Tabasco sauce
1/4 cup Worcestershire sauce
2 tablespoons molasses
2 tablespoons sugar
1 clove garlic, chopped
2 tablespoons red wine vinegar

METHOD
In a large saucepan, combine all of the sauce ingredients and warm over low heat.
Do not allow to simmer or bubble.
Remove the sauce from the heat and set aside to cool until ready to use.
Prepare a hardwood charcoal fire. Add soaked hickory wood or mesquite wood chips for a distinctly smoky flavor. Place the sauce in an old metal pot and set close to the smoking fire to absorb the smoke flavor.

Note: The sauce on the side of the fire will continue to absorb the smoke which acts as a preservative. Stored airtight in the refrigerator, the sauce will keep for weeks.

The sauce may be used for 4 pounds of ribs (single or rack), a 4-pound brisket, or 3 halved or quartered chickens.

Makes approximately 5 cups

BARBECUED RIBS OR CHICKEN

METHOD
When preparing ribs for the grill, weave the cut ribs on a spit. If using a rack of ribs, coat the meat with the sauce before placing the rack directly on the grill.
Baste the meats frequently during cooking. The ribs should be placed about 6 to 8 inches above the coals and grilled for 40 to 45 minutes or until evenly browned. Watch carefully and do not over char. Adjust the level of the grill accordingly.
When grilling chicken, follow the basting method above.

Evenly brown the cut chicken, skin side down, for
    7 to 8 minutes on each side. Place the chicken
    pieces in an oven preheated to 350° F for 10 to
    15 minutes, depending on the size of the pieces.

To "barbecue" in the oven:
Preheat the oven to 325° F.
Place the ribs in a shallow baking pan and cover
    with half the sauce.
Bake the ribs in the center of the oven for 45 to 60
    minutes, depending on the size of the ribs.
Baste frequently and serve with the remaining
    barbecue sauce.

OVEN-BRAISED BARBECUED BRISKET

INGREDIENTS
4 to 5 pound brisket, covered with 1/4 inch of fat
Kosher salt and freshly milled pepper
2 cups chicken or beef stock (see Basics, page 332)
    or canned low-sodium chicken or beef broth
5 cups Hank Coleman's Barbecue Sauce

METHOD
Preheat the oven to 325° F.
Let the brisket come to room temperature.
Salt and pepper the meat.
Heat a large heavy skillet over moderately
    high heat.
Brown the brisket, fat-side down, for 3 to 4 minutes,
    or until a crust is formed.
Turn and brown the other side.
Place the brisket in a shallow baking pan with the
    chicken stock and bake for 2 hours.
Generously coat the brisket on both sides with half
    of the sauce.
Return to the oven and continue to bake for 2 to 3
    hours, or until tender.
Remove and let the brisket rest for 10 minutes
    before slicing.
Serve with the remaining barbecue sauce.

Lemonade

Lemonade is probably the most refreshing thirst-
quencher I can think of for the hot months of July
and August. It is a beverage I associate with
summers, laziness, reading a book, or doing
nothing—a part of civilized life. It should always be
made with pure lemon juice and sugar syrup—
tangy and not sweet. The tongue should smart
with more sour than sweet and the jaw should
squeak a little when you drink it.

LEMONADE

INGREDIENTS
4 cups simple syrup (see Basics, page 337)
3 cups lemon juice strained, approximately
    12 large lemons, strained
3 cups soda water
Mint sprigs

METHOD
Prepare the simple syrup.
Cool and refrigerate in a covered container.
In a large pitcher, combine 1 1/2 cups lemon juice
    with 1 cup simple syrup and 3 cups cold water.
Mix and pour into ice cube trays and freeze.
When ready to serve, combine the remaining
    lemon juice, simple syrup, and 3 cups soda
    water or ice water and mix. Pour over lemonade
    ice cubes.
Add a mint sprig, a straw, and serve.

Makes approximately 6 glasses

Thanksgiving

○

APPLE AND BUTTERNUT SQUASH SOUP

ROAST TURKEY WITH PAN GRAVY

CREAMED ONIONS

RUTABAGA AND APPLE PUREE

MASHED POTATOES

CRANBERRY AND KUMQUAT CONSERVE

NUT CONSERVE

WARM RED CHARD SALAD

MAYTAG IOWA BLUE CHEESE

CAPRIOLE FARMS INDIANA GOAT CHEESE

COWGIRL CREAMERY CALIFORNIA "MT. TAM"

SHELBURNE FARMS VERMONT CHEDDAR

PUMPKIN MOUSSE WITH CRYSTALIZED GINGER

HOT MINCEMEAT (See page 210) WITH RUM HARD SAUCE (See Basics, page 336)

○

A to Z Pinot Gris, Willamette Valley, Oregon
Stag's Leap Cabernet Sauvignon, California
Iron Horse Classic Vintage Brut, Sonoma, California

The tying of a few ears of maize to our doorways is a homey touch passed on to us by the American Indians, symbolizing the celebration of the harvest. In November of each year, our country stops to reflect and give thanks. We do it all with family and friends, more often than not dining on a big turkey. I like to think of those comforting smells wafting through the house. It is the one day when most of us are eating nearly the same celebratory meal, and usually too much of it. I love the idea of the proud golden bird brought to the table in succulent splendor. I like even more turning the leftover turkey into sandwiches, hash, and soup.

This meal is a rather odd assemblage of foods: creamed and puréed root vegetables, sweet relishes, and savory pies. Trying to match it with wines that complement the changing tastes of all these dishes is often difficult for the host. I suggest serving a white and a red and let your guests take their pick. Or you can serve a dry sparkling wine or champagne throughout the entire meal.

APPLE AND BUTTERNUT SQUASH SOUP

INGREDIENTS

2 tablespoons unsalted butter
2 large onions, chopped
2 tablespoons good quality curry powder
1 teaspoon chili powder
5 cups chicken stock, (see Basics, page 332) or canned low-sodium chicken stock
1 large butternut squash (approximately 8 cups peeled, seeded, and chopped)
3 firm, tart apples
Salt and freshly ground black pepper
1/2 cup heavy cream
1 tablespoon fresh parsley or fresh cilantro, chopped

METHOD

In a heavy skillet, melt the butter over medium heat.
Add the onions and sauté until translucent, approximately 5 minutes.
Add the curry and chili power and cook for another 5 minutes.
Add half the stock and bring to a boil.
Transfer the mixtures to a soup kettle, and add the squash and apples.
Bring to a boil, reduce the heat, and simmer for 45 minutes, or until the squash is tender.

Stir occasionally to prevent the vegetables from sticking to the pan.
Strain the soup and reserve the liquid.
Place the pulp in the bowl of a food processor and pulse until puréed.
Return the purée, reserved liquid, cream, and the remaining chicken stock to a clean soup kettle.
Season with salt and pepper and bring to a simmer.
Ladle the soup into warm soup bowls and sprinkle with chopped parsley or cilantro.

Note: The soup recipe can be doubled and made a day ahead or frozen without the cream.

Serves 10

ROAST TURKEY WITH PAN GRAVY

Note: If using the brine method, first follow the instructions on page 188.

INGREDIENTS

12- to 14-pound turkey, brined (see page 188)
6 to 8 cups stuffing (see page 150)
Making stock:
2 celery ribs, chopped
1 medium carrot, chopped
1/2 onion, chopped
2 parsley sprigs

For roasting the turkey:
Vegetable oil or unsalted butter, for coating
the bird
2 celery ribs, cut in half
1 medium carrot, washed and cut lengthwise
1 1/2 onions, peeled and halved
1 cup black coffee for basting

For the gravy:
1/4 cup all-purpose flour (preferably Wondra)
Salt and freshly milled pepper

METHOD
Remove the bird from the brine and rinse,
then dry, thoroughly.
Remove the wing tips and chop the reserved
gizzard and heart.
In a small saucepan, combine the wing tips, neck,
gizzard, and heart, along with the vegetables for
the stock.
Add water to cover.
Bring to a boil over high heat, skim, and reduce
the heat to a simmer.
Continue to simmer for 1 1/2 hours or until the neck
and bones have fallen apart.
Add water as necessary to keep the ingredients
covered with liquid.
When the stock is cooked, strain and discard
the solids.
There will be about 2 cups of stock.
Meanwhile, stuff and truss the turkey.
Preheat oven to 450° F.
Coat the bird with oil or butter and place on a
rack in a roasting pan, and surround it with the
roasting vegetables.
Place in the oven and immediately reduce the
heat to 325° F.
After the first 30 minutes, baste the bird every 20
minutes or so with the pan drippings and spoon
a little of the coffee over the skin.
Cover with a large sheet of foil after the
first basting.
Continue to roast and baste with the pan juices
and coffee every 20 minutes.
Cook 15 to 20 minutes per pound, or until the
internal temperature reaches 165° F, or until the
juices run clear after piercing the leg joint with a
kitchen fork. (Use an instant-read thermometer
to determine the internal temperature of
the turkey.)
Remove the foil during the last 30 minutes to brown
the bird.
Remove the bird from the oven and let rest while
you prepare the pan gravy.
Pour off all but 2 tablespoons of fat from the
roasting pan and blend in the flour and cook,
scraping up the crusty bits.
Add 2 cups of strained stock and cook, whisking
constantly until the gravy is smooth,
approximately 8 to 10 minutes.
Season to taste with salt and pepper.
Strain the gravy into a saucepan and keep warm
until ready to serve with the bird.

Note: For a 12- to 14-pound turkey you will need 6
to 8 cups of stuffing. If making the cornbread
stuffing, triple the recipe; if making the sausage
stuffing, double the recipe. This menu works nicely
for 12 to 24 people. Rather than preparing an
enormous bird, two smaller birds of 12 pounds
each are more delicious and give you a choice of
two stuffings. As time consuming as it is, a well-
basted bird will be the most tender.

Serves 10 to 12

BRINING INGREDIENTS
Note: If following the brine method, do not use
a Kosher or self-basting turkey. These birds are
already processed and would not respond well
to brining.
For the Brine:
2 cups Kosher salt
2 gallons cold water
Leftover celery and onion trimmings
Leftover parsley and herb trimmings
12 peppercorns, crushed
2 allspice berries, crushed

SPECIAL TOOLS
6 to 8 gallon stockpot (or substitute a large picnic
cooler) for brining the turkey

Instant-read cooking thermometer

BRINING METHOD

Overnight brining method:

In a large stockpot, dissolve the salt in the water, stirring occasionally.

Add the remaining ingredients and set aside.

Remove the giblets from the turkey and reserve.

Wash the turkey thoroughly under cold running water and drain.

Submerge the turkey in the brine, cover with waxed paper and refrigerate overnight or for 8 to 12 hours, turning over once.

Note: At holiday time refrigerator space is at a premium. If you do not have room in your refrigerator to brine the turkey overnight, proceed using the method that follows.

4-hour brining method:

Prepare the brine with an additional cup of salt.

Line a picnic cooler with a white plastic trash bag.

Set the turkey inside the bag and pour the brine over the bird.

Tie the bag closed, add a few frozen gel-packs, and fill the cooler with more ice before closing.

Place the cooler in a basement or garage where the temperature is in the 40s or below.

Remove the bird from the brine after 4 hours.

Note: The primary benefit of brining is to keep the bird moist. The turkey absorbs water during the brining process and may cook faster. This process also ensures that all parts of the turkey are at the same temperature if you are working with a frozen bird that you have thawed.

RUTABAGA AND APPLE PUREE

INGREDIENTS

2 large rutabagas, trimmed and cut into cubes

2 tart apples

1 tablespoon lemon juice

Salt and freshly milled white pepper

2 tablespoons unsalted butter (optional)

METHOD

Place the cubed rutabaga in a saucepan and cover with cold water.

Bring to a boil over high heat and cook until tender, approximately 20 to 25 minutes.

While the rutabaga is cooking, peel, halve, and core the apples.

Cut into 1-inch slices, place in a small saucepan with lemon juice, and cook over low heat until the apples are soft.

Stir from time to time to avoid the apples sticking to the pan.

Drain the rutabaga and place them in the bowl of a food processor with the softened apples.

Process until smooth, season, and fold in the butter.

Keep hot in a double boiler of simmering water until ready to serve.

Note: Turnips can be cooked and prepared in a similar way, substituting a cooked pear for the apples. A pound of turnips serve 7 to 8. The addition of the fruit sweetens these vegetables and softens their slightly bitter taste.

Serves 10

MASHED POTATOES

INGREDIENTS

5-pounds Yukon Gold or Idaho potatoes

$1^{3}/4$ cups milk

$2/3$ cup heavy cream

10 ounces (2 sticks) unsalted butter

Salt and freshly milled white pepper

$1/3$ cup of fresh herbs—any combination of parsley, sage, thyme, and tarragon (optional)

METHOD

Peel and quarter the potatoes and wash thoroughly in cold water.

Place the potatoes in a large stockpot and add enough cold water to cover by 3 inches.

Bring to a boil, and cook about 25 minutes or until their centers can be pierced easily with a pairing knife. Drain the potatoes, return them to the dry pot, and place a clean kitchen towel or a few layers of paper towel in the pot to absorb the steam.

Cover tightly and set aside.

In a saucepan scald the milk and cream.

Add the butter and allow the butter to melt over low heat.

Using an electric mixer with the paddle attachment, or a potato masher, break up the potatoes.

When they begin to break up, gradually add the milk mixture to the potatoes, increasing the speed until the potatoes are puréed, or whip them using a sturdy wooden spoon.

Depending on how dry the potatoes are, you may not require all of the milk mixture.

Season with salt and pepper and fold in the herbs.

Place the potatoes in the mixing bowl over a pot of simmering water.

Cover the bowl and keep warm over the hot water as you continue preparing the dinner.

When ready to serve, whip the potatoes with a large wooden spoon or metal whisk and, if necessary, add a little more milk and butter mixture to loosen the purée.

Serves 10 to 12

CRANBERRY AND KUMQUAT CONSERVE

INGREDIENTS

20 medium kumquats, seeded and chopped
1 pound fresh cranberries, washed and drained (approximately 4 cups)
3/4 cup maple syrup

METHOD

Combine all the ingredients in a heavy saucepan and bring to a simmer over moderate heat.

When the berries begin to pop, reduce the heat to very low and cover.

Continue to cook for 10 minutes, stirring occasionally to prevent sticking.

Remove from the heat and serve. The relish is a nice accompaniment with flapjacks, buckwheat cakes, game meats, birds, or sausages.

Makes approximately 3 cups

NUT CONSERVE

INGREDIENTS

9 navel oranges, cut in half and thinly sliced
2 lemons, cut in half, thinly sliced, and seeds removed
1 1/2 cups golden raisins
4 cups chopped walnuts
1 1/2 cups white grape juice
1/4 cup bourbon

METHOD

Combine all the ingredients in a large heavy saucepan.

Bring to a boil and immediately reduce the heat to a simmer.

Cook, stirring occasionally, for 1/2 hour, or until the mixture is the consistency of marmalade.

When cool, purée the conserve briefly in a food processor, pulsing on and off to produce a rough texture

Serve as an accompaniment to game meats and birds.

Makes approximately 2 quarts

PUMPKIN MOUSSE WITH CRYSTALIZED GINGER

INGREDIENTS

1 teaspoon unflavored gelatin
1/4 cup dark rum
6 eggs separated (set aside 2 yolks for another use)
1/2 cup sugar
1 cup pumpkin purée (a 2- to 3-pound pie pumpkin will yield 2 1/2 to 3 cups of pumpkin purée)

¹/4 teaspoon cinnamon

¹/4 teaspoon ground mace

¹/3 teaspoon ground cloves

1 cup heavy cream, whipped

¹/4 cup crystallized ginger, cut into julienne,
  for decoration

Whipped heavy cream, for decorating and serving

METHOD

In a double boiler, dissolve the gelatin in the rum
  over simmering water.

Remove from the heat and set aside.

Whisk 4 of the egg yolks with ¹/4 cup sugar until
  lemony in color and the mixture falls in ribbons
  from the whisk.

In a mixing bowl, combine the pumpkin purée, the
  dissolved gelatin and rum, and the spices.

Blend well and fold in to the yolk mixture.

Beat the 6 egg whites in an electric mixer.

When they begin to stiffen, gradually add the
remaining ¹/4 cup sugar, continuing to beat until
  the whites form stiff glossy peaks.

Whisk ¹/3 of the meringue into the pumpkin
  mixture and blend thoroughly.

Fold in the remaining meringue and whipped
  cream and mix lightly. Do not overblend,
  allowing some of the white to show through.

Turn the mixture into a serving bowl and freeze for
  20 minutes, or until set.

Place the bowl in the refrigerator for 4 hours, or
  until thoroughly chilled.

To serve, sprinkle with the ginger julienne or
  decorate with additional whipped cream, piped
  in a lattice fashion (using a pastry bag
  with a star tip).

Serve with additional unsweetened
  whipped cream.

Serves 6 to 8

NORTHERN REGIONS

NORTHERN REGIONS

The promise of big game was an irresistible lure to trappers and fur traders. These mountain men moved north, leaving behind the buffalo of the Great Plains. The mountains of the northern regions were rife with beaver, porcupine, rabbit, hare, black bear, elk, antelope, and moose. When the Lewis and Clark expedition reached the Yellowstone River in the spring of 1805, Lewis recorded, "We can scarcely cast our eyes in any direction without perceiving a deer, elk, buffalo, or antelope." In the warmer months a mountain dweller could easily dine on trout, fiddlehead ferns (from which they made a sort of bread), and an abundance of wild mushrooms. The territory was brilliant with summer's currants—red, yellow, black, and purple—which grew sweet in the valleys and tart along the craggy cliffs of the mountains. Summer was an explosion of wild raspberries, blackberries, and choke-cherries, and apple and plum branches were heavy with fruit. Pioneers dried as much food as they could to provide for them in the long winter months ahead. Fruits, of course, were saved along with walnuts, hazelnuts, and butternuts. In lean times, the dried cherries, apples, and nuts were mixed with a little flour and boiling water either to produce a rude fruitcake or to dress a boiled bird or hare. Many sustained themselves on roots alone, including the wild artichoke (similar to the Jerusalem artichoke) and the prairie turnip (or "prairie potato"), eaten raw or cooked. Elk and antelope were dried and jerked like the Plains buffalo, and early explorers found it leathery, but excellent for strengthening teeth, although they rarely commended the taste.

The Great Lakes offered walleyed pike, whitefish, chub, lake herring, perch, eel, and catfish; the Snake, Clearwater, and Salmon Rivers, stretching from Wyoming to Idaho, ran with trout, bass, and salmon. The parasite lampreys, introduced to these waters by clinging to the hulls of ships entering the St. Lawrence Seaway, wreaked havoc in the Great Lakes. Elvars killed most of the Lakes' Mackinaw trout and cutthroat trout. Today these trout thrive in Jenny Lake, just outside Jackson Hole, where they were stocked as a precaution after their alarming decline in the Great Lakes. They are a chief delight for that seasonal sport, ice fishing. The success of these transplanted trout is similar to that of the coho salmon, native to the Pacific Northwest, introduced to Lakes Michigan and Superior in the late 1960s, where it has done very well indeed. The Great Lakes' waterfowl and game birds once included all manner of ducks, geese, grouse, pheasants, quail, woodcock, snipe, larks, and the sage hen. Some of the best sage hen hunting continues in Wyoming today. (Larger than a chicken, but smaller than a turkey, this fragrant bird feeds principally off wild sage.)

The "good berry" is the Chippewa Indian name for what is known as wild rice, one of North America's great luxuries. Wild rice is not actually rice at all, but rather a kernel from aquatic grasses that grow in shallow lake water. Minnesota became a preeminent reaper of this grain, and 90 percent of Minnesota wild rice is harvested just as the American Indians have done for centuries. Skiffs and canoes slide through the tall grasses. The berries ripening at the tops of the reeds are hit with sticks and the loose grains shower into the boats. Many fall back into the marsh, seeding next year's crop, as well as feeding fish and fowl. These days, commercially grown wild rice farms use mechanical harvesters, equipped with wooden flails that knock the kernels into motorized skiffs. Wild rice is perishable and must be processed immediately. Roasting the grains gives them a dark, nutty color after the chaff has been separated by the polishing process. And because the grains ripen first at the very top of the stalk, the same plants must be harvested several times. It is no surprise, considering time and labor, that wild rice is perhaps the most expensive grain.

Early trappers were a fearless breed whose wanderlust drove them into the mountain regions for whole years at a time. Their comforts didn't exceed the usual supplies of flour, sugar, meal, coffee, whiskey, and tobacco, and they relied on their guns to provide meat. In summer, most trappers traveled down to the plains of Idaho and Utah and to Jackson Hole to sell their bundles of pelts to the fur merchants who journeyed from St. Louis to buy them. The 1840s saw a wave of German immigrants fleeing one of the European potato famines. Their first stop was Ohio, with many continuing on to Wisconsin and to the harsher climes of Minnesota and the Dakotas. The Germans were followed by Scandinavians, Austrians, and Swiss. These immigrants brought with them a penchant for simple meals of potatoes: boiled, steamed, fried, or spooned into dumplings, and flavored with parsley, onion, and chopped bacon. They brought their sauerkraut to accompany a variety of wursts (which by 1910 would accommodate the growing American popularity of the meal on the run). Wisconsin has more varieties of excellent bratwurst and sausage than anywhere else in the nation, and wurst cook-offs attract as many devotees as Texas chili competitions. The Swiss made a variation of their rosti potatoes, cakes of moist shredded potatoes, caramelized with the smoky, dark maple syrup made by New Englanders gone west. The Swedes of Wisconsin would dish out *pitti panna*, a highly-seasoned hash of ground ham and beef served with a raw yolk cradled in its shell.

Around 1850, the occasional log cabin appeared in the foothills of these mountain ranges, and the plains of Nebraska and the

Dakotas sprouted sod houses built with blocks of matted grass, roots, and mud. Some of these primitive domiciles were built into hillsides, incorporating the natural embankment as one or more of the walls. Since settlements were far removed from one another, isolation was a way of life and winter survival demanded self-sufficiency. One young pioneer woman commented on her life, "While I'm young this sort of life will be exciting, and when I get old I'll be used to it." Four generations later another young woman said, "Life in this part of the world has its rewards. We don't get to see many people. We will get in a car on a good day and drive 400 miles to the nearest French restaurant, just for a change."

The grasses of spring and summer have always produced quality cattle feed for prime quality beef at market. Lush grass and abundant water make the northern valley a natural haven for cattle and other livestock, but life in river country above the plains could be as devastating as in any other part of the wilderness. Spring's high-running waters were a constant threat to farm, livestock, homesteads, and the settlers themselves. The rushing waters pulled out bridges and tore away protective dams. Rivers and streams could change their course practically overnight, abruptly leaving settlers on isolated islands, their livelihood destroyed.

Ranchers along Wyoming's Snake River buy their calves in early spring. Today, vaccinated, branded, and fed on hay as winter recedes, the calves are turned out to feed on grass before sale in the fall. The cattle are rounded up before dawn, as quietly as possible so as not to excite them, because once their adrenaline gets going, they lose weight. The cattle are weighed, four or five at a time, at the ranch weighing shed. Buyers and sellers drink hot coffee and eat doughnuts, joking with one another and betting on the weight of the cows as the animals are prodded onto the scales. The cattle are trucked to Idaho feed lots, where they will be fattened on corn. The grass-fed steer is tougher and less fatty than the grain-fed variety, but is also sweeter with a more distinct flavor.

Fall is the season to pickle and preserve the summer's harvest. The growing season is short; spring rushes into summer, and by September winter is back. Thimbleberries, gooseberries, huckleberries, and plums are hastily put up in jams and conserves, along with sweet and pickled cherries, and Utah's peaches and pears. Garden vegetables and tomatoes are blanched, salted, and packed, and the wild mushroom hunter lays by a stock of cèpes, chanterelles, and morels.

An important source of food for many who live here is big game. Many a family lives off the elk, antelope, black bear, and deer that are taken in autumn. Snow has already covered the ground when the hunting begins. The hunter makes his way through the woods on cross-country skis; it's easier going for the hunter, but also easier for the prey to hear the approaching danger. Perhaps this makes for an even match at the outset, but carting home the kill is hard work. The good hunter rarely shoots his game if he has seen the animal run more than 100 feet; fear causes an animal's adrenaline to peak; to kill it then would lend the meat a sour or "gamey" taste. There is more to hunting than proper aging and butchering. An elk herd is one of the greatest sights in the northern valleys. On the drive from the airport to Jackson Hole during the winter, one might glimpse the herd of some 8,000 elk on the range, fed by the Fish and Game Preserve. The Preserve became a necessity because so many elk perished during the bitter winters. The starving creatures moved into the range, and the kindness of many nineteenth-century farmers kept some of the elk alive. It is not rare, either, for a moose to come lumbering through the snow up to the back door.

Big game is dressed immediately after shooting. Heart and liver are drained and cooled, then usually prepared and eaten fresh. The livers are roasted or made into sausages and pâtés, and the hearts grilled, or perhaps stuffed with dried fruits and nuts and roasted with a rich game sauce. Deer, elk, moose, and mountain sheep carcasses are aged for about a week before cutting and wrapping for the freezer. (Animals under a year old don't require aging.) Bull elk and bull moose are aged for a period of two weeks, and antelope prepared within three days of the kill will avoid the mushy texture typical of this meat. Immediate butchering and freezing are necessary for carcasses shot in warm weather, as well as for animals that were stressed prior to shooting or suffered extensive wounds.

In butchering virtually all fat is trimmed from the animal to avoid a "turn." (The meat can later be larded with pork fat.) Wild game fat quickly turns rancid, and this accounts for some of the "gamey" tang people seem to find so objectionable; in game that has been properly butchered this needn't occur. There is a "best cooking method" for every cut of meat. As with game birds, marinades tenderize these meats and can enhance or, if desired, even disguise the flavor. Big game cuts should be cooked according to the principles applied to the cow; the cuts are similar, if not the same. The shank, neck, and shoulder are for stewing; the chuck, shoulder, leg, and breast are for braising; rib steaks and loin chops are for broiling, pan sautéing, and grilling; and the whole loin and rib roasts are for roasting. Braising and stewing should be done on low heat or low temperature for two or three hours to achieve a tender dish. Steaks and chops need only to be browned and basted, and roasts need to be basted frequently at a temperature of 300° F to 350° F. Choice cuts such as these are best served very rare (when the internal temperature reaches 105° F on a meat thermometer). Game flesh is tougher and leaner than domestic, and cooking these princely cuts rare will result in a tastier and juicier dish. Always defrost game meat in the refrigerator, and always serve it very hot or very cold. Small game birds are treated in the same way as big game. Hunters freeze the viscerated birds with feathers intact, just as they freeze fish in water with scales still on and, more often than not, ungutted; the result is a fresher taste. For the devoted hunter who loves to cook his prey, this remains the best way to retain freshness and taste. The tradition of the trapper lives on in these regions. Bearskins and beaver pelts still bring in good prices, and local artisans make jackets, gloves, and shirts from deer, elk, and antelope hides.

Breakfast

FLAPJACKS ○ MAPLE SYRUP ○ CRANBERRY-APPLE CONSERVE ○ COFFEE, HONEY, AND CREAM

The flapjack was a breakfast food that traveled from New England straight across the country with the pioneers. Cranberries and the maple tree were indigenous not only to New England, but also thrived in the northern regions, especially around Minnesota. Cranberries were served with the flapjacks as a winter fruit.

FLAPJACKS

INGREDIENTS
1 1/2 cups all-purpose flour
1 teaspoon salt
2 tablespoons sugar
2 teaspoons baking powder
1 1/4 cups milk
2 eggs, lightly beaten
3 tablespoons melted butter
Butter, for cooking
Unsalted butter, warmed maple syrup, and
   cranberry apple conserve, for accompaniments

METHOD
In large mixing bowl, combine all of the
   dry ingredients.
Add the milk, eggs, and melted butter, and
   mix together.
Set aside.
Melt 1 tablespoon butter in a large skillet, tilting
   to coat the entire bottom of the pan or use
   a griddle.
Using a 2-ounce ladle, pour circles of pancake
   batter into the pan.
When the pancakes bubble, flip them over with
   a spatula and brown the other side.
Serve with additional melted butter, warmed
   maple syrup, and cranberry-apple conserve.

Makes sixteen 4-inch pancakes

CRANBERRY-APPLE CONSERVE

INGREDIENTS
4 large apples (such as Matsu, Braeburn, or
   Jonagold), peeled, cored, and sliced
1 tablespoon granulated sugar
2 tablespoons water
1 cup maple syrup
2 cups fresh cranberries
1 tablespoon orange zest, grated

METHOD
Place the apples, sugar, and 2 tablespoons water
   in a saucepan over medium heat and steam for
   5 minutes.
Shake the pan to prevent the apples from sticking
   to the bottom.
Mix in the syrup, cranberries, and zest.
When the berries begin to pop, reduce the heat
   to low.
Cover and cook for 10 minutes, stirring
   occasionally to prevent sticking.

Makes approximately 3 cups

Rabbit Shortcake Supper

POTATO, LEEK, AND HAM SOUP ○ RABBIT SHORTCAKE ○ Chateau Montelena
Chardonnay, CA, Navarro Pinot Noir, CA or Capital Blonde Doppelbock, WI

Long before the Idaho strain became prince of all potatoes, mountain settlers relied on the prairie potato, wild turnips, burdocks, cattails, ramps, and wild onions to make soups and flavor dishes. This creamy stew with bits of ham in it is a Swedish variation. Although rabbit has more nutritional value than chicken, it is often met with resistance. It can be a sweet, tender meat if properly cooked.

POTATO, LEEK, AND HAM SOUP

INGREDIENTS

4 cups milk

1 ham bone or ham knuckle with ham

3 cups diced potatoes (if possible, use a
  combination of Idaho, Yukon Gold, and purple
  peruvian potatoes)

1/4 pound butter or 1/2 cup bacon fat

4 leeks, washed, spit, and the white part cut
  into 2-inch julienne

1 cup celery and celery leaves, chopped

2 tablespoons mustard seed, crushed

Salt and freshly milled black pepper

2 tablespoons all-purpose flour mixed with
  2 tablespoons softened, unsalted butter

METHOD

In a soup kettle, simmer the milk with the ham
  bone and potatoes for 30 minutes, or until the
  potatoes are almost tender.

Meanwhile, melt the butter in a large sauté pan or
  skillet over moderate heat.

Add the leeks and cook until wilted.

Add the leeks, celery, and mustard to the milk
  mixture and cook for 15 minutes.

Season to taste with salt and pepper.

Whisk in the flour and butter.

Remove the ham bone and flake off the ham.

Fold it into the soup and stir.

Continue to simmer for 10 minutes, or until the flour
  is completely dissolved.

Serves 4 to 5

Freshly grated nutmeg

Salt and freshly milled black pepper

1/4 cup fresh parsley, chopped

RABBIT SHORTCAKE

INGREDIENTS

Dough:

4 cups all-purpose flour

2 teaspoons salt

2 tablespoons baking powder

2 scant teaspoons sugar

2 cups heavy cream

Rabbit:

1 large rabbit (approximately 4 to 5 pounds)

1/2 cup all-purpose flour

Salt and freshly milled black pepper

12 shallots, halved

1 cup fresh cranberries

4 medium parsnips, peeled and cut into
2-inch julienne

Sauce:

1 cup dry vermouth

2 cups brown sauce (see Basics, page 333),
reduced to 1 cup, or 1/2 cup demi-glace (see
Sources, page 344) mixed with 1/2 cup water

3 cups sour cream

1/2 cup heavy cream

1/4 cup plus 1 tablespoon honey mustard

METHOD

Prepare the dough:

In a mixing bowl, sift together the dry ingredients
and fold in the cream.

Wrap in waxed paper and chill until needed.

Preheat the oven to 350° F.

Prepare the rabbit:

Cut the rabbit into small serving pieces.

Remove all of the fat and place it in a shallow
ovenproof casserole.

Place the casserole in the hot oven to render
the fat.

Season the flour with salt and pepper and dredge
the rabbit pieces in it.

Pour the rendered fat into a large heavy skillet set
over moderate heat.

When the fat is hot, add the shallots and rabbit
pieces and cook until browned on all sides.

Transfer the rabbit and shallots to the
casserole.

Add the cranberries and parsnip julienne.

Prepare the sauce:

Remove any excess fat from the skillet and place
the skillet over moderate heat.

Add the vermouth and deglaze the pan, scraping
up the browned bits that cling to the bottom.

Add the reduced brown sauce or demi-glace, sour
cream, heavy cream, and honey mustard.

Blend well and simmer.

Season to taste with nutmeg, salt, and pepper.

Cook the sauce until reduced slightly and pour
over the rabbit.

Sprinkle with parsley.

Assemble the shortcake:

Either spoon the dough over the rabbit and sauce
to cover, or on a floured surface, use your fingers
to pat out the dough 1/2-inch thick, shaped to fit
the casserole, and set the dough in place.

Bake for approximately 45 minutes or until golden
and serve.

Serves 8 to 10

Game Pie Dinner

SMOKED LAKE TROUT WITH SAUTÉED PEPPERS ○ GAME PIE ○ PICKLED SOUR CHERRIES ○ PEAR SNOW ○ CHOCOLATE POTATO CAKE ○ New Glarus Brewing Co. Belgian Red Ale, WI

Any old campaigner or trapper knew more about the art of survival and cooking in the wild than most hunters do today. At the end of the day, it was the fault of the hunter or his gun if he hadn't bagged a brace of birds. The smart hunter dried spring morels, boletus, and chanterelle mushrooms, packing them alongside his provisions of dried fruits, salt, lard, and whiskey. This is a genuine woodsman's game pie, following the hunter's adage that game is best put forth with the foods the animal itself eats. A brown sauce rich with the addition of game bones is added after the pie is baked, avoiding yet another soggy crust. Fluffy pear snow is complemented by put-up fruits from the last of summer's harvest. The cake is rich, dense, and very chocolatey, using potatoes, a traditional extender for the white flour that was expensive and so hard to come by.

SMOKED LAKE TROUT WITH SAUTÉED PEPPERS

INGREDIENTS
4 sweet green frying peppers
8 yellow mildly hot peppers, like Hungarian Yellow
Olive oil
Salt and freshly milled black pepper
4 smoked trout, preferably boned with head and
    tail intact (6 to 8 ounces each)
2 to 3 lemons, halved
Freshly grated horseradish

METHOD
Preheat the oven to 300° F.
Cut the peppers lengthwise and remove the seeds
    and veins.
Lightly coat a heavy skillet with olive oil.
Sauté the peppers until they give off their juices
    and wilt.
Season to taste with salt and pepper.
Place the trout on a baking sheet and heat in the
    oven for 10 minutes.
Serve with the peppers, fresh lemon wedges, and
    freshly grated horseradish.

Serves 4

GAME PIE

INGREDIENTS
Dried ingredients:
1 cup dried morels
1/2 cup dried cherries
Birds:
4 partridges (each about 1 1/2 pounds) or
    6 pounds of pheasant, quail, or Canadian
    goose breast
Salt and freshly milled black pepper
1/4 pound unsalted butter
Stock for Game Pie:
Reserved bones from the birds

2 quarts chicken stock (see Basics, page 332) or canned low-sodium chicken broth

Necks, gizzards, and hearts, from the birds

1 celery rib, coarsely chopped

1 carrot, coarsely chopped

1 bay leaf

6 peppercorns, crushed

5 juniper berries, bruised

1/3 cup demi-glace (see Sources, page 344)

Vegetables and fruit:

1 leek, including some of the pale green leaves, washed, split, and cut into 2-inch julienne; reserve the dark green leaves

24 pearl onions

2 large carrots, peeled and sliced diagonally 1/4-inch thick

2 small white turnips, peeled and cut into 1/2-inch cubes

2 hard pears, peeled, cored, diced into 1/2-inch cubes, and tossed with the juice of 1/2 lemon

2 recipes pie dough, made with lard (see Basics, page 335)

1 egg, beaten with 2 tablespoons cold water, for egg wash

SPECIAL TOOLS

Fine sieve

9-inch loose-bottomed tart pan with 2-inch sides, or a 9-inch, deep-dish pie pan

METHOD

The dried ingredients:

In separate bowls, soak the dried morels and the dried cherries in enough warm water to cover.

Let the morels soak for 2 hours and the cherries for one hour.

Drain and reserve the soaking liquid.

Prepare the birds:

Wash the birds and pat dry with paper towels.

Lightly salt and pepper the cavities of the birds.

Melt the butter in a large heavy ovenproof skillet.

Brown the birds evenly on all sides.

The meat will be rare.

Set aside to cool.

Remove the meat from the bones.

Reserve the bones for the stock.

To remove the meat:

Using poultry shears or a cleaver, cut the birds lengthwise in half, splitting the breast.

Cut away the backbone.

Remove the wingtips and feet with a chopping knife or cleaver.

Remove the upper wing bone from the breast portion.

Remove the thighs and legs from the frames with a sharp boning knife.

Cut the legs from the thighs and remove the meat.

Remove the breast meat from the frame.

Reserve all the bones and cut the meat into bite-sized pieces.

Cover and set the meat aside.

Prepare the game stock and vegetables:

Place the bones in a stockpot with all the remaining stock ingredients.

Add the soaking water from the dried morels and cherries.

Add the reserved dark green leek ends, salt, and pepper.

Bring to a boil.

Skim, reduce the heat, and simmer for 1 hour, or until reduced by half.

Strain the sauce through a fine sieve into a saucepan; discard the solids and reserve the sauce.

In a saucepan filled with boiling water, blanch the vegetables separately for 1 minute each.

Start with the leeks first, then the onions, then the carrots, and end with the turnips.

Cool under cold running water and drain

Set aside with the pears.

To assemble the pie:

Preheat the oven to 400° F.

Divide the pie dough in half.

On a floured surface, roll out one half of the pie dough about ¹/₄-inch thick.

Line the tart pan with the dough.

Toss the meat with the blanched vegetables, drained morels and cherries, and the pears.

Fill the pan with the mixture.

Roll out the top crust.

Moisten the sides of the dough with egg wash and set the top crust in place.

Trim and crimp the dough, pressing down lightly on the edges of the pan.

If you wish, roll the pastry scraps and make a braid to fit around the exterior rim. Make leaves and berries from the rest of the dough scraps to decorate the top of the crust.

Brush the top of the pie with the egg wash and cut a small round hole in the center of the pie.

Decorate the hole with more braid and coat the decoration with egg wash.

Set the pie on a baking sheet and bake for 50 minutes or until golden.

If the crust browns too quickly, cover loosely with foil.

Allow to rest before removing the sides of the pan, leaving the bottom in place.

Reheat the game sauce.

Set the pie on a serving platter and funnel hot game sauce through the opening on top.

Serves 6

PEAR SNOW

INGREDIENTS

5 cups pears, preferably Anjou (approximately 5 large pears), peeled, cored, and cubed

Juice of ¹/₂ lemon

¹/₂ cup sugar

12 peppercorns, crushed, wrapped, and tied in

a double thickness of cheesecloth

1 tablespoon unflavored gelatin

2 tablespoons Aquavit or Kirschwasser

3 egg whites, at room temperature

SPECIAL TOOLS

5-quart decorative mold

Food processor or food mill

METHOD

Place the pears in a large pot with the lemon juice and enough cold water to cover.

Add the sugar and peppercorns and simmer over moderate heat until tender. Cool thoroughly.

Meanwhile, place a 5-quart mold in the freezer to chill.

In a double boiler over hot water, combine the gelatin, Aquavit, and 2 tablespoons of the pear liquid.

Cook just until the gelatin dissolves.

Set aside to cool.

Drain the pears of their liquid.

Remove and discard the peppercorns and purée the pears in a food processor or food mill until velvety and smooth.

In a bowl, beat the egg whites until stiff, but not dry.

Beat the gelatin mixture into the pear purée, then gently fold in the beaten egg whites.

Turn the mixture into the chilled mold and freeze for 15 minutes or until set, then move to the refrigerator and chill the snow for 4 hours, or until ready to serve.

Unmold and serve with the chocolate potato cake and the put-up fruits.

Serves 10

CHOCOLATE POTATO CAKE

INGREDIENTS

Butter and flour, for preparing the loaf pans
1/2 pound unsalted butter, at room temperature
2 cups sugar
1/4 cup unsweetened cocoa powder
4 ounces unsweetened chocolate, melted
3 eggs
1 cup cooked mashed potatoes (approximately
　2 medium potatoes)
1 teaspoon vanilla extract
1 cup milk
2 1/2 cups all-purpose flour, sifted
2 teaspoons baking powder

METHOD

Butter 2 medium loaf pans and dust with flour,
　tapping out any excess.
Preheat the oven to 350° F.
In a mixing bowl, cream the butter and sugar with
　an electric mixer.
Add the cocoa powder and blend.
Stir in the melted chocolate.
One at a time, add the eggs and beat
　until smooth.
Add the mashed potatoes and blend well.
Add the vanilla and blend well.
Sift together the flour and baking powder.
Alternately add the milk and dry ingredients until
　the mixture is smooth.
Divide the batter between the prepared loaf pans.
Bake for 35 to 40 minutes, or until the cake pulls
　away from the sides of the pans.
Unmold onto a cooling rack and cool thoroughly
　before slicing.
Cover and refrigerate any leftovers.

Makes 2 loaves

Hunter's Dinner

FRESH FRIED TROUT ○ ELK ROAST WITH
WILD RICE ○ CRANBERRY-AND-
JERUSALEM-ARTICHOKE FRITTERS ○ WILD
CURRANT JAM ○ VENISON MINCEMEAT
WITH CANDIED FRUITS ○ RUM HARD
SAUCE (See Basics, page 336) ○ PORT
AND COFFEE ○ Ste. Chapelle
Winemaker's Series Cabernet Sauvignon,
ID or Big Sky Moose Drool Brown Ale, MT

*Game supports many a northern family, and is
put away in freezers or sometimes frozen
outside and used as the winter wears on. Fresh-
caught trout deserve a quick fry in butter.
Catching a 5 to 6 pound trout is not unusual
here, and it is such a meaty fish that often it is
served as a main course. The finer cuts of elk,
antelope, moose, or deer should be served rare;
short cooking time results in more tender meat.
It's difficult to get a good head of lettuce up
north in winter, but with put-up fruits,
vegetables, and preserves, you're not as limited
as you might think. The Jerusalem artichoke is
a versatile tuber that can be shaved directly
into salads or boiled and dressed with
hollandaise; here it's grated into a fritter batter
with cranberries. Homemade mincemeat is
sturdy enough to last a season or two under
refrigeration, and homemade candied fruit
retains more zest than any store-bought variety.*

CRANBERRY-AND-JERUSALEM-ARTICHOKE FRITTERS

INGREDIENTS
Fritter Batter:
2 eggs, separated
$1/4$ teaspoon salt
2 tablespoons granulated sugar
$3/4$ cup milk
$1\,1/3$ cups all-purpose flour
3 to 4 gratings of nutmeg
2 cups fresh cranberries
Confectioners' sugar, to coat the berries
1 cup Jerusalem artichoke, peeled, grated, and
    soaked in water with 2 tablespoons lemon juice
Vegetable oil, for frying
Granulated sugar, for serving (optional)

SPECIAL TOOLS
Deep-frying thermometer

METHOD
In a mixing bowl, beat the egg yolks until creamy.
Add salt, 2 tablespoons granulated sugar, milk,
    flour, and nutmeg, and mix well.
Set aside for 1 hour.
Coat the berries in confectioners' sugar.
When ready to make the fritters, beat the egg
    whites until soft peaks form and fold into the
    batter mixture.
Stir the berries and drained, grated Jerusalem
    artichoke into the batter.
In a large heavy skillet, heat $1\,1/2$ inches of oil until
    almost smoking (365° F).
Using a teaspoon, drop the fritter batter into the
    hot vegetable oil and cook for 3 to 4 minutes, or
    until golden brown.
Sprinkle with granulated sugar if desired, and serve.

Makes $2\,1/2$ to 3 dozen fritters

VENISON MINCEMEAT WITH CANDIED FRUITS

INGREDIENTS
Venison and Stock:
4 pounds neck or shoulder of venison
1 bay leaf
8 to 10 whole cloves
8 peppercorns
4 juniper berries
3 cups apple cider
1 cup cider vinegar
Candied Citrus Peel:
Peel of 6 oranges
Peel of 8 lemons
Peel of 8 limes
$2\,1/4$ cups water
$4\,1/2$ cups sugar
Mincemeat:
1 pound suet, minced or ground
1 quince, peeled, cored, and diced
4 apples, peeled, cored, and diced
2 pounds currants
1 cup candied lemon peel, reserved from above
1 cup candied orange peel, reserved from above
4 cups dry sherry
1 cup Cognac
1 tablespoon ground cloves
$1\,1/2$ teaspoon freshly grated nutmeg

METHOD
Prepare the venison:
In a large stockpot, simmer the venison with all of
    the stock ingredients and water to cover until
    tender, approximately $1\,1/2$ hours.
Drain, reserving the liquid.
Shred the meat or pulse in a food processor.
Prepare the citrus peel:
Cut the orange peel into $1/4$-inch squares.
Place the peel in a saucepan with water to cover
    and boil for 15 minutes.
Drain and repeat the process 3 more times.
In a medium saucepan, combine $3/4$ cup water
    and $1\,1/2$ cups of sugar. Cook until the sugar
    dissolves and add the orange peel.

Cook for approximately 15 minutes, or
  until translucent.
Remove the peel with a slotted spoon to a sheet
  of waxed paper and cool.
Reserve the sugar syrup for the mincemeat
  mixture.
Repeat the process with the remaining fruits
  and peels.
When all of the peels are dry, reserve $1/4$ cup of
  each to serve with the completed mincemeat.

Prepare the mincemeat:

In a heated bowl, combine the shredded or
  ground venison with the suet, $3 1/2$ cups of the
  reserved meat juice, and the remaining
  mincemeat ingredients.
The mixture should be loose; if necessary, add an
  additional cup or two of Cognac.
Create a makeshift double boiler by placing the

bowl over a pot of boiling water, and cook the
  mixture for approximately 4 hours, until thick.
Place the mincemeat in a crock, cover, and allow
  to stand in a refrigerated place for a month or
  longer before using. Mincemeat will keep for a
  year or more in covered containers.
Check the mincemeat from time to time. If too
  much liquid is absorbed and the mincemeat is
  dry, add additional sherry or a combination of
  sherry and Cognac.
To serve, heat in a double boiler and serve with
  rum hard sauce and candied fruit peels, or serve
  hot in miniature tart shells.

Note: For tart shells, see Basics, page 336. For rum
hard sauce, see Basics, page 337.

Makes approximately 6 quarts

Festive Dinner

GAME SOUP WITH PEARS ○ PAGE'S WILD RICE WAFFLES ○ ROAST PHEASANTS WITH BUFFALO SAUSAGES AND SPARKLING CIDER SAUERKRAUT ○ MICHIGAN POTATO CAKE ○ CARAMEL DUMPLINGS ○ L. Mawby Cremant Brut, MI or Great Lakes Brewing Co. Edmund Fitzgerald Porter

It's a foolish cook who throws the carcass in the garbage. Crush the bones and store them in the freezer until you have enough to make a good, rich stock—the base for a variety of game soups and sauces. Although the sauerkraut can be prepared with cider, a sparkling cider is drier and less sweet. A handful of ranchers raise buffalo, and the meat of grass-fed buffalo is as sweet and lean as that of grass-fed cattle before they've been sent to the corn feedlots. This sausage makes a nice change from pork. Flour dumplings reflect the influence of the northern Europeans. Steamed with sugar and spices, coated with caramel syrup, and garnished with a grating of lemon and orange zest for relief, they make a nice lift, if a desperate one.

GAME SOUP WITH PEARS

INGREDIENTS

Stock:

3 pheasant carcasses or 6 partridge carcasses

3 celery ribs, roughly chopped

3 carrots, roughly chopped

10 peppercorns, crushed

2 bay leaves

1 teaspoon thyme

1 teaspoon sage

1 teaspoon rosemary

8 juniper berries, bruised

4 sprigs fresh parsley

3 quarts chicken stock (see Basics, page 332)
   or canned low-sodium chicken broth

Salt

2 medium onions, halved

Soup:

3 carrots, peeled and cut into 2-inch julienne

3 medium leeks, tough green parts removed,
   washed well and cut into 2-inch julienne

2 hard winter pears, such as Bosc or Seckle

METHOD

Prepare the stock:

Break up the carcasses of the birds and place
   them in a large soup kettle.

Add all of the remaining stock ingredients except
   the onions and bring the stock to a boil over
   high heat.

Place a black cast-iron skillet over high heat.

Add the halved onions, flat side down, and cook
   until blackened and caramelized.

Remove the skillet from the heat and add the
   onions to the soup kettle.

Reduce the heat to low and simmer for 1 hour.

Strain the stock into a clean pot and bring to a
   simmer over moderately high heat.

Add the carrots and the leeks.

Thinly slice the pears from stem to base.

Add the pear slices to the soup.

Simmer for 3 to 4 minutes, or until the pears begin
   to wilt and serve hot.

Serves 6

PAGE'S WILD RICE WAFFLES

INGREDIENTS

$1/2$ cup all-purpose flour

$1/2$ cup whole wheat flour

1 tablespoon sugar

2 teaspoons baking powder

$1/2$ teaspoon baking soda

$1/4$ teaspoon salt

$1 3/4$ cups cooked wild rice, well drained

$1 1/2$ cups buttermilk

2 large eggs

$1/4$ cup unsalted butter, melted

METHOD

Sift the dry ingredients into a large mixing bowl.

Add the cooked wild rice to the dry ingredients
   and mix thoroughly.

In another bowl whisk together the buttermilk,
   eggs and melted butter.

Add buttermilk mixture to dry ingredients and
   stir well.

(The waffle batter can be made up to 2 hours
   ahead of time, and refrigerated.)

Ladle the batter into a preheated waffle iron.

Cook until browned and crisp.

Keep warm in a 200° F oven until ready to serve.

Serves 6

ROAST PHEASANTS WITH BUFFALO SAUSAGES AND SPARKLING CIDER SAUERKRAUT

INGREDIENTS

3 thick slices smoked bacon

1 medium-sized yellow onion, diced

1 tart apple, diced

1 tablespoon caraway seeds

6 pounds sauerkraut, washed in cold water to remove brine and squeezed dry

2 quarts sparkling cider

2 pheasants (each approximately 3 pounds)

1/4 pound unsalted butter

8 juniper berries, bruised

2 fresh or dried sage sprigs

2 pounds buffalo sausage links

1/4 cup finely chopped fresh parsley

METHOD

Preheat the oven to 325° F.

In a large skillet or saucepan, render the bacon fat but do not allow the bacon to crisp or brown.

Transfer the bacon to an ovenproof casserole.

Add the onions to the rendered fat and sauté until wilted.

Add the apple, caraway seeds, and the sauerkraut and toss to combine.

Pour in the sparkling cider and bring to a boil over moderate heat.

Transfer the sauerkraut mixture to the casserole with the bacon.

Cover the casserole and bake for 3 hours, tossing the mixture every hour.

Remove from the oven and keep covered.

To cook the pheasants:

Preheat the oven to 425° F.

Melt the butter in a heavy ovenproof skillet.

Divide the juniper berries and sage between the cavities of both birds.

Truss the birds.

Brown the birds evenly on all sides.

Place the skillet in the oven and roast for 30 to 40 minutes, until the juices run pale pink.

While the birds are cooking, prick the sausages and cook them in a heavy skillet with approximately 1/2 cup water until the water evaporates and the sausages brown.

To serve, cut up one or both pheasants.

Arrange the meats attractively over the sauerkraut and dust with the chopped parsley.

Note: The sauerkraut can be prepared up to a day in advance. Bring to room temperature and reheat when ready to serve.

Serves 6

MICHIGAN POTATO CAKE

INGREDIENTS

10 large Idaho potatoes

1 pound unsalted butter, clarified (see Basics, page 333), or a combination of butter and lard

Salt and freshly milled black pepper

1/2 cup maple syrup

1/4 cup chopped fresh parsley

METHOD

Boil the potatoes in their skins in lightly salted water.

Cook for approximately 20 minutes, or until a paring knife easily pierces the center of the potato.

Drain, cool, and refrigerate.

Peel the potatoes and shred coarsely, using a grater.

Pour half of the butter into a 15-inch skillet.

Heat the butter over moderately high heat and add the shredded potatoes. Sprinkle liberally with salt and pepper.

Push the shreds in from the rim of the pan and pat the top into a large pancake.

Reduce the heat and cook, shaking and rotating

the pan to loosen the potatoes.

Drizzle a few tablespoons of butter around the inner rim of the pan.

Continue to cook for 15 minutes.

Place a large plate, face down, over the top of the skillet and invert the skillet to turn the pancake out onto the plate.

Slide the pancake back into the skillet, cooked-side up, and drizzle the remaining butter around the inner rim.

Drizzle the syrup in the same manner.

Continue to cook until the bottom has formed a crust and the potatoes are cooked through.

Shake the skillet from time to time to ensure that the potatoes do not stick to the pan.

Use a spatula to lift the pancake from the edge when checking for doneness.

Sprinkle with the parsley and serve.

Serves 6 to 8

CARAMEL DUMPLINGS

INGREDIENTS

Dough:

1 cup all-purpose flour, sifted

2 teaspoons baking powder

1/8 teaspoon salt

Grated zest of 1 lemon

1 egg, beaten

1/3 cup milk

1 tablespoon unsalted butter, melted

Poaching Liquid:

1 1/2 cups brown sugar

2 tablespoons unsalted butter

2 cups water

Caramel Sauce:

1 1/2 cups granulated sugar

1/2 cup heavy cream

3 tablespoons unsalted butter

For Serving:

Grated zest of 1 lemon

Grated zest of 1 orange

METHOD

Prepare the dumpling dough:

In a mixing bowl, combine the dry dough ingredients with lemon zest.

Mix in the egg, milk, and melted butter and beat just until the batter is smooth.

Prepare the poaching liquid:

In a large saucepan, dissolve the brown sugar and butter in 2 cups water and bring to a simmer over moderate heat.

Prepare the caramel sauce:

Place the granulated sugar in a heavy saucepan and melt over low heat, stirring constantly with a wooden spoon until the sugar is dissolved and starts to become a golden brown.

Swirl the sugar in the pan to color the mixture evenly.

Do not let the sugar become too dark.

When the sugar is a uniform golden brown, remove the pan from the heat. Carefully add the heavy cream, stir in the butter, and mix until smooth. Set aside.

Prepare the dumplings:

Working in batches if necessary, use a large oval soup spoon to drop the dough by spoonfuls into the poaching liquid.

Cover and cook for 5 minutes.

Turn the dumplings over and cook, covered, for 3 to 5 minutes more.

Remove the dumplings with a slotted spoon and continue until all of the dumplings are cooked.

Keep warm.

To serve, place one dumpling on each serving plate, spoon the caramel over, and sprinkle with the lemon and orange zests.

Makes 8 to 10 dumplings

Winter Picnic

WILD MUSHROOM SOUP ○ SMOKED TROUT SCONES ○ CHOCOLATE SNOW ○
APPLES AND RAT CHEESE ○ LENA'S GLOGG ○ Bell's Expedition Stout

Expeditions into the woods by dogsled, skis, snowshoes, and snowmobiles can become pretty elaborate. Fires are built, steaks are grilled, potatoes are fried; but I prefer not cooking at all and find packing up scones flecked with smoked trout, thermoses of hot spiced wine and wild mushroom soup, some apples, and dependable store-bought rat cheese equally satisfying. Chocolate snow is one of winter's pleasures, not unlike the hot maple syrup New Englanders drizzle into snowbanks where the syrup hardens into crystalline webs.

WILD MUSHROOM SOUP

INGREDIENTS

1 pound fresh morels or boletus mushrooms
   (American cêpes), or substitute 2 ounces dried
   morels, 2 ounces dried cêpes, and 3/4 pound
   fresh button mushrooms
3 cups chicken stock (see Basics, page 332), or
   canned low-sodium chicken broth
1 cup heavy cream
2 tablespoons all-purpose flour mixed with
   2 tablespoons softened, unsalted butter
Salt and freshly milled pepper

METHOD

If using dried mushrooms, plump them in the stock
   for approximately 1 hour before cooking.
In a large heavy saucepan, place the stock and
   the mushrooms over moderate heat.
Bring to a simmer and continue to cook for
   approximately 15 minutes.

Drain the mushrooms, reserving the stock.
Strain the stock through a double thickness of
   dampened cheesecloth and return the stock to
   the saucepan.
Coarsely chop the mushrooms in a food processor,
   pulsing 4 or 5 times.
Do not puree; they should be chunky.
Return the chopped mushrooms to the stock and
   add the cream.
Bring to a simmer over moderately low heat and
   whisk in the flour-butter mixture.
Season to taste with salt and pepper and cook for
   about 10 minutes, or until the flour dissolves and
   the soup has thickened.
Serve immediately.

Serves 4 to 5

SMOKED TROUT SCONES

INGREDIENTS

8 ounces smoked trout, finely flaked
1/4 cup finely chopped scallions, including some
 of the green
Grated zest of 2 lemons
2 cups all-purpose flour
2 tablespoons baking powder
2 tablespoons cold, unsalted butter
2 eggs, lightly beaten
1/2 cup heavy cream
1 egg, beaten with 1 tablespoon cold water,
 for egg wash

METHOD

Preheat the oven to 400° F.
In a bowl, combine the trout, scallions, and half of
 the lemon zest.
Set aside.
Sift the flour and baking powder into the
 mixing bowl.
Cut the butter into bits and rub it into the flour by
 hand or with an electric mixer.
Combine the eggs, cream, and the remaining zest,
 and mix into the flour mixture. Do not overmix.
Divide the dough in half.

On a lightly floured surface, roll out each portion of
 dough 1/3-inch thick.
Cut 1 piece of dough into triangles that measure
 3 inches a side.
Place 1 tablespoon of the trout mixture in the
 center of each triangle.
Paint the edges of each triangle with the
 egg wash.
Cut the remaining dough into triangles.
Top each of the filled triangles with dough and
 crimp the edges with a fork. Brush the top of
 each scone with the egg wash.
Place the scones 2 inches apart on baking sheets
 and bake for 15 to 20 minutes, or until golden.

Makes 8 scones

CHOCOLATE SNOW

INGREDIENTS

8 ounces semisweet chocolate

METHOD

Chop the chocolate into small pieces and place
 them in the top of a double boiler.

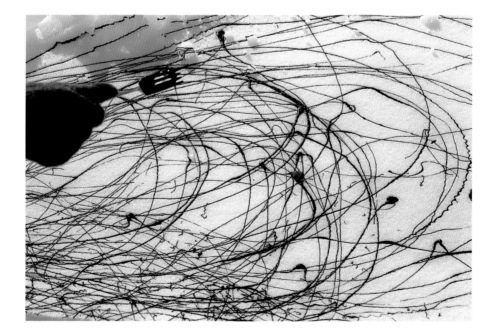

Set over moderately high heat and bring the water to a simmer.

When the chocolate melts, remove from the heat.

Dip a fork into the chocolate and flick the chocolate over the snow in a back and forth motion.

Do this several times to make a lattice of chocolate over the snow.

Carefully pick up the lattice from the top of the snow and eat.

Note: This may be prepared in a long-handled pan over a campfire.

LENA'S GLOGG

INGREDIENTS
2 bottles dry red wine
8 cardamom pods
5 whole cloves
1 small cinnamon stick
Zest of 1 navel orange cut into strips
Zest of 1 lemon cut into strips
1 cup sugar
12 to 18 whole blanched almonds
$1/4$ cup raisins
6 to 8 ounces Aquavit

SPECIAL TOOLS
1 dozen 4-ounce glasses
1 dozen small silver spoons

METHOD
In a large kettle, combine the wine with the cardamom, cloves, cinnamon, orange zest, and lemon zest.

Stir to mix and set aside to steep overnight.

The next day, add the sugar and warm the mixture over very low heat until the sugar has dissolved and the mixture is hot, approximately 15 minutes.

Place 1 almond and 2 or 3 raisins in each glass.

Add approximately 1 tablespoon of Aquavit to each glass and place a silver spoon in each.

Pour the hot wine into the glass and serve.

Makes 12 to 18 servings

Range Food

Beef Jerky

Jerky was never meant to be incorporated into a dish. The meat (elk, antelope, deer, or beef) is cut into ribbons, salted, and left out in the sun to dry. Dishes such as creamed dried beef came along later, using meat cured by a process that was much less severe. This was saddlebag food that sustained the woodsman from the North and the cowboy of the Panhandle. When you hold a piece of this meat in your hand, you say to yourself, "My God, how unappealing," and then as you actually begin to chew it, it all juices up, becomes quite delicious, and makes a lot of sense.

SOUTHWEST

SOUTHWEST

The old-time cowboy was a rough-and-tumble loner who smelled of his horses and cattle, and whose sweaty life was romanticized until it became the stuff of dreams. He was a different breed of settler, drawn west by the promise of work, inheriting the horse and longhorn steer from the Conquistadors before him. In the 1830s, the cowboy worked miles from the ranch, making his home with the herd on a range millions of acres wide. He packed his saddlebags with *charqui* (Spanish for leathery American Indian jerky that passed for countless meals) and carried his staples of coffee, tobacco, ammunition, and a treasured keg of sourdough starter. Sourdough traveled well and could take the pounding abuse of long days in the saddle. These basics sustained the lone horseman until he rejoined his outfit. A chuck wagon followed the herd, a veritable pantry on wheels stocked with flour, cornmeal, salt, cured pork, lard, sugar, coffee, cane sugar syrup, and dried legumes. The round-the-clock beverage was coffee, made black and strong enough to "float a horseshoe." Meals offered pretty much the same unchanging bill of fare for breakfast, lunch, or dinner: bacon, steaks from a steer slaughtered on the range fried in lard, and *chicharrones*—fried pork rinds, which today are packaged like potato chips.

Chuck wagon cooks always managed to drum up some variety for the boys, even after the best cuts of meat went to the foreman and owners. A notorious fiery stew was made from beef tripe, marrow, brains, kidneys, lungs, and heart, boiled together with spicy chiles. It is a very Texan dish, known as "cowboy stew" in polite society, although cowhands referred to it only as "son of a bitch." There were beans ad infinitum—pinto, red, pea, and lima—often all cooked up into a heavy porridge and sopped up with biscuits or cornbreads produced in makeshift Dutch ovens. At meal's end, a keg of smoky cane sugar syrup was passed around to be poured over the last of the bread. On rare occasion a proper dessert might be put forth—perhaps an egg pie, sweetened with molasses, in a sourdough crust. Stick-to-the-ribs meals answered the demand of heavy work in 115-degree heat. Most dishes reflected, even if just subtly, the influence of the Spanish and the American

Indians. The barbecue, one of many Latin American methods adopted by the Spanish, would become popular on the range, as the cowboys often worked too far away to get back to the ranch.

The longhorns were driven from the grasslands of southern Texas to markets in the Panhandle, Oklahoma, and southwestern Kansas, a journey that took months. The more slowly the steer crossed these territories, grazing on rich summer grasses as they went, the fatter they would be when they reached the rowdy cow towns of Wichita, Dodge City, and Abilene. This trip was perilous, with the likelihood of ambush by American Indians, cattle rustlers, horse thieves, and rattlesnakes. Dangers not withstanding, the demand for beef in the East spurred Texas to achieve an even stronger foothold as the nation's cattle domain. The cowboy's long cattle drive ended with the sale of the herd in one of the cow towns, where most hands squandered their hard-earned wages on drink and roughhousing to celebrate the end of the drive. By 1900, the heyday of the cattle drive was over, and railroads were shipping "cattle-on-the-hoof" to Chicago and New York, where demands for meat verged on gluttonous. The cattle barons were rolling in money, and were trailed wherever they went by bank robbers and train robbers who found waistcoated entrepreneurs easy targets.

Texas can be thought of as one big country made up of four regions: east, central, south, and west. Each area champions its own ways in the kitchen, so it's easy to see how Texans might disagree on the definition of "authentic" barbecue or chili. Almost everyone has the

best recipe. Most agree that typical barbecue meats include pork back ribs, short beef ribs, brisket, chicken, sausage, pork loin, and baby pig, but as for method, accompaniments, and sauces, the field is open to dispute. In east Texas, they like to brush the meat with a thick, sweet barbecue sauce before cooking it over oak and hickory. This smacks of the South, particularly when accompanied by black-eyed peas, baked beans with ham hocks, or beans cooked to mush with hot sauce á la Creole. Central Texas favors mesquite and charcoal in addition to oak and hickory, and their beans-and-sausage comes to the table with sliced tomatoes, onions, and pickles. Mesquite is something of a buzzword; like green oak, it gives off extraordinary heat. The wood comes from a succulent tree, whose roots absorb nearly every drop of water from the surrounding soil. Mesquite fuel results in a moist heat that flavors meat distinctly but doesn't dry it out. The wood is taken for granted in Texas, where it is simply regarded as a local convenience, but is prized as a status fuel around the rest of the country. Fortunately there are not enough barbecue pits in America to exhaust the supply. South Texans like barbecue cooked only on mesquite, with the sauce hot and not too thick. Their beans are spicy Mexican brown beans or Ranch beans, served with pico de gallo, a combination of tomatoes, onions, garlic, and chopped jalapeños in oil. (Beans are of humble repute. At one hastily called White House dinner given by President Johnson for a rather celestial group of cabinet members, the president tucked a napkin under his chin and put away a bowl of black-eyed peas while the others waited for the meal to commence.)

Texas boasts an eclectic bounty: her rivers run thick with trout, perch, and catfish, and the Gulf waters from Padre Island to Port Arthur supply red snapper, king mackerel, speckled sea trout, redfish, shrimp, flounder, crabs, and oysters. Pecan producers here are second only to those in Georgia, and the pralines of south Texas and pecan pies of east Texas bespeak a southern influence. The lower Rio Grande valley grows some of the finest pink grapefruit in the land, in addition to juicy fragrant honeydews, cantaloupes, and watermelons. Tiny figs thrive as far north as the irrigated gardens of Dallas and Fort Worth and are made into tarts and rich, syrupy conserves.

Tex-Mex cooking developed in San Antonio and Austin, to the far western corner of El Paso where they serve the best Mexican food in the state. Tex-Mex started out as cheap and trashy food, using inexpensive cuts of meat and chicken parts smothered in spices to seem more appealing. In early days, the meats were shredded and spooned into corn tortillas with hot sauces, but by the 1930s, ground meats were being used in fillings.

Southwestern style finds its heritage in the food known to American Indian tribes. The Southwest's endless horizon reaches over rock, mesas, desert, and the verdant vein that runs along the Rio Grande as it weaves through New Mexico. For millennia people have lived here in caves and cliff dwellings on the face of the mesas. Tiered level on level, these dwellings were connected with wooden ladders, making

a sort of primitive cityscape that afforded a 180-degree view of possible attack. Pueblo Indians' culture sprang up in near-total isolation. Their handmade silver, turquoise, pottery, and wool are among the most exquisite objects and designs dreamed up by any civilization. Maize was the grain that sustained this native agrarian society, so much so that elders admonished young men to love and cherish their corn as they love and cherish their women. Understandably fearful of droughts, the Pueblos built dams and irrigated the Rio Grande valleys as far north as Taos. Their maize was many-colored: red, white, blue, yellow, purple, and black. Breads and tortillas were made from a meal of ground kernels. Posole was their version of hominy, the tough corn casings removed with a lye made from wood ash. The Pueblos made

a pleasant, fresh-tasting dish from dried sweet corn kernels called *chicos*; nowadays those kernels are salted and packaged as a crunchy snack. When the Coronado expedition reached Pueblo country in 1540, they came upon fields thick with maize and storerooms stocked with a seven-year supply from just one season's harvest. Archeologists are still sweeping fragments of ancient kernels and cobs from the cliff and cave dwellings. American Indians of the Southwest, like their Eastern brothers, told their own corn myths. The Navajos believed that when the wild turkey hen came flying from the direction of the Morning Star, she shook her feathers and freed an ear of blue corn, which fell to earth. The Hopis of Arizona believed that the color of corn they planted was an indication to the corn god of the color wanted back; if blue and white corn were planted close together, the mixed colors that grew on some of the ears were the result of the deity's confusion. We in turn have almost succeeded in creating a striated red, white, and blue patriotic variety. There was once a feeble, although well-thought-out, suggestion made in the nineteenth century: substitute corn for the olive branch held in the claw of the eagle on the United States seal, in recognition of our debt of gratitude.

When the Spanish arrived they noted with astonishment that the Pueblo Indians were cultivating all manner of beans, squash, melons, wild berries (including strawberries), avocados, and the American plum. The American Indians were not great meat eaters, but did keep turkeys and prairie hens penned. This tribe rarely bothered with game, excepting the occasional rabbit; big game was left for the warring Apaches. Nuts from the piñon, a native low-growing pine, were used in salads and ground into paste for moles. The piñon wood itself warms the cold desert nights, and as cooking fuel, it imbues meats and fowl with an elusive piney flavor. There is a lovely local habit of lighting a small green piñon branch and walking it through the house, scenting the air more gently than any scented candle ever could. Wild oregano, garlic, and onions lent pungent flavor to many Pueblo dishes such as trout from the river, which were wrapped in cornhusks and baked over mesquite or piñon coals.

The Pueblo Indians made yeast from fermented corn and the wild potato root to raise breads. The *horno* (an outdoor beehive-shaped adobe oven of Spanish-Moorish origin that came with the Spanish) established itself as the preferred way of baking and cooking. Today, the Pueblo bride is still trained by her mother in the traditional cooking skills of her ancestors, and prepares foods for the tribe's many feasts. Custom dictates that they must welcome and feed all the guests, even those who arrive uninvited. This presents no small problem when hordes of tourists descend to sample the native food as though it were just another church supper.

The introduction of chile peppers—fresh and dried, sweet to hot—has brought about a cooking style particular to the Rio Grande valley. It is unlike the Mexican-influenced cookery of the Texas and Arizona borders and the Anglo-influences of neighboring Colorado and much of the West. Here the exchange of customs with the Indians and Spanish resulted in a type of cooking proudly called New Mexican. The Pueblos use masa prepared from wet kernels of dried, then cooked, corn. Tortillas are often made with blue corn *masa harina*, to be stuffed with fillings for enchiladas and burritos, fried into tostadas for scooping salsa and guacamole, and stacked like elaborate club sandwiches layered with tomato, lettuce, avocado, and Anaheim or bell peppers and topped with mild Chihuahua cheese.

By the eighteenth century, the Spanish missions were well established and cultivating olives and grapes. Spain's political influence was declining—her empire on the wane. The legacy of that influence would change the eating and drinking habits of the entire country two centuries later.

Breakfast

BROILED GRAPEFRUIT WITH HONEY ○ YEAST-RAISED WAFFLES WITH CREAMED DRIED BEEF ○ COFFEE ○ Gruet Methode Champenoise NV Brut, NM

I doubt any cowboy ever bothered to grill his grapefruit, but halved and sectioned grapefruit smeared with honey and set under the broiler to char makes a warm opening to a meal. Dried beef is an offshoot of American Indian preserved meats that have included elk, antelope, buffalo, and cow. The same drying method prevails, and creamed dried beef was often the horror of every soldier's tin plate. What was hell for the enlisted man became a craze in the kitchens of the 1930s, and then a chic dish at the New York restaurant "21." Served up on toast, baked potatoes, or waffles, it's a good dish.

YEAST-RAISED WAFFLES

Start this recipe the night before you plan to make the waffles.

INGREDIENTS
1 package dry yeast
1/2 cup warm water
2 cups milk
1/2 cup (1 stick) butter
1 teaspoon salt
1 teaspoon sugar
2 cups all-purpose flour
2 eggs
1/4 teaspoon baking powder

SPECIAL TOOLS
Waffle iron

METHOD
In a medium bowl, combine the yeast with the warm water and let stand until dissolved.
Warm the milk slightly over low heat.
Add the milk, butter, salt, sugar and flour to the yeast mixture and beat until smooth. Cover the bowl with plastic wrap and let stand overnight at room temperature.
The next morning, or just before cooking the waffles, beat in the eggs, add the baking powder and mix together well. The batter will not be very thick.
Ladle the waffle batter onto a hot waffle iron and cook until golden.

Makes approximately 8 waffles

CREAMED DRIED BEEF

INGREDIENTS
1 cup milk
1 cup heavy cream
2 tablespoons bourbon
1 teaspoon Dijon-style mustard
2 tablespoons unsalted butter, at room temperature
2 tablespoons all-purpose flour
2 ounces sharp cheddar cheese, grated
Cayenne pepper
Freshly milled white pepper
1 teaspoon grated fresh horseradish
1 pound dried beef, cut into 1/2-inch slivers

METHOD
In a heavy saucepan over high heat, bring the milk, cream, bourbon, and mustard to a boil.
Reduce the heat and simmer for 10 minutes.
In a bowl, cream together the butter and flour.
Whisk the paste into the hot mixture and bring to a boil.
Fold in the cheese and simmer for 5 minutes.
Season with cayenne and white pepper to taste.
Fold the horseradish and beef into the cream mixture and heat thoroughly.
Spoon over hot waffles.
Serve immediately.

Serves 6

Round-up Lunch

CHICKEN-FRIED STEAK AND CREAM GRAVY ○ DOUBLE-DUSTED FRIED CHICKEN ○
BLACK-EYED PEAS ○ LEAH DARBY'S CHOWCHOW ○ STEWED CORN ○ CANDIED
SWEET POTATOES ○ MARY PERRY'S FIVE-FINGER CORN BREAD ○ MASHED POTATOES ○
BUTTERED PEAS ○ TOMATO AND ONION SALAD ○ GRITS ○ PICKLES ○ BANANA
PUDDING ○ ICED TEA ○ Pabst Blue Ribbon Lager, TX

As one rancher said, "We don't know how he does it. Every fall, our old foreman sniffs the air one day and then gives us just a week's warning that on such and such a day the temperature's going to drop and it will have to be the day to round up the herd." For the next three or four days the cowboys saddle up at 4 a.m. and break at noon. The real thrill of their day is to stop in the heat of it all and eat this huge lunch. Typical of many chuck wagon meals, these recipes are actually two

days' eating. The chicken-fried steak and the crusty fried chicken are particular specialties of south Texas, where the food smacks more of the South than of the Southwest. Five-Finger Cornbread is yet another expression of the inventive cook. There are endless cornbread variations, and this recipe might be unheard of just 20 miles away where the ranch cook learned a different variation from her great-grandmother. She makes a kind of cornmeal mush, scoops up a little cake of it, pats it in the palm of her hand, and fries it. The imprint of her fingers is left on the cake, thus the name. The cowboys eat their beans with forkfuls of chowchow, not the cooked, put-up variety, but fresh chopped vegetables in vinegar. And still, they find room for dessert! Cornbread is sopped up with thick and sticky cane syrup, and they love that Texan specialty, banana pudding. You can't beat fresh bananas and you can't beat vanilla wafers. I don't see any point in going through the effort of making the wafers yourself; the pudding just wouldn't be the same. Nabisco wafers do very well, thank you.

CHICKEN-FRIED STEAK
AND CREAM GRAVY

INGREDIENTS

5 pounds top or bottom round of beef, sliced
    1/2-inch thick
3 cups milk
Salt and freshly milled black pepper
5 cups all-purpose flour
2 eggs, lightly beaten
1 quart vegetable oil, for frying
2 cups heavy cream

METHOD

In a shallow dish, steep the sliced steak in 2 cups of
    the milk for 1 hour.
Drain and dry with paper towels.
Season the meat with salt and pepper.
Sprinkle lightly with 2 tablespoons of the flour and
    pound 1/4-inch thick with a meat pounder.
In a shallow bowl, combine the eggs and the
    remaining cup of milk.

Lightly dip the meat in the egg mixture.
Dredge in the remaining flour, reserving
    2 tablespoons, and dredge twice more, shaking
    away any excess.
In a large cast-iron skillet, pour in 1 inch of oil.
Heat the oil until hot and fry the steak in batches
    until golden brown on each side. (The oil will
    have to be changed at least once for this
    amount of meat.)
Continue frying until all the floured meat is cooked.
When the meat is cooked, pour off all but
    1 tablespoon of the oil.
Off the heat, stir in 2 tablespoons flour and mix
    with the oil.
Return to low heat and add the cream.
Bring to a simmer, stirring constantly and scraping
    up the browned bits that cling to the bottom of
    the pan, until the cream gravy thickens.
Season with salt and pepper to taste and
    serve hot.

Serves 8 to 10

DOUBLE-DUSTED FRIED CHICKEN

INGREDIENTS

3 chickens (each approximately 3 1/2 pounds),
  cut into serving pieces with livers, gizzards, and
  hearts reserved
6 cups all-purpose flour
2 tablespoons baking powder
1/4 cup salt
2 tablespoons freshly milled black pepper
1 tablespoon paprika
2 tablespoons dried oregano
2 teaspoons dried thyme
Approximately 1 quart vegetable oil
2 eggs, lightly beaten

SPECIAL TOOLS
Deep-frying thermometer

METHOD
Wash the chicken pieces and pat dry with
  paper towels.
Mix the flour, baking powder, and seasonings
  together and divide between two paper bags.
Heat 1 1/2 inches of oil in a large heavy skillet.
Place the chicken pieces in a large bowl and toss
  with the eggs.
Place 4 to 5 pieces in one bag and shake well.
Repeat until all the chicken has been floured.
Quickly drop the chicken pieces in a bowl of
  ice water, remove, and then place in the
  second bag.
Shake well.
Fry in the hot oil (365° F), turning occasionally,
  cooking slowly until the chicken is golden brown,
  10 to 12 minutes for breasts and thighs, a few
  minutes longer for legs.
Remove the giblets once they turn golden.
Depending on the size of the skillet, the oil will have
  to be changed at least twice.

Note: Cream gravy is often a traditional
accompaniment to this dish. Follow the directions
in the recipe on the previous page.

Serves 8 to 9

BLACK-EYED PEAS

INGREDIENTS

5 pounds fresh black-eyed peas, shelled or 1
  pound dried, soaked in water overnight
1/2 pound fresh pork fatback, cut into
  1-inch cubes
6 small yellow onions, peeled
Salt and freshly milled black pepper

METHOD
Place the peas, fatback, and onions in a large pot
  and add water to cover.
Bring to a boil, reduce the heat, and simmer for
  2 to 2 1/2 hours, or until the peas are tender.
Season with salt and pepper.
Serve with chowchow.

Serves 8

LEAH DARBY'S CHOWCHOW

INGREDIENTS
4 medium-sized firm tomatoes, seeded
1 medium yellow onion
2 cucumbers, peeled, cut lengthwise, and seeded
5 tablespoons cider vinegar
Salt and freshly milled black pepper

METHOD
Roughly chop the vegetables.
Sprinkle with 2 1/2 tablespoons of the vinegar and
  lightly season with salt and pepper.
Continue chopping until the vegetables take on
  the consistency of a relish.
Add the remaining vinegar and seasonings.
Spoon the chowchow into a bowl, cover, and chill
  for 1 hour.
Serve with black-eyed peas.

Serves 6 to 8

CANDIED SWEET POTATOES

INGREDIENTS
4 pounds sweet potatoes, peeled and quartered
1 1/2 cups sugar
4 tablespoons butter

METHOD
Place the potatoes and sugar in a large pot and
add water to cover.
Bring to a boil, reduce the heat, and simmer
until tender.
Using a slotted spoon, remove the potatoes and
place in a serving bowl.
Dot with butter and serve immediately.

Serves 8

MARY PERRY'S FIVE-FINGER CORN BREAD

INGREDIENTS
4 cups white cornmeal
1 tablespoon salt
2 tablespoons sugar
4 to 5 cups boiling water
2 eggs
Vegetable oil, for frying

METHOD
In a large mixing bowl, combine the cornmeal,
salt, and sugar.
Lightly mix with 4 cups of the boiling water.
If the consistency is dry and lumpy, immediately
add 1/2 to 1 cup of cold water.
Add the eggs and mix.
Heat 1 1/2 inches of oil in a large heavy skillet.
When the oil is very hot, dip your fingers into a
bowl of cold water.
Take approximately 1/4 cup of the cornmeal
mixture and pat it between your fingers into
3-inch long ovals. (You should see the imprint of
your fingers.)
Immediately slip the ovals into the hot oil.

STEWED CORN

INGREDIENTS
20 ears fresh sweet corn
1 cup milk
1/4 pound butter
1/2 cup water
Salt and freshly milled pepper

METHOD
Remove the kernels from the cobs with a sharp
knife and set aside in a pot.
With a soupspoon, scrape the milk from the cobs
into the pot, over the corn kernels.
Add the milk, butter, and water.
Place the pot over moderate heat and bring
to a boil.
Reduce the heat and simmer for 1 hour.
Taste for seasonings and serve hot.

Serves 8 to 10

Turn the cornbread when golden and continue to cook the other side.

Remove with a slotted spoon and drain on paper towels.

Note: Corn bread is traditionally served with pure cane syrup at the end of the meal. It can be reheated and served for breakfast the next morning.

Makes 2¹/₂ dozen

BANANA PUDDING

INGREDIENTS

1 cup plus 6 tablespoons sugar
6 cups milk
¹/₃ cup arrowroot
¹/₄ cup bourbon
8 egg yolks
6 ripe bananas, peeled and sliced ¹/₄-inch thick
3 dozen vanilla wafers
3 egg whites

SPECIAL TOOLS
2¹/₂-quart ovenproof bowl

METHOD

In a large heavy saucepan, combine 1 cup of sugar and all of the milk and bring to a simmer over moderate heat.

In a small mixing bowl, dissolve the arrowroot in the bourbon.

Whisk the yolks together and add the bourbon mixture.

Measure out ¹/₂ cup of the simmering milk and whisk it into the egg mixture.

Whisk the mixture into the saucepan of simmering milk.

Stir constantly until the pudding bubbles and thickens enough to coat the back of the spoon.

Remove from the heat, place a sheet of plastic wrap directly on top of the surface, and cool in an ice water bath. Chill until you are ready to assemble the pudding.

To assemble:

In a large ovenproof bowl, alternate layers of bananas and pudding, lining the sides of the bowl with the vanilla wafers as you fill the bowl.

Cover the pudding with plastic wrap and chill thoroughly until you are ready to add the meringue.

Preheat the oven to 400° F.

With an electric mixer, beat the 3 egg whites until frothy.

Gradually add the remaining 6 tablespoons sugar and beat until stiff and glossy.

Spread the meringue over the pudding and bake for 10 minutes, or until the meringue is golden brown.

Serves 8 to 10

Chili Dinner

CHILI ○ GRAPEFRUIT-AND-CHAMPAGNE SORBET ○ Becker Vineyards Cabernet
Sauvignon, TX or Live Oak Pilsner, TX

*There are chili recipes, chili cooks, chili contests, chili cook-offs, and people eat quarts of the stuff
at big weekend chili-fests all across the state. Some people make it with steak and shun beans; some
people say even hamburger meat is too good for chili, and they cook it forever. I'll bite the bullet
and give you my own recipe.*

CHILI

INGREDIENTS

3/4 pound salt pork, diced

7 pounds top round of beef, sliced 1/4-inch thick
and diced

8 Spanish onions, finely diced

10 cloves garlic, minced

12 ripe tomatoes, peeled, seeded, and chopped
with the juices reserved

1 can (6 ounces) tomato paste

3/4 cup chili powder

1/2 cup ground cumin

1 tablespoon chopped fresh oregano

3 tablespoons crushed red pepper flakes

3 whole poblano chili peppers, seeded
and chopped

2 tablespoons salt

2 tablespoons *masa harina* or fine cornmeal

2 bunches scallions, including some of the green,
thinly sliced

1 pound cheddar cheese, shredded, to
accompany the chili

In a large heavy skillet, render 2/3 of the salt pork over moderate heat.

Remove the salt pork and place it in a large pot.

Working in batches, brown the meat in the skillet and transfer the meat to the pot.

Render the remaining salt pork in the skillet.

Add the onions and sauté over a moderately low heat until caramelized.

When caramelized, add the garlic and cook for a few minutes.

Turn the mixture into the pot.

Add the tomatoes and their juices and cook for 5 to 7 minutes.

Add the tomato paste and stir it into the meat.

Add the seasonings, chile peppers, and salt, and mix thoroughly.

Mix the *masa harina* with 2 tablespoons of water and fold into the chili.

Simmer over moderately low heat for 3 1/2 to 4 hours, stirring occasionally and checking to be sure the chili does not stick to the bottom of the pot.

Before serving, check the seasonings.

Depending on the freshness of the chili powder, the strength may vary. You may want additional seasonings.

Serve with sliced scallions and shredded cheddar cheese.

Note: This chili develops its flavor best over time. Make it ahead of time and chill. The next day, skim off the fat and reheat.

Serves 12

GRAPEFRUIT-AND-CHAMPAGNE SORBET

INGREDIENTS

2 cups fresh grapefruit juice, strained and chilled

1 cup champagne, chilled

1/2 cup simple syrup (see Basics, page 337), chilled

1 tablespoon vodka, chilled

1/2 cup pomegranate seeds

SPECIAL TOOLS

Ice cream maker

METHOD

In a bowl, mix the grapefruit juice, champagne, and simple syrup.

Turn on the ice cream maker and add the chilled vodka while the machine is running.

Pour the grapefruit mixture into the ice cream maker.

Chill according to the manufacturer's directions.

When the sorbet is frozen, remove, cover, and place in freezer.

When ready to serve, sprinkle with the pomegranate seeds.

Note: If the sorbet becomes too hard, place it in the refrigerator for 20 minutes or so to soften up before serving. The addition of vodka softens the texture and consistency.

Makes approximately 1 quart

Breakfast

SOPAIPILLAS ○ HUEVOS RANCHEROS ○ COFFEE

Like pillows of air, sopaipillas are a New Mexican favorite that have established themselves throughout the Southwest. Like the beignets in the Deep South and the doughnuts in the East, these puffed pastries are best served piping hot, with jam, honey, or a dusting of powdered sugar. Try them the way the locals do: poke a hole into the pastry and pour a stream of honey into the warm interior. Huevos Rancheros also go with the territory.

SOPAIPILLAS

INGREDIENTS

1 3/4 cup all-purpose flour
2 teaspoons baking powder
1 teaspoon salt
2 tablespoons shortening
2/3 cup water
1 quart vegetable oil, for frying

SPECIAL TOOLS

Pastry wheel
Deep fryer or deep heavy pot
Deep-frying thermometer

METHOD

In a mixing bowl, combine the flour, baking
    powder, and salt.
Cut in the shortening until the mixture resembles
    the consistency of cornmeal.
Gradually blend in 2/3 cup water.
Knead the dough on a clean surface for 5 minutes,
    or until smooth.
Divide the dough into 3 equal parts.
Roll out each portion of dough into a 1/8-inch-
    thick circle.
Using a pastry wheel, cut each circle into quarters.
While the dough is resting, heat the oil in a deep
    heavy pot until it reaches 350° F.
Working in batches, fry the sopaipillas, turning with
    a slotted spoon, for 2 to 3 minutes, or until a pale
    golden color.
Drain on paper towels and serve hot.

Makes 1 dozen

HUEVOS RANCHEROS

INGREDIENTS

2 fresh green New Mexican, Poblano or Anaheim
    chile peppers
1 small green jalapeño chile pepper
4 tomatillos
1 small garlic clove, peeled and minced
I small yellow onion, roughly chopped
2 tablespoons olive oil, peanut or canola
2 large ripe tomatoes, about 2 pounds, cored
    and chopped
Salt and freshly milled black pepper to taste
6 eggs
Chopped cilantro to taste

METHOD

Roast, seed, and peel the chiles
    (see Basics, page 338).
To prepare the tomatillos, remove the papery husk
    and rinse them.
Place them in a saucepan with just enough water
    to cover.
Bring to a simmer and cook for 8 to 10 minutes until
    soft and translucent. Drain.
Put the chiles, tomatillos, garlic, and onion into the
    bowl of a food processor and pulse on and off
    to create a rough puree.
In a medium skillet, heat the oil and sauté the chile
    mixture until the onion is translucent.
Add the tomatoes and cook for about 5 minutes,
    or until the tomatoes soften.
Season with salt and pepper and keep warm while
    you prepare the eggs to your liking—poached,
    scrambled, or fried.
Pour the sauce over the eggs and sprinkle with
    a little chopped cilantro.
Serve with warm tortillas. (An accompaniment of
    refried beans is also traditional.)

Serves 2 to 3

Menudo Lunch

MENUDO (TRIPE SOUP) WITH PIQUANT TAMALES ○ GRILLED CHICKEN SALAD ○ CANTALOUPE WITH TEQUILA LIME SYRUP ○ Alamosa Wine Cellars Viognier, TX or Ponderosa Vineyards Riesling, NM

This menu is a cacophony of spices and herbs used in New Mexican cooking. The tripe soup should cook at a lazy bubble on the back of the stove while you prepare the tamales and the salad. Tamales date to the days before Columbus; practically every culture used stuffed leaves or bark to steam or roast their food. Tamales are little steamed puddings—blue-corn flour filled with vegetables, tied up like tiny packages. All of the salad components bear witness to the fruitful bounty of the Rio Grande valley, including the sturdy but obliging iceberg lettuce, which becomes quite special when shredded. Tequila combined with limes in a sweet syrup enhances ripe melon.

MENUDO (TRIPE SOUP)

INGREDIENTS

2 pounds fresh honeycomb tripe

2 tablespoons olive oil

1 large onion, peeled and chopped

2 garlic cloves, crushed

3 whole cloves

5 peppercorns, crushed

1 1/2 to 2 quarts beef stock, as needed (see Basics, page 332) or canned low sodium beef broth

1/4 cup fresh green Poblano or Anaheim chili peppers, deveined, seeded, and chopped

3 large ripe tomatoes, peeled, seeded and chopped

1 tablespoon fresh oregano, chopped

1/2 cup scallions, chopped, including some of the green

3 tablespoon fresh cilantro, chopped

Salt

METHOD

Trim and wash the tripe under cold running water.

Place the tripe in a saucepan with salted cold water. Cover and refrigerate overnight.

Drain the tripe and place in a large kettle of salted boiling water to cover. Bring to a boil and cook 5 minutes. Rinse the tripe under cold running water. You may blanch the tripe two or three more times to rid it of its tripe-iness.

Using sharp kitchen shears, cut the tripe into 1-inch wide strips, and cut the strips into 1-inch squares.

Blanch again, and cool under cold running water and drain.

In a large soup kettle that will comfortably hold the tripe, heat the oil over medium heat.

Add the onions and sauté for 5 minutes or until wilted.

Add the garlic, cloves, and peppercorns.

Add 2 quarts of boiling water and fold in the tripe.

Bring to a boil, reduce the heat to a simmer, cover the pot and cook for 30 minutes.

Add the 1 1/2 quarts of stock and continue to simmer for 2 1/2 hours covered, or until the tripe is very tender.

Check the liquid level from time to time making sure the tripe is covered, adding more stock if necessary. The texture of the tripe should be as tender as soft gristle.

Add the tomatoes, peppers, herbs and scallions and simmer for 15 to 20 minutes.

Check the seasonings and serve in heated soup bowls and sprinkle a little chopped cilantro over the soup.

Serves 6

PIQUANT TAMALES

INGREDIENTS

3 dozen dried cornhusks (available at Hispanic
   markets, see Sources, page 344)

Vegetable Filling:

3 tablespoons olive oil

3/4 cup finely diced onion

1 clove garlic, minced

1 small eggplant, finely diced, approximately 1 cup

3/4 cup finely diced zucchini

1/2 cup tomato, peeled, seeded, and chopped

2 tablespoons finely diced green jalapeño peppers

1 teaspoon cornmeal

Masa Mixture:

1/4 cup lard

3 cups blue corn *masa harina*

1 1/4 teaspoons salt

SPECIAL TOOLS

Steamer

METHOD

Prepare the cornhusks:

Submerge the husks in a pan of warm water for
   2 to 3 hours.

Prepare the vegetable filling:

In a medium skillet, heat the oil over moderate
   heat and sauté the onions and garlic until wilted.

Add the eggplant and sauté for 5 minutes.

Add the zucchini, tomatoes, and diced jalapeño
   peppers and sauté for 3 minutes.

Stir in the cornmeal and set aside to cool.

Prepare the masa mixture:

In a mixing bowl, beat the lard with a wooden
   spoon or electric mixer until soft and light.

Add the *masa harina* and salt and mix thoroughly.

Add enough water to make the mixture
   spreadable but firm.

The amount of water will depend on the
   coarseness of the masa.

Assemble the tamales:

Drain the cornhusks.

Using 3 or 4 of the split husks, pull off 1/4-inch strips
   going with the grain of the husks to use to tie the
   tamales and reserve.

With scissors, cut off 1 inch of the pointed smaller
   end of each husk and discard.

Place the husks on a flat working surface; there will
   be about 1 1/2 dozen.

Place a rounded teaspoon of the masa mixture in
   the center of the husk and spread it out about
   1/8 inch thick.

Spoon 1 teaspoon of the vegetable mixture into
   the center of the masa mixture.

Carefully wrap the husks around the masa and
   filling, pulling the sides around first and folding
   the top and bottom of the husks toward the
   center of the tamale to make a neat package.

Tie each tamale closed with a cornhusk strip.

In a steamer, bring 2 cups of water to a boil.

Cover the base of the steamer container with a
   layer of the remaining cornhusks, and set the
   tamales over the husks.

Cover and steam for 45 minutes, or until the masa
   mixture pulls away from the husks of the tamale.

Makes 1 1/2 dozen

GRILLED CHICKEN SALAD

INGREDIENTS

3 large whole chicken breasts, split

Oil

Marinade:

1/4 cup olive oil

1/2 cup fresh lime juice

1 medium onion, thinly sliced

6 cloves garlic, minced

Salt and freshly milled black pepper

Dressing:

1/3 cup fresh lime juice

1/4 cup olive oil

1/4 cup vegetable oil

1 teaspoon chopped fresh mint

Salt and freshly milled black pepper

Salad:

1 medium head iceberg lettuce, cored and thinly
   sliced with the outer leaves discarded

3 ripe avocados

3 large ripe tomatoes, peeled, seeded
    and chopped
6 green poblano peppers, roasted, seeded,
    deveined, and chopped (see Basics, page 338)
1/2 cup piñon nuts, toasted (see Basics, page 337)

METHOD
Place the chicken breasts in a shallow bowl.
Combine all the ingredients for the marinade and
    pour over the chicken breasts.
Cover and refrigerate for 6 hours, turning the
    breasts at least once.
Prepare a fire in a charcoal grill using hardwood
    charcoal, piñon, or fruit wood.
When the coals reach a dusty red glow, brush the
    grill with oil.
Place the breasts on the grill, skin side down.
Grill on one side for approximately 10 minutes.
Turn breasts over and grill for approximately
    15 more minutes, or until cooked through.
    Do not overcook.
Remove from the heat and set aside to cool
    for 30 minutes.
Mix the dressing, cover and set aside.
Remove the chicken from the bone with a sharp
    slicing knife.
Cut into long, thin, slices including the skin.
Place the shredded lettuce in a large bowl.
Peel the avocados and slice into long, thin strips.
Arrange the tomatoes, peppers, nuts, avocados,
    and chicken over the lettuce.
Add the dressing and toss the salad at the table,
    or each ingredient may be placed individually
    on chilled plates, with the dressing served on
    the side.

Serves 6

CANTALOUPE WITH
TEQUILA LIME SYRUP

INGREDIENTS
4 limes
1 cup sugar
1/4 cup tequila

2 ripe cantaloupes, chilled
Fresh mint

METHOD
Using a vegetable peeler, remove the zest from the
    limes in long strips.
Cut the zest into fine, needle-thin julienne.
Place the lime julienne in a medium saucepan and
    add cold water to cover.
Bring to a boil for 8 minutes.
Repeat the process again with fresh water.
Drain thoroughly and set the lime zest aside.
Section the limes and discard the pith and
    membrane. Reserve.
In a medium saucepan, combine the sugar with 1
    cup of water and bring to a boil over high heat.
Add the lime julienne and continue boiling for
    5 minutes.
Add the tequila to the syrup and cool.
Halve and seed the melons.
Cut into long 1-inch-wide strips.
Remove the melon rind with a sharp paring knife.
Arrange the melon slices on a platter or serving
    dish. Sprinkle the lime sections over the melon.
Pour the syrup over the fruits and serve with
    the mint.

Serves 6

Posole

POSOLE STEW ○ VEGETABLE CORN BREAD ○ GREEN MANGO WITH SALT AND LIME ○
Dos Cabezas Cabernet Sauvignon, NM or Sierra Blanca Nut Brown Beer, NM

Every region produces a dish that is reminiscent of a similar dish made elsewhere. Posole is the Southwestern version of hominy, not unlike large kernels of samp. Simply boiled it sustained the Pueblo community. Posole is a generic term both for the dry treated kernel and for this stew. Over the years, each incoming settlement added an ingredient to the recipe for posole: a bone, morsels of meat, culminating with the addition of sausage and saffron. When it came to sweets, not every region depended on sugar. Honey was easily available, but in these arid regions they developed a habit of salting sweet fruits.

POSOLE STEW

INGREDIENTS

3 thick slices slab bacon
3/4 pound pork shoulder or neck, cut into
    1-inch cubes
3/4 pound lamb shoulder or neck, cut into
    1-inch cubes
Salt and freshly milled pepper
2 medium onions, chopped
4 cloves garlic, minced
3 to 4 quarts chicken stock, as needed (see Basics,
    page 332) or canned low-sodium chicken broth
2 pounds dried posole (or hominy)
10 fresh green New Mexican, Poblano or Anaheim
    chile peppers, peeled, seeded, deveined,
    and chopped
2 teaspoons chopped fresh oregano
2 pinches saffron threads
3/4 pound Linguiça sausage
3/4 pound chorizo or Italian sweet sausage
1 tablespoon chopped fresh cilantro or parsley

METHOD

In a heavy skillet, render the bacon.
Drain on paper towels when crisp.
Season the pork and lamb with salt and pepper.
Brown the meat in the bacon fat over moderately
    high heat. Remove and set aside.

Cover and refrigerate.
Add the onions and garlic to the bacon fat in the
    skillet and sauté until translucent and set aside.
Add 1/2 cup of the chicken stock to the skillet and
    deglaze the pan, scraping up the brown bits that
    cling to the bottom.
Pour the liquid into a large kettle.
Add approximately 3 quarts of the chicken stock,
    the posole, green chile peppers, oregano,
    saffron, and 1 teaspoon salt.
Bring to a boil, reduce the heat, and simmer for 2
    hours, stirring from time to time and adding more
    chicken stock or water as needed.
Add the pork and lamb, and continue to cook for
    1 to 1 1/2 hours, until the posole is tender.
Twenty minutes before the posole is ready to serve,
    prepare the sausages.
Poach the Linguiça sausages in a pot of simmering
    water for 15 minutes.
In a medium skillet filled with 1/4 inch of water,
    cook the chorizo over moderately high heat until
    the water evaporates and the sausages brown.
Place the posole in a heated crock or bowl.
Arrange the sausages in the posole.
Dust with the chopped cilantro or parsley and serve.

Serves 8 to 10

VEGETABLE CORN BREAD

INGREDIENTS

2 tablespoons butter, for greasing the baking pan

1 1/3 cups yellow cornmeal

1 teaspoon baking powder

2 teaspoons salt

3/4 cup buttermilk

2 eggs, lightly beaten

1/4 cup vegetable oil or rendered bacon fat

1 cup grated zucchini

1/2 cup tomatoes, peeled, seeded, and chopped

1/4 cup sweet red bell pepper, seeded, deveined, and chopped

1 tablespoon jalapeño peppers, chopped

1 ear fresh, sweet corn, kernels removed

METHOD

Preheat the oven to 350° F.

Butter a 9-inch square baking pan.

In a mixing bowl, combine the dry ingredients.

Add the liquid ingredients and mix well.

Fold in the vegetables.

Pour the batter into the pan and bake for 35 minutes, or until the edges turn golden and pull away from the sides of the pan.

Note: Any combination of leftover vegetables may be used. Timing here is set for low altitude cooking. In a high altitude, bake at 400° F for 45 minutes.

Serves 8 to 10

GREEN MANGO WITH SALT AND LIME

INGREDIENTS

4 medium-size tart mangoes

4 to 8 limes, halved

Sea or kosher salt

METHOD

Cut the mangoes flush against the pit on each side. (Reserve any leftover mango for chutney or another recipe.)

With a small sharp paring knife, score the fruit in a grid pattern; do not pierce the skin.

Squeeze the lime juice over the fruit and sprinkle with salt.

To eat the fruit, hold it in your hands, flesh side up, and push up in the center from the skin side to allow the grid-patterned flesh to protrude.

Serves 8

Mole Supper

SQUASH BLOSSOM SOUP ○ TURKEY MOLE ○ BLUE-CORN PANCAKES ○ HOT MANGO
SALSA ○ FLAN WITH COCONUT CREAM ○ St. Clair Vineyards Chardonnay, NM

*Squash blossoms are frequently available in markets and farm stands in late spring through most
of the summer. If you grow this prolific vegetable in your own garden, be sure to pluck only the
male flowers (armed with pistils). This is a very delicate soup, a creamy prelude to the mole.
Chocolate in its unsweetened form is used to enrich the flavor of many dishes. Our tendency to
recoil when chocolate is used in a savory dish is based purely on our assumption that all chocolate
is sweet. From Mexico to the Southwest, turkey and mole go hand in hand. Shredded and served
on buttered blue-corn pancakes with fresh mango salsa hot with chile peppers, the turkey becomes
anything but ordinary.*

SQUASH BLOSSOM SOUP

INGREDIENTS

1 pound squash blossoms (approximately 60
   blossoms), reserve 8 of the choicest blossoms
   for decoration
2 tablespoons unsalted butter
1 bunch scallions, including some of the green,
   cut lengthwise and thinly sliced
1 1/2 quarts chicken stock (see Basics, page 332),
   reduced by half, or canned low-sodium
   chicken broth
1 1/2 to 2 pounds baby zucchini and yellow
   squash, chopped
2 cups heavy cream
Salt and freshly milled white pepper

METHOD

Remove the blossoms from the squash.
In a medium kettle or saucepan, melt the butter.
Sauté the scallions until wilted.
Add the reduced stock and bring to a simmer.
Add the blossoms and squash to the stock.
Simmer for 10 minutes.
Meanwhile, in a separate pan, reduce the
   cream by half.

Strain the broth into a clean saucepan, reserving
   the solids.
Puree the solids in a food processor or food mill.
Fold the puree into the broth and add the cream.
Season to taste and chill for 1 hour.
When ready to serve, decorate each plate with a
   reserved squash blossom.

Serves 8

TURKEY MOLE

INGREDIENTS

18 dried red New Mexican or Ancho chile peppers

$^3/_4$ cup lard or substitute corn oil

1 boneless turkey breast (approximately 4 pounds)

3 tablespoons raisins

2 tablespoons skinless peanuts

5 cloves garlic

$^1/_8$ teaspoon coriander seed

$^1/_4$ teaspoon cinnamon

$^1/_4$ teaspoon anise seed

1 teaspoon sesame seeds

1 large ripe tomato, halved and seeded

1 ounce Mexican or unsweetened chocolate, chopped

1 quart chicken or turkey stock (see Basics, page 332) or canned low-sodium chicken broth

METHOD

Remove the stems and seeds from the dried chile peppers.

Reserve 2 tablespoons of the seeds.

In a large skillet, melt $^1/_4$ cup of the lard (if using corn oil, warm the pan and add $^1/_4$-cup of the oil to heat) and briefly sauté the chili peppers until they turn dark red.

With a slotted spoon move the chili peppers to a bowl of warm water, and soak for 20 minutes.

Add $^1/_4$ cup lard or oil to the skillet and brown the turkey breast, skin-side down, for 10 minutes.

Turn and brown the other side for 10 minutes.

Refrigerate until you are done making the sauce.

Drain the peppers and puree in a food processor until they make a smooth paste.

Add some of the soaking liquid, if necessary, to loosen the mixture.

In a large skillet, melt 2 tablespoons of lard or oil over moderate heat.

Add the puree and simmer for 5 minutes.

Remove the puree to the bowl of a food processor.

In the skillet, melt the remaining 2 tablespoons of lard or oil.

Add the raisins and simmer until they plump.

Remove with a slotted spoon and put into the

bowl of the food processor with the
pureed chiles.

Over low heat, lightly toast the peanuts, garlic,
spices, and the reserved chile seeds in a clean
cast iron skillet. Add the toasted ingredients and
the tomato to the bowl of the food processor
and process the mixture until smooth.

In a large saucepan add the puree and cook over
moderate heat, stirring constantly, for 10 minutes.

Add the chocolate and stir until melted.

Add the broth a little at a time, bring to a simmer
and cook for 10 minutes.

Set aside and keep warm.

Remove the skin from the chilled turkey.

Cut the turkey breast into long, 1/2-inch strips and
add to the mole sauce.

Prepare the pancake batter and make
the pancakes

Bring the turkey and mole sauce to a simmer until
heated through and serve, ladling the turkey
over each stack of 3 blue-corn pancakes.

Serves 8

BLUE-CORN PANCAKES

INGREDIENTS

1 1/2 cups blue or yellow cornmeal
1/2 cup all-purpose flour
1 teaspoon salt
1 tablespoon plus 1 teaspoon baking powder
2 eggs, lightly beaten

1 1/2 cups milk
4 tablespoons melted butter
Unsalted butter, for the griddle

METHOD

Sift the dry ingredients into a mixing bowl.
Add the eggs, milk, and butter and mix thoroughly.
Cook the pancakes on a hot, buttered grill or
   skillet, using 2 tablespoons of batter for
   each pancake.
Keep the pancakes warm in a low oven until ready
   to serve.

Note: Blue cornmeal is milled dry blue corn. Blue-
corn *masa harina* is fresh corn masa that has been
dried and then powdered for use in making
traditional tortillas and tamales.

Makes approximately 25 small pancakes

HOT MANGO SALSA

INGREDIENTS

1 dried red New Mexican or Ancho chile pepper
   pod, soaked in warm water for 20 minutes
2 large ripe mangoes, peeled and cut into
   1/2-inch slices
1 tablespoon tequila
1 teaspoon sugar
2 tablespoons piñon nuts, toasted
   (see Basics, page 338)

METHOD

Remove the stem, seeds, and veins from the chile
   peppers and cut into needle-thin julienne.
In a saucepan, combine the mangoes, tequila,
   and sugar over moderate heat.
Stir with a wooden spoon until the sugar dissolves
   and the mangoes begin to give off their juice.
Add the chile julienne and cook for another 2 to 3
   minutes. Set aside to cool.
When the mixture has cooled, fold in the
   piñon nuts.
Serve at room temperature with the turkey mole.

Makes approximately 2 cups

FLAN WITH COCONUT CREAM

INGREDIENTS

3/4 cup sugar
2 cups heavy cream
2 cups milk
4 egg yolks, lightly beaten
5 whole eggs, lightly beaten

SPECIAL TOOLS

9-inch flan mold or deep-dish glass pie plate

METHOD

Preheat the oven to 350° F.
Place 1/2 cup of the sugar in a heavy skillet.
Melt the sugar over moderately high heat.
When the sugar begins to dissolve, stir constantly
   with a wooden spoon to prevent scorching.
When the sugar melts and begins to turn a
   light golden color, remove from the heat and
   immediately pour into the flan mold.
Lift the mold with a dry kitchen towel or hot pads
   and turn it until the bottom surface and sides are
   well coated with the caramelized sugar.
   Set aside.
In a heavy saucepan, scald the cream and the
   milk over moderately high heat.
Add the remaining 1/4 cup sugar.
When the sugar dissolves, remove from the heat
   and whisk in the egg yolks and eggs one at
   a time.
Pour the mixture into the prepared mold, and
   place the mold in a large pan.
Add hot water to come halfway up the sides of
   the mold. Place the pan in the preheated oven
   and bake for 45 minutes to 1 hour, or until a knife
   comes out clean when inserted in the center of
   the flan.
Remove from the oven for at least 2 hours
   before unmolding.
Briefly return to a warm water bath to loosen
   the caramel.
Invert the pan on a platter and serve with the
   Coconut Cream.

Serves 8

COCONUT CREAM

INGREDIENTS

1 fresh coconut or $1/2$ cup prepared grated
    coconut and $1/2$ cup of unsweetened
    coconut milk, or substitute canned

$1/2$ cup heavy cream

$1/4$ cup sugar

3 egg yolks, lightly beaten

METHOD

Prepare the coconut:

Preheat the oven to 350° F.

With a large nail or screwdriver, poke the 3 eyes of
    the coconut. Drain the milk and reserve.

Place the coconut in the oven and bake for
    10 minutes.

Remove the coconut and reduce the oven
    temperature to 275° F.

Hit the coconut firmly with a hammer.

Peel the meat out of the shell.

With a vegetable peeler, peel off the outer
    brown skin.

Grate the flesh.

On a baking sheet, spread out $1/4$ cup of the
    grated coconut and bake, tossing, until golden;
    reserve the remaining coconut for another use.

Prepare the sauce:

Strain the coconut milk into a saucepan and add
    the heavy cream and sugar.

Bring to a simmer, stirring until the sugar dissolves.

Remove from the heat and whisk half of the liquid
    into the eggs.

Return the mixture to the saucepan, and cook,
    stirring constantly, until it thickens slightly.

Fold in the fresh toasted coconut, and serve at
    room temperature with the flan.

Makes 1 cup

Piñon-Grilled Dinner

MARINATED GRILLED BEEF HEARTS WITH SALSA RENA ○ HOT NEW MEXICAN SALAD ○ TORTILLAS ○ SQUASH PUREE ○ COCADA WITH FRESH CORN ○ TEQUILA WITH SALSA ○ Milagro Vineyards Cabernet Sauvignon, NM

Beef hearts are a chuck wagon legacy. The dish has a very aromatic blend of spices and herbs and a simple preparation. The vegetable salad and squash puree are almost bland accompaniments, offset by the New Mexican habit of washing down fiery pureed dried pepper salsa with tequila. The cooling corn-and-coconut dessert helps to extinguish the fire.

MARINATED GRILLED BEEF HEARTS

INGREDIENTS

1 beef heart (3 to 4 pounds), fat and nerves
   removed, cut into 1-inch cubes
12 cloves garlic, chopped
1 red onion, thinly sliced
1/4 cup fresh oregano, chopped
2 teaspoons ground cumin
Freshly milled black pepper
1 bottle dry red wine
Salt, for grilling

METHOD

Place the cubed beef heart in a mixing bowl.
Add all the ingredients and mix.
Cover and refrigerate for 24 hours.
Prepare a fire in a charcoal grill using hardwood
   charcoal, piñon, or fruit wood.
Drain the beef hearts, reserving the marinade.
Thread the cubes onto skewers and season
   with salt.
When the coals reach a dusty red glow, grill the

hearts, turning often and basting with the
   remaining marinade.
Beef hearts are best served rare with salsa.

Serves 8 to 10

SALSA RENA

INGREDIENTS

12 dried red New Mexican or Ancho chile peppers
1 tablespoon fresh oregano, chopped
Salt
2 to 3 tablespoons olive oil

METHOD

Remove the stems and seeds from the chili
   peppers and soak in a bowl of warm water for
   20 minutes.
Drain the peppers and process them in a food
   processor, pulsing on and off until they begin
   to puree.
Add the oregano and a generous amount of salt.
Turn the processor on and gradually add the oil.

For a very hot sauce, add chili seeds to suit your taste.

Serve with grilled beef hearts with tequila as a chaser.

Makes $^1/_2$ to $^3/_4$ cup

HOT NEW MEXICAN SALSA

INGREDIENTS

3 medium tomatoes, peeled, seeded, and finely chopped

3 ears sweet corn, blanched and the kernels cut off the cobs

2 green bell peppers, seeded, deveined, and finely chopped

1 sweet red bell pepper, seeded, deveined, and finely chopped

2 medium zucchini, finely chopped

2 slices smoked slab bacon, cut $^1/_4$-inch thick and diced

2 teaspoons chili powder

$^1/_3$ cup cider vinegar

$^1/_4$ cup fresh parsley, chopped

2 tablespoons cilantro, chopped

METHOD

In a large bowl, toss all of the vegetables together, cover, and set aside.

Do not refrigerate.

When ready to serve, render the bacon in a large skillet and cook until lightly crisp.

Stir in the chili powder, add the vinegar, and bring to a simmer.

Fold in the herbs and pour the dressing over the vegetables and toss.

Serves 8 to 10

SQUASH PUREE

INGREDIENTS

2 butternut squash

Salt and freshly milled black pepper

Freshly grated nutmeg

2 tablespoons butter, at room temperature

METHOD

Place the squash in one or two large kettles of salted cold water, and bring to a boil.

Reduce the heat and simmer until tender, approximately 30 minutes.

Drain.

Cut each squash in half and remove the seeds.

Scoop out the pulp from the skin and puree the pulp in a food processor, or use a potato masher or food mill.

Season the puree, and stir in the nutmeg and butter.

Serve hot.

Serves 8 to 10

COCADA WITH FRESH CORN

INGREDIENTS

1 1/2 cups sugar

1 vanilla bean, split

1/2 cup fresh coconut milk, or substitute canned

2 1/2 cups shredded coconut

2 1/2 cups milk

2 eggs, separated

1 cup fresh corn kernels, cooked (approximately 2 ears)

1/4 cup toasted coconut

METHOD

In a heavy saucepan, combine 1 cup of the sugar, vanilla bean, and coconut milk.

Simmer over moderate heat until the sugar dissolves.

Add the shredded coconut and cook for 7 to 8 minutes to extract the flavors.

Pour in the milk and bring to a boil.

Reduce the heat, and simmer, stirring often, for about 20 minutes, until the mixture thickens.

Whisk in the egg yolks.

When blended, cook for 1 to 2 minutes before removing from the heat and adding the corn kernels.

Turn the cocada into a bowl and refrigerate for 2 hours.

Before serving, beat the egg whites until soft peaks form, then beat in the remaining 1/2 cup of sugar until mixture forms stiff, glossy peaks.

Fold the whites into the custard mixture.

Turn into a serving dish and sprinkle with the toasted coconut.

Serves 8 to 10

Tequila

Tequila, like any liquor, can be of the best or worst quality. Made from the Agave cactus, it has influenced drinking habits from Mexico to the Southwest, and in most Spanish-speaking enclaves in our big cities. The Mexicans take it with lime and salt to combat the tequila's fire. The rugged ranchero laps up salsa from a little tumbler, and shoots it down with a jigger of tequila. Here, the tequila puts out the fire of the chile peppers.

Green Chile Lunch

GREEN CHILE STEW ○ MICHELLE NARANJO'S INDIAN BREAD ○ GREEN SALAD WITH WATERMELON ○ ONION-AND-DILL VINAIGRETTE ○ PIÑON BRITTLE ○ Callaghan Vineyards, Lisa's Cuvee, AZ or Nimbus Pale Ale, AZ

The typical Southwesterner has a lusty passion for chile peppers. For the uninitiated, chiles are an education. In this case, a pile of hot chile peppers and a little meat spiked with lemon zest make a refreshingly unexplosive stew. Fruit with salad greens was a Spanish combination, common here long before the Californians took it up. Be certain to serve this dense Indian bread hot from the oven. Piñon nuts make a brittle that's as sweet and crunchy as one made from peanuts.

GREEN CHILE STEW

INGREDIENTS

2 tablespoons lard or vegetable oil

Salt and freshly milled black pepper

1 1/2 pounds lamb shoulder, trimmed and cut into
1-inch cubes

1 1/2 pounds pork shoulder, trimmed and cut into
1-inch cubes

18 long, medium-hot, green Poblano or Anaheim
chile peppers, peeled, stemmed, seeded,
and deveined

1 1/2 to 2 cups chicken stock (see Basics,
page 332)or canned low-sodium chicken broth

Grated zest of 1 lemon

METHOD

In a large heavy skillet, melt the lard over
moderately high heat.

Lightly salt and pepper the lamb.

Brown the lamb on all sides and set aside.

Lightly salt and pepper the pork.

Brown the pork on all sides and set aside.

Cut the peppers into long 1/2-inch strips,
depending on their size.

Lightly sauté the peppers in the lard until they
begin to wilt.

Add the stock to the skillet.

Bring to a boil and reduce the heat.

Add the meats and simmer until tender, about
1 1/2 hours.

Add the peppers and cook until heated through.

Fold in the zest and serve.

Serves 6

MICHELLE NARANJO'S
INDIAN BREAD

INGREDIENTS

7 cups all-purpose flour

1/2 teaspoon salt

1/3 cup lard

1 teaspoon active dry yeast

1 1/2 cups lukewarm water

1/2 teaspoon sugar

METHOD

In a large bowl, combine the flour and salt and cut
in the lard, using a fork, your fingers, or a pastry
blender, until the mixture is crumbly.

In a small bowl, combine the yeast, lukewarm water, and sugar.

Set aside until the yeast and sugar dissolve and the mixture is foamy.

Mix the dissolved yeast mixture with the flour and lard.

Knead the dough until it becomes elastic and pliable, approximately 7 minutes.

Place the dough in a greased bowl.

Cover the bowl and place it in a warm, draft-free place to rise until doubled, approximately 4 hours.

Punch down the dough and divide in half.

Shape the dough into 2 free-form loaves and place them on an ungreased baking sheet, or place each loaf in a medium-size bread pan.

Cover the loaves and let rise again in a warm, draft-free place for another 2 hours.

Preheat the oven to 375° F.

Place the loaves on a preheated pizza stone and bake them for 45 to 60 minutes, or until the bottom of each loaf sounds hollow when tapped.

Makes 2 loaves

ONION-AND-DILL VINAIGRETTE

INGREDIENTS
Basic Vinaigrette (see Basics, page 334)
2 tablespoons finely chopped red onion
1 tablespoon chopped dill
1 clove garlic, minced

METHOD
Prepare the vinaigrette and whisk in the onion, dill, and garlic.

Cover and refrigerate for 30 minutes.

Whisk the vinaigrette before using.

Note: Toss the vinaigrette with a salad of ruby red lettuce leaves and cubed and seeded watermelon, and serve as an accompaniment.

Makes approximately 1 1/4 cups

PIÑON BRITTLE

INGREDIENTS
Vegetable oil
2 cups sugar
1 cup light corn syrup
1/4 cup water
2 tablespoons unsalted butter
2 1/2 cups roasted piñon nuts (see Basics, page 338)
1 teaspoon baking soda

SPECIAL TOOLS
Candy thermometer

METHOD
Lightly coat the baking sheet with oil.

In a heavy saucepan, combine the sugar and corn syrup with 1/4 cup water.

Bring to a boil and cook until the mixture reaches the hard ball stage (250° F). Off the heat add the butter and nuts. Return to the heat and cook to the hard crack stage (295° F).

Remove from the heat.

Stir in the baking soda.

Pour the brittle quickly over the oiled pan and spread as thin as possible with a spatula.

Cool completely and break into pieces.

Store in airtight containers.

Puye Picnic

GAZPACHO ○ AVOCADO SANDWICHES ○ JALAPEÑO PIE ○ PEANUT SHORTBREAD ○
SPICED POACHED PEACHES ○ Full Moon Pale Rye Ale, TX

This picnic is set on a mesa in the Puye ruins of New Mexico. Gazpacho traveled with the conquistadors from Spain to the Southwest. The best time to make gazpacho is when tomatoes are bursting with flavor and ripeness and the vegetable garden is at its peak. The sandwiches are a sophisticated B.L.T. to be eaten with the soup. Jalapeño pie is a flavorful baked custard, and the peaches have a hint of peppery taste. Shortbread sneaked into the territory with the Scots, and I've sneaked peanuts into the shortbread.

GAZPACHO

INGREDIENTS

2 quarts homemade tomato juice or good quality
    bottled juice

4 to 5 cloves of garlic, minced

1 1/2 bunches scallions, including some of the
    green, split lengthwise and finely chopped

1 large sweet red bell pepper, seeded, deveined,
    and finely diced

2 green bell peppers, seeded, deveined, and
    finely diced

3 medium zucchini, grated (approximately 4 cups)

1 celery heart, finely diced

2 medium cucumbers, peeled, seeded,
    and chopped

1/4 cup fresh lime juice

1/4 cup tequila (optional)

2 teaspoons ground cumin

Salt and freshly milled black pepper

METHOD

In a large bowl, mix together all of the ingredients
    and chill for 4 hours.

Serve with the avocado sandwiches.

Serves 10

AVOCADO SANDWICHES

INGREDIENTS

$^1/_4$ pound unsalted butter, at room temperature

1 teaspoon finely chopped cilantro

1 large ripe tomato, peeled, seeded,
  and chopped

6 slices crisp cooked bacon, chopped

2 medium-sized ripe avocados

20 thin slices wheat or grain bread

METHOD

In a small bowl, cream the butter with the cilantro.

Lightly butter each slice of bread.

Spread a little of the tomato on 10 slices of the
  bread and dust with the bacon.

Thinly slice the avocados and arrange over
  the bacon.

Top each sandwich with a slice of buttered bread.

Trim the crusts and cut in half diagonally.

Pack in an airtight container, covered with damp
  paper towels.

Close tight and refirgerate until ready to serve.

Makes 20 half-sandwiches

JALAPEÑO PIE

INGREDIENTS

Cornmeal Crust:

$^1/_3$ cups yellow or white cornmeal

$^2/_3$ cups all-purpose flour

$^1/_2$ teaspoon salt

$^1/_2$ cup lard

$^1/_4$ cup cold water

Filling:

1 $^1/_2$ cups heavy cream

1 $^1/_2$ cups milk

4 whole eggs, lightly beaten

3 egg yolks, lightly beaten

Salt, freshly milled pepper, and freshly
  grated nutmeg

1 cup grated Chihuahua, Queso Blanco or
  Monterey Jack cheese

7 fresh jalapeño peppers, seeded, deveined, and
  cut into $^1/_4$-inch strips

METHOD

Prepare the cornmeal crust:

Preheat the oven to 350° F.

In a mixing bowl, mix the cornmeal, flour, and salt.

Cut in the lard, using a fork, your fingers, or a
  pastry blender.

Add the cold water and mix.

Wrap the dough in waxed paper and refrigerate
  for at least 30 minutes.

Roll out the dough on a lightly floured surface.

Place the dough in a 10-inch tart pan, fitting it
  evenly over the bottom of the pan and pressing
  it against the inside edges.

Trim off excess dough by rolling a rolling pin over
  the top of the tart pan.

Cover the pastry with aluminum foil and weight
  down with dried beans or aluminum
  baking weights.

Bake for 15 to 20 minutes, until the sides are set.

Remove the weights and foil and continue baking
  for 15 to 20 minutes, until light golden.

Set aside; leave the oven on.

Prepare the filling:

In a large bowl, combine the heavy cream, milk,
  whole eggs, and egg yolks.

Blend thoroughly.

Season to taste with salt, pepper, and nutmeg.

Sprinkle the cheese over the bottom of the
tart shell.

Arrange the strips of jalapeño over the cheese.

Pour the filling mixture into the shell.

Bake for about 40 minutes, or until the custard sets.

Allow to cool for at least 2 hours before cutting.

Serves 10

PEANUT SHORTBREAD

INGREDIENTS

$^1/_2$ pound unsalted butter at room temperature

$^1/_2$ cup sugar

2 cups all-purpose flour

$^3/_4$ cup skinless roasted peanuts

METHOD

In a mixing bowl, cream the butter and sugar.

Blend in the flour.

Stir in the peanuts.

On a lightly dusted board, roll out the dough
about $^1/_2$-inch thick. Cut into approximately
$^1/_2$- by 2-inch rectangles.

Transfer the cookies to baking sheets.

Score the tops of the cookies in grid fashion with
the edge of a paring knife.

Place the baking sheets in the refrigerator for
45 minutes.

Meanwhile, preheat the oven to 375° F.

Place the baking sheets in the oven and reduce
the temperature to 325° F.

Bake for approximately 25 minutes or until the
bottoms are golden.

Cool.

Serves 8 to 10

SPICED POACHED PEACHES

INGREDIENTS

10 small, firm, ripe peaches

1 bottle zinfandel or other robust red wine

1 cup cold water

2 cups sugar

1 lemon sliced

12 black pepper corns, slightly crushed

3 whole cloves

2-inch cinnamon stick

1 sprig fresh thyme

METHOD

In a large pot of boiling water, blanch the
peaches, then cool under running water

In a large saucepan, combine the wine, water,
sugar, lemon, spices, and thyme sprig. Bring to a
boil, reduce the heat, and simmer for 10 minutes.

Meanwhile remove the skins from the peaches.

Bring the wine mixture to a simmer, add the
peaches and poach for 8 to 10 minutes, or
until the peaches can easily be pierced with a
sharp pairing knife. To check for doneness,
pierce the flesh to the pit and if a knife slips in
easily, the peaches are cooked. Remove
peaches to another bowl.

Increase the heat and simmer the wine syrup for
30 minutes or until reduced by half.

When the syrup is cool, pour it over the peaches,
cover with plastic wrap and reserve.

Peaches can be made a day ahead of time.

Serve at room temperature with some of the syrup.

Note: To use pears instead, peel 10 small- to
medium-sized, firm ripe pears, add to the
simmering wine mixture syrup, and poach for 20
minutes or until the pears can easily be pierced
with a sharp pairing knife. Remove the pears from
the wine syrup and proceed as above.

Serves 10

Street Food

Frito Pie

Never underestimate the imagination of a fast food vendor, and never doubt that when hunger strikes, we want food now. It's just a little bag of corn chips, cut along the side, but a creative vendor can dump chili, cheese, and onions into this pouch and hand you a plastic fork and you will go to town.

GUACAMOLE WITH TOSTADOS

INGREDIENTS
4 ripe avocados
2 small ripe tomatoes, peeled, seeded, and chopped
1/4 cup chopped cilantro
2 to 3 fresh green jalapeño peppers, deveined, seeded, and chopped
2 tablespoons fresh lime juice
2 cloves garlic, minced
1 small onion, minced (approximately 1/4 cup)
Tostados, for serving

METHOD
Mash the avocados in a bowl.
Add the remaining ingredients and mix together thoroughly.
Serve with the tostados.

Makes approximately 3 cups

RED SALSA

INGREDIENTS
12 dried red New Mexican chili peppers
1/2 cup vegetable oil
3 cloves garlic
1 teaspoon chopped fresh oregano
6 large ripe tomatoes, peeled and seeded
Salt
2 tablespoons lime juice
Tostados, for serving

METHOD
Cut the chili peppers in half and devein and seed them.
In a heavy skillet, heat the oil and fry the peppers quickly until they begin to turn a brighter shade of red.
Remove with a slotted spoon and place in a bowl of warm water.

Margarita

If ever a regional drink complemented the region's food, it is the margarita, the champagne of the Southwest. Inevitably, drinks arrive with an assortment of velvety guacamole, hot salsa, and chicos fried up like popped corn.

MARGARITA

INGREDIENTS
1 lime slice
Kosher salt
Ice cubes
3 ounces tequila
1 ounce Triple Sec
2 ounces fresh lime juice

METHOD
Rub the rim of the glass with the lime.
Pour a little salt in a flat dish and dip the glass in the salt to form a light coating around the rim.
Fill a small pitcher or cocktail shaker with 6 to 8 ice cubes.
Add the tequila, Triple Sec, and lime juice and stir or shake briskly.
Strain into the salt-rimmed glass and serve.

Serves 1

Let the peppers soak for 30 minutes.
In the skillet with the hot oil, toast the garlic cloves until golden.
Place the garlic in a food processor along with the drained peppers, the oregano, and the tomatoes and chop coarsely.
Transfer the salsa to a bowl and set aside at room temperature for 2 hours.
Before serving, season to taste with salt and add the lime juice
Serve with tostados.

Makes 2 to 2 1/2 cups

WEST COAST

WEST COAST

Los Angeles in 1820 was just a small town, numbering only a few thousand people. It was populated for the most part by the Spanish, Mexicans, and American Indians whose lives revolved around the Franciscan missions that devoted their efforts to prayer, evangelizing the natives, and tilling the land. The friars brought their European olive, grape, and fig cuttings to these fertile valleys where the climate, so similar to the Mediterranean, was ideal. The sun-drenched soil produced wine grapes, table grapes, dates, figs, and pistachios. In the arid land of southern California, citrus and semitropical fruits included limes, oranges, grapefruits, mangoes, papayas, apricots, and plums. English walnuts, artichokes, garlic, and berries flourished in the moist earth of northern California. At the time the Franciscans began building their missions in 1769, the nomadic tribes who inhabited the desert land of California and Nevada depended on the acorn as their staple; acorns, hulled and ground, were made into bread or gruel, just as hominy had been used in the Southwest. The cooking method preferred by these tribes was a full day's project. Baskets sunk in shallow pits were filled with water and hot stones. The food was added to the basket where it absorbed the stones' heat, and the cool stones were replaced with newly heated ones until the food was cooked. Unlike so many other ingenious cooking techniques devised by natives across the country, this was one the settlers never really accepted.

By the 1850s, much of what is now Orange County was settled by Southerners—first by the gold diggers, their pockets heavy with the dust of the Sierra Nevada lode, and later by refugees of the war-ravaged South. In their "transplanted" southern gardens, magnolia and jasmine bloomed next to pomegranates, avocados, quince, and cherimoya (the creamy, vanilla-fragrant fruit native to this arid soil). In the canyons, artichokes grew wild alongside cactus, whose leaves were used to pepper stews and were also thrown together with garden chard and beet greens to be boiled up with pork scraps for pot liquor. Southerners continued to feast on familiar fried hominy, pancakes studded with corn kernels, and fried apple rings, and the pig continued to play a major role. From New England to

California, the pork barrel followed the settler right across the country.

Los Angeles boasted a population of 100,000 by the turn of the century. During the summer months, fashionable families would have their trunks packed onto the small, independently run railroad cars that chugged to the seashore in Santa Monica. Little cups of steaming samp and sausages could be purchased from carts, and figs and guavas were plucked fresh from the trees lining the driveways.

The discovery of gold nearly emptied some of the Western states in 1851 as pioneers moved out to California. Fortune-seekers from every corner of the Union were joined by English, French, and Germans who sailed to Panama and up the Pacific coast to California.

Many went north to seek excitement in San Francisco, and others packed off to the Sierras to join the frantic hunt for gold. "Hangtown," the commonly used name of Placerville, was the gold miners' unofficial headquarters where saloons, boarding houses, dance halls, gambling houses, and bordellos were eager to accommodate the flood of business. Streets were littered with empty bottles, sardine boxes, and old chicken bones. Dry goods stores and outfitters offered essential supplies at inflated prices to speculators. Boarding houses shoveled up greasy steaks, salt pork, pickles, and bad coffee to the customers who sit at the oilcloth-covered tables, but the price of a square meal in a local eatery far exceeded its style. A plate of fried oysters, eggs, and bacon was bought with raw gold, and the infamy of this town is remembered not for its hotheaded vigilantes, but for this commonplace oyster fry, the "Hangtown Fry."

San Francisco, in contrast to dusty Los Angeles, was a makeshift town of plank and mud streets. Housing, such as it was, consisted of canvas tents, corrugated iron shacks, and prefabricated cottages complete with flimsy shutters. Immigrant-filled boats passing through the Golden Gate in the 1880s—a last wave from starving Europe—were greeted by what was described by the adventuring Scotsman J. D. Borthwick as a "ready-made population of active and capable men of every trade and profession."

Of the many nationalities to be found in San Francisco, each left its mark. The Chinese, who came to work the railroads, entrenched themselves in their own quarter. Their shops were filled with dried fish, glazed dried ducks, strange-looking vegetables, and foreign smelling tea. Their "100-year-old eggs" and rumors of rat pies didn't stir a sense of culinary adventure in the general public. By midcentury, sections of San Francisco were completely French, others completely Italian. There were French-speaking theatres, and Italian operas, concerts, and masquerades. San Francisco was becoming rather elegant, for an outpost. Restaurants provided excellent fare but encountered competition in the feasts offered by many bars and saloons—a groaning board set with sumptuous meats, fishes, and soups was available at no charge, the expectation being that the diner would make his contribution by purchasing some kind of punch, "sling," or cocktail. At home, San Franciscans could indulge in the basic, unelaborate American fare of cornbread, buckwheat cakes, pickles, molasses, and pies. And although many ethnic cooks entered the service of the wealthy, the Chinese cook was preeminent. Some employers didn't necessarily like to "eat Chinese," but their approach, using finely cut, briefly cooked vegetables and meats would bring about an awareness of their cuisine and establish San Francisco as one of the capitals of Chinese cookery in America.

The city market was one enormous larder of deer, rabbit, and little quail hailed as the most delectable in the country (fetching an impressive $4 per dozen during the Gold Rush). Cabbages, turnips, potatoes, and onions were as fine as any grown, and broccoli, zucchini, artichokes, and garlic, along with the profusion of wild and cultivated herbs, comforted the European. California farming was big thinking right from the start, producing remarkably large, succulent vegetables and fruits. A beetroot weighing in at 100 pounds was not thought too freakish (but finding a pot to fit it would be a mean feat). What would the first farmers think of today's sudden affection for miniature this and miniature that?

The Sacramento River ran with excellent salmon and sturgeon during the spawning months in spring and fall. The Pacific coast was fished mainly by Italians whose cuisine was familiar from popular Italian restaurants as well as the fish shacks along the wharf where hot cauldrons simmered with an invention called *cioppino*—a stew of Dungeness crabs, mussels, clams, and cod simmered in stock, tomatoes, oil, and herbs. Perhaps sweetest of all treats was batter-fried abalone. (Abalone is now making something of

a comeback after the ravages of pollution and the greedy sea otter.)

On the drive through the San Joaquin, or Central Valley, in spring, the land is already burnished with hip-high grasses shimmering in shades of copper brown to gold. This valley is a technological masterwork, an overwhelming achievement of farming. Imagine it as a series of huge cultivated tracts—for example, 20-mile stretches of bell-pepper fields bordering 1,000 acres of strawberries. Miles of pipeline and wheels dizzily spout thousands of gallons of water, coaxing the plants from the desert. The agribusiness man or "desktop farmer" has left the pickup truck in favor of air-conditioned, stereo-equipped cabs that sit on huge tractors. These farmers go to any length to increase production, even bringing in bees to pollinate stone fruits, pistachios, almonds, and walnuts. Walnuts, for instance, illustrate America's methodical approach to crop raising. In France, the typical walnut grower hopes for three weeks of clear weather to dry his three-acre crop. In northern California, monstrous farms dry theirs artificially in a couple of days. It's hard to imagine that production on such a huge scale can give us an equally delicious walnut, when a single California grower outstrips the whole of France's annual harvest by 160 million pounds.

On vegetable farms, migrant workers arrive before dawn, and the moment the sun peeks over the distant hills the day's picking begins. The workers are paid by the pound, and pick as fast as they possibly can, filling canvas bags that are transported by conveyor belt to wheeled gondolas. Produce is hand-sorted and packaged in nearby packing sheds. By midday the light is white and the heat typically reaches a mean of 100 degrees. During the hell of summer, picking continues through the night with tractors floodlighting the fields as pickers work through a heavy rain of insects. Onions and garlic are harvested and sacked right in the fields and left there until they dry. The lack of moisture is no enemy here. In vineyards, plastic hoses run down the rows, dripping precisely controlled amounts of water to produce the perfect-looking table grape. Large-scale farming would hardly be possible without today's scientific manipulation. When 80 percent of a grape stem has bloomed, a spray is applied to thin out the buds, and eventually elongate the grape. Later, second and third sprayings stretch the maturing grape to achieve a larger size. These sprays increase the beauty of each bunch, as well as the yield per acre. These sprays are water-soluble and although the chemicals don't enter the fruit, they do produce a tougher skin. We habitually wash fruits purchased from the market in cold water, but the pickers choose to dip theirs first in hot, then cold water before eating the fruit.

Although the table-grape grower can manipulate his fruit with chemicals, he must carefully harvest and pack the fruit by hand. However, the wine-grape grower demonstrates his embrace of the trends of modern agriculture with a mechanical harvester that straddles the vine and shakes off the grapes, sucking up the leaves and stems with a fan and setting the clusters in the gondolas. A couple of workers sit on the harvester's wings, pulling out unwanted branches and debris. Yet like most of the handpicked produce of the valley, handpicked wine grapes fetch a higher price, since they carry more weight, and less debris.

Eighty percent of this region's produce is shipped east, and most of the remaining tonnage is sent to the canning factories and markets of California. The yield is simply astonishing, a legacy of Luther Burbank, who left New England for the west in the 1920s and will be remembered as one of America's greatest horticulturists. During the peak picking season, the strain of round-the-clock work is felt night and day at the little Mexican fondas that keep the workers going, dishing out burritos and refried beans with store-bought tacos, or at the cozy diners where they still serve stacks of pancakes, fresh farm eggs, sausages, grits, and good coffee with fresh cream.

In the late nineteenth century, the United States government brought a number of Basque sheep farmers from France to encourage the raising of sheep in the western states. The Basques settled from Idaho to the San Joaquin Valley, and Bakersfield today is a melting pot of Basques, Mexicans, farmers, and cowboys. Although it may be a city in some respects, more than anything else Bakersfield is a farm town, with farm ethics and the good fun of racecar heats and rodeos. Despite the oil derricks pumping away right in the middle of farmland, it has a Midwestern feel. Local farmers permit Basque flocks to come down from the hills in winter and forage for whatever they can find in the harvested fields, and in exchange, the shepherd gives up one of his lambs.

On Sunday nights, the local Basque restaurant is crowded with farmers, families in tow, all speaking French. First they have a drink of fizzy Picon punch, and then the doors open onto a room with long tables. A battery of dishes appears, one following the other: tureens of vegetable soup, cold veal's tongue with vinaigrette and onions, beef stew with noodles, grilled chicken with fried potatoes, leafy salads, brie and bread, crème caramel to polish it off, and big bottles of plonk red to wash it all down. These farmers defy the dictates of California cooking today, that to eat cool is to stay cool, and the whole occasion is a throwback to the nineteenth century.

America's native grape, *Vitis labrusca*, didn't flourish west of the Rockies until about 1770 when Franciscan friars planted these vines in California. At about the same time, Padre Junipero Serra, a Franciscan monk, brought the Mission grape to San Diego from Baja. Missionaries produced as many as 50,000 gallons of wine a year, using local American Indians to trample the grapes, then storing the wine in barrels and cowhide bags to ferment. In the 1830s, when the Mexican government stripped California's 21 missions of their religious authority, winemaking in the region became a secular concern. Although the grapes grown in California may have been good at that time, winemaking techniques were not, so neither was the wine for many long years.

It is Bordeaux-born Jean Louis Vignes who is often considered the father of California wine. By 1840, he was cultivating 100 acres (mostly Mission vines with some French varieties as well), which today lie beneath Union Station in Los Angeles. Vignes aged his wine 8 to 10 years, unheard–of devotion at that time, and induced

a considerable number of Frenchmen to emigrate to California and enter the wine industry.

The French in California were soon joined by Germans, Hungarians, and Italians who established vineyards of their own. But Prohibition in the 1920s devastated the burgeoning industry. Many wineries closed their doors and some were able to operate making sacramental wines or selling grapes to the home winemaker. It was not until the early 1940s that large-scale California winemaking began to take a foothold in the valleys of Napa, Sonoma, and Mendocino. The wines produced here were inexpensive table wines, but competition among vineyards and a growing public awareness of good wine encouraged the older, larger wineries to turn from jug wine to more reputable labels. Today the many boutique wineries produce wines that are elegant competition for any of the world's contenders. The drive to compete with international producers, and to create wines on par with those of the French in particular, prompted California vintners to purchase oak aging barrels from the forests of Limousin and Nevers, France. Over the years California winemakers have experimented with native California oak or redwood, but prefer the imported wood.

A leisurely drive from San Francisco takes you to the narrow, fertile valleys with rows upon rows of vines carefully pruned and protected by tree-covered mountain ranges. The sun-drenched hills are reminiscent of summer days in Provence; the smell of lavender, the wild orange poppies poking up along paths, and patches of untrammeled land gives a sense of peace and anticipation of things to come. The people are very friendly and the generosity of the winemakers and their eagerness to please and educate and present their wines to visitors are the ingredients of a magical experience. The geography alone has resulted in California becoming one of the greatest tourist attractions in the United States, but it is the wine and food that is the main event. Over the years, I have seen the valleys become more developed, and wine is now big business. As well, it is a playground for San Francisco and LA residents who want their second homes nestled near the vineyards or hidden in the hills. Thankfully, the Agricultural Preserve keeps farmland from being sold and developed, so the valleys retain their original beauty.

California cooking is a very clear derivative of American cooking, done with the raw materials California has made her own. In no other part of the country do we have such a strong feeling that the food and wine wholly complement each other. This is a new experience for Americans, to visit an area and dine on its local goat cheeses, salads dressed in olive oils produced by some of the most notable vineyards, and farm-grown organic vegetables, local lamb and quail, desserts made of fresh almonds and walnuts, and pomegranates and persimmon sorbets, all accompanied by a true *vin du region*.

Not one of these valleys was developed by a single nationality but by blends of Finns, Czechs, Germans, Hungarians, Spaniards, French, and Italians. The result is totally American.

Shepherd's Lunch

LAMB MEATBALLS WITH LEMON-GARLIC TOAST ○ ICED FRESH FRUIT ○ FRESH ALMONDS
○ Edna Valley Pinot Gris, CA or Sierra Nevada Pale Ale, Peju Province Syrah, CA

Every spring the shepherds send down buckets of lamb fries, nipped from would-be rams. This delicacy rarely goes beyond the rancher's kitchen, but spring lamb meatballs make a nice substitute. Sun-ripened fruits are refreshed in bowls of ice. Branches of green almonds, picked almost before they are ready to be harvested, are heavy with silken nutmeats. You can break the velvety outer skin with your teeth to reach the inner shell, full of soft, pungent almond fruit. Eating almonds while they're still green was as new to the local growers as it was to me when I was first served them in Corsica.

LAMB MEATBALLS

INGREDIENTS

1/2 cup breadcrumbs
1/4 cup milk
1 1/2 pounds trimmed lamb shoulder, ground
1 cup cooked spinach, squeezed dry
    and chopped
1 cup cooked brown lentils
1 cup blanched almonds, toasted, cooled,
    and ground in a food processer
2 tablespoons onion, minced
1 clove garlic, finely chopped
1/4 teaspoon grated orange zest
1 large egg, lightly beaten
Salt and freshly ground pepper
Fresh lemon wedges

METHOD

Preheat oven to 350° F.
In a small bowl soak the breadcrumbs with
    the milk.
In a large mixing bowl, combine the lamb,
    spinach, lentils, almonds, onion, garlic, zest,
    and egg.
Add the moistened breadcrumbs to the
    lamb mixture.
Mix thoroughly and season with salt and pepper.
Roll the mixture into small balls, approximately the
size of a ping pong ball, using the palms of your
    hands and set aside.
Heat the remaining oil in an ovenproof or cast
    iron pan.
Place the meatballs in a single layer in the pan
    and quickly sear them over medium heat until
    nicely browned.
Place the pan in the oven and cook until the
    meatballs are firm to the touch and browned on
    all sides, approximately 10 minutes.
Serve immediately with lemon wedges and
    garlic toast.

Serves 6

Grilled on Grapevines

GRILLED BUTTERFLIED LEG OF LAMB ○
GRILLED VEGETABLES ○ POTATO TART ○
SOURDOUGH BREAD (See page 289) ○
PLUM TART ○ Cakebread Cellars
Sauvignon Blanc, CA or Joseph Phelps
Insignia, CA

Young lamb does not require marinating, but does require constant basting when grilled. Brush the meat as it grills with a "broom" made of wild rosemary and thyme branches, dipped in a bowl of local olive oil. If you are lucky enough to live near a vineyard, use the vine trimmings to start the grill and add a few near the end of the cooking to flare up the fire and perfume the meat.

GRILLED BUTTERFLIED LEG OF LAMB

INGREDIENTS

1 leg of lamb (5 to 6 pounds), butterflied
1 1/4 cups olive oil
2 teaspoons fresh rosemary, chopped
1 teaspoon lemon thyme leaves
1 tablespoon red pepper flakes
Salt and freshly milled pepper
3 cloves garlic, minced
Zest of 1/2 navel orange, grated
12 large basil leaves, torn

METHOD

Place the leg of lamb in a shallow baking pan.
In a bowl, combine the olive oil, rosemary, lemon thyme, and red pepper flakes.
Pour the oil mixture over the lamb, turning the meat from side to side until well coated.
Cover and marinate for 2 hours: 1 hour in the refrigerator and 1 hour at room temperature.
Prepare a hardwood charcoal fire and preheat the oven to 250° F.
When the coals reach a dusty red glow, brush the grill with olive oil.
Season the meat with salt.
Place the meat on the grill and cook for 15 minutes on each side.
Transfer the meat to a baking pan and place in the oven for 10 minutes, or until internal temperature is 125° F for rare meat.
Allow the lamb to rest for 10 minutes before slicing.
While the meat is in the oven, grill the vegetables lightly on each side.
Serve rare.
To assemble:
Thinly slice the meat
Sprinkle with a little minced garlic, orange zest, and basil.

Serves 10 to 12

GRILLED VEGETABLES

INGREDIENTS

6 long Japanese or other small eggplant
3 each of red, yellow, and purple bell peppers
3 heads of garlic
6 ears of young sweet corn
12 zucchini and yellow squashes with blossoms
6 small pattypan squashes with blossoms or any combination of colorful sweet and hot peppers, small eggplant, corn, zucchini, and squash
1 cup olive oil
Salt and freshly milled black pepper

METHOD

Prepare a hardwood charcoal fire.
Thinly slice the larger eggplants up to the stem and fan out the slices.
The smallest eggplants can be grilled whole.
Halve the peppers and remove the stems, seeds, and veins.
Cut a small slice off the stem and root ends of the garlic.
Cut the bulb horizontally in half.
Pull back the husks from the corn, leaving them attached at the bottom.
Remove the silk and pull a double layer of husks back up around the corn, and remove the remaining husks.
Soak the ears in cold water before grilling.
Brush all of the vegetables with olive oil and lightly sprinkle with salt and pepper.
When the coals have reached a dusty red glow, place the vegetables on the grill, cooking on each side until tender and slightly charred.
Served with sliced grilled lamb.

Serves 6 to 8

POTATO TART

INGREDIENTS
6 large Idaho potatoes, peeled
1 cup clarified butter (see Basics, page 333)
Salt and freshly milled black pepper

SPECIAL TOOLS
10-inch pie pan, 2-inches deep (preferably glass)

METHOD
Preheat the oven to 500° F.

Thinly slice the potatoes approximately $1/8$-inch thick on a mandolin and wash them thoroughly in cold running water.

Drain and place them in a bowl of lightly salted ice water for up to 1 hour.

Drain and thoroughly dry the slices with paper towels.

Coat the pie pan with 3 tablespoons of the butter.

Arrange the potatoes in an overlapping spiral on the bottom of the pan.

Season the first layer with salt and pepper and coat with butter.

Continue making layers, alternating potatoes, seasonings, and butter until the pan is filled, ending with a layer of potatoes.

Place a clean kitchen towel over the pan and weigh down with a second pan and a heavy weight for 10 minutes.

Remove the weights, pan, and towel, and coat the tart with the remaining butter.

Bake for 45 minutes, or until the bottom crust is golden.

Let the tart rest for 5 minutes.

Place a serving platter over the tart and invert.

If the potatoes do not immediately release, run a metal spatula around the rim of the pan.

Slice into pie wedges and serve hot.

Note: The tart can be prepared and weighed down and refrigerated for up to 1 hour before baking. A glass pie pan allows one to check the degree of doneness of the tart.

Serves 6 to 8

PLUM TART

INGREDIENTS
1 recipe pie dough, made with butter
  (see Basics, page 335)
12 to 16 ripe red plums
Grated zest and juice of 1 lemon
3 tablespoons sugar

METHOD
On a lightly floured surface, roll out the pastry dough to form a large rectangle, approximately $1/4$-inch thick, 10-inches wide, and 24-inches long.

Place the dough on a baking sheet.

Cover with waxed paper and refrigerate while you prepare the plums.

Preheat the oven to 400° F.

Cut the plums in half, remove the pits, and cut each half into quarters.

Toss the plums with the lemon juice and zest.

Starting at the center and working out to within 1 inch of the sides, arrange the plums on the pie dough, slightly overlapping the pieces.

Roll in the edges of the dough to meet the plums.

Dust with the sugar and bake for 30 to 40 minutes, or until the outer crust is crisp and golden.

Cool on a rack.

Serve slightly warm.

Serves 10 to 12

Samp Dinner

SAMP WITH FRESH LIMA BEANS AND SMOKED WHITEFISH ○ POUSSIN WITH OLIVE PUREE AND SWEET PEPPERS ○ PARKER HOUSE ROLLS (See Basics, page 336) ○ LEMON MERINGUE PIE ○ Trefethen Chardonnay, CA or Ridge "Lytton Springs", CA

Samp found its way west from the coastal towns of New England, Long Island, and the South. It was the Southerners who brought it to Los Angeles and cooked it up with bits of meat and shanks. It became the custom at the southern tip of Long Island to add a little smoked eel to the cooked kernels. Here, we used smoked whitefish. Poussin is a little chicken—not to be confused with a game hen or a Cornish hen—that weighs a pound or less, and is best when simply roasted. Local ripe olives pureed with garlic and oil, similar to the southern French tapenade, are stuffed between the skin and the flesh to infuse the chicken with pungent olive flavor.

SAMP WITH FRESH LIMA BEANS AND SMOKED WHITEFISH

INGREDIENTS

1 1/2 cups samp (coarse hominy)
1 quart chicken stock (see Basics, page 332)
   or canned low-sodium chicken broth
2 cups heavy cream
1 cup fresh lima beans, shelled
1 smoked whitefish, peeled, and flaked from the
   bone (approximately 1 1/2 cups)
1 tablespoon unsalted butter
2 to 3 gratings of nutmeg
Salt and freshly milled pepper

METHOD

In a large bowl or pot, cover the samp with 3 quarts of water and soak for 12 hours or overnight.

Drain and place the samp into a stockpot with the chicken stock.

Add water to cover and simmer until tender, adding more water or stock as needed.

When tender, drain and return the samp to the pot.

Add the heavy cream and place over low heat.

In a pot of lightly salted water, cook the lima beans until tender.

Drain and fold into the samp mixture.

Fold in the flaked whitefish.

Add the butter and seasonings to taste and serve hot.

Note: The samp will take 2 to 3 hours of watchful cooking; add additional liquid as necessary, stirring often.

Serves 4 to 6

POUSSIN WITH OLIVE PUREE AND SWEET PEPPERS

INGREDIENTS

Olive Puree:

1 cup salt-cured black olive, pitted

1 clove garlic, crushed

1 1/2 tablespoons olive oil

Poussin:

4 poussins or very young chickens (each
   approximately 1 1/4 pounds)

Salt and freshly milled black pepper

Olive oil

2 sweet red bell peppers and 2 yellow bell
   peppers, cored, seeded, deveined, and cut into
   1-inch strips

3 tablespoons olive oil

1/2 cup dry white wine

1 cup chicken stock (see Basics, page 333)
   or canned low-sodium chicken broth

METHOD

Prepare the olive puree:

Blend the olives, garlic, and oil in a food processor
   or mortar and pestle until smooth.

If too dry, add an additional tablespoon of oil.

Prepare the poussin:

Preheat the oven to 400° F.

Remove the fat from the cavities of the birds.

Salt and pepper the cavities.

Using your index finger, carefully loosen the skin from
   the breasts. Spread a little of the olive puree into
   the pockets.

Truss the birds and brush with olive oil. Set the birds
   on a rack in a roasting pan and roast, basting
   frequently, for 30 to 40 minutes, or until the juices
   run clear when the legs are pierced.

Meanwhile, in a large skillet, sauté the red and
   yellow bell peppers in the olive oil over low heat,
   until they wilt and are tender.

Season with salt and pepper.

Transfer the birds to a warm platter.

Spoon off any excess fat from the roasting pan.

Add the wine and stock and deglaze the pan over
   high heat, scraping up any brown bits that cling
   to the bottom of the pan.

Season the sauce and cook until reduced by 1/3.

Strain and reserve the sauce over low heat.

Serve the birds with sautéed peppers and
   the sauce.

Serves 4

LEMON MERINGUE PIE

INGREDIENTS

Pastry:

1 cup all-purpose flour

1 tablespoon granulated sugar

$1/8$ teaspoon salt

$1/2$ teaspoon grated lemon zest

8 tablespoons unsalted butter, cut into bits

Approximately 1 $1/2$ tablespoons butter

Lemon Filling:

Grated zest of 2 lemons

$1/3$ cup lemon juice (approximately
   2 lemons), strained

3 eggs, separated (reserve whites for meringue)

1 egg

$1/3$ cup sugar

2 tablespoons heavy cream

$1/3$ teaspoon cornstarch

5 $1/2$ tablespoons unsalted butter, cut into bits

Meringue:

3 egg whites (reserved from the filling)

$1/2$ teaspoon lemon juice

$1/2$ teaspoon vanilla extract

$3/4$ cup plus 1 teaspoon granulated sugar

METHOD

Prepare the tart shell:

Mix together the flour, sugar, salt, and lemon zest.

Add the butter and mix together with your fingers,
   a fork, or a pastry blender until well-blended, but
   pea-sized pieces of butter remain.

Add the water and toss together with your hands
   until the pastry starts to hold together.

Form into a flat disk, wrap in plastic wrap and let
   rest in the refrigerator for at least 30 minutes.

Preheat the oven to 375° F.

On a lightly floured surface, roll out the dough into
   a 12-inch circle about $1/8$-inch thick.

Roll up the pastry loosely around the rolling pin,
   then unroll it over a 9-inch pie pan.

Ease the pastry into the pie pan and lightly press
   into the contours of the pan.

Cut the pastry approximately $1/2$ inch beyond
   the edge of the pan and crimp the edges with
   a fork.

Refrigerate for 15 minutes or until ready to bake.

Bake for 20 minutes or until lightly golden.

Remove from the oven and let cool.

(The pie shell can be made ahead and frozen at
   this point, wrapped tightly in several layers of
   plastic wrap.)

Prepare the lemon filling:

Combine the lemon juice and zest in a small bowl
   and set aside.

In a saucepan, beat the egg yolks and egg with
   the sugar until thick and lemony in color.

Combine the cream and cornstarch in a small
   bowl and add to the egg mixture.

Whisk in the lemon mixture and place the pan over
   medium heat.

Add the butter bit by bit, whisking constantly until it
   thickens and coats the whisk.

Pour the lemon filling into a bowl and whisk again.

Cover with plastic wrap and chill.

(The filling will keep for 2 weeks.)

Prepare the meringue:

With an electric mixer, beat the whites until frothy
   in a greaseless bowl.

Beat in the lemon juice and vanilla extract.

Increase the speed, slowly add $3/4$ cup of sugar,
   and beat until the meringue forms glossy,
   stiff peaks.

Mound the meringue over the filling and swirl
   into peaks.

Sprinkle with the remaining teaspoon of sugar
   and bake for 15 minutes or until the meringue is
   lightly browned.

Let cool to room temperature, then refrigerate for
   at least 2 hours before serving.

Serves 8

Sashimi Supper

SASHIMI NAPOLEON ○ FRESH FRUIT WITH TRIPLE SEC CREAM ○ Chappellet Chenin Blanc, Napa Valley or Scharfenberger Brut Rosé, CA

Possibly the freshest fish to be found in Los Angeles comes from the markets of Little Tokyo where the best sushi bars are also found. If the French borrowed the Japanese aesthetic in creating nouvelle cuisine, the Japanese in turn have embraced the principles of French cooking. The stark look of these Los Angeles eateries—the straightforward lighting, the marble, the neon—is an American touch, but the dishes are an amalgam of East and West.

SASHIMI NAPOLEON

INGREDIENTS

Dressing:

3 tablespoons sherry vinegar

$1/8$ teaspoon wasabi, or to taste

1 tablespoon soy sauce

$1/3$ cup mild olive oil

Fish:

$1/2$ pound fresh tuna

$1/2$ pound smoked salmon

$1/2$ pound fresh halibut or sea bass or striped bass fillets, with skin intact

Wontons:

8 fresh wonton skins

$1/2$ cup clarified butter (see Basics, page 333)

Vegetables:

4 shiso leaves (sometimes called "beefsteak")

$1/4$ of a whole daikon (Japanese white radish), peeled, cut into needle-thin julienne, and soaked in ice water

1 bunch radish sprouts, roots trimmed

8 long fresh chives

METHOD

Prepare the dressing:

In a small bowl, whisk together the vinegar, wasabi, and soy sauce until dissolved.

Gradually whisk in the olive oil.

Prepare the fish:

With a sharp thin-bladed knife, thinly slice the fish against the grain.

When cutting the halibut or bass, slice against the skin as you would smoked salmon.

Reserve.

Prepare the wontons:

Cut the wonton skins in half, making 16 pieces.

In a skillet, heat $1/4$ cup of the clarified butter over moderate heat.

Fry the wonton skins until golden on each side, adding more butter as needed.

Remove and drain on paper towels.

To assemble:

Place a fried wonton skin on each of four plates.

Place a layer of fish on top of the wonton skin, and continue to assemble the Napoleon, ending with a layer of fish.

Tuck a shiso leaf under the corner of each Napoleon.

Drain and dry the daikon julienne and scatter it over the top of the Napoleon along with the radish sprouts and chives.

Sprinkle with the dressing and serve.

Serves 4

FRESH FRUIT WITH TRIPLE SEC CREAM

INGREDIENTS

Fruit:

Choose any combination of strawberries, raspberries, and figs; orange, grapefruit, or lime sections; sliced starfruit; and peeled and quartered kiwi fruit

Triple Sec Cream:

4 egg yolks, at room temperature

$1/2$ cup sugar

$1/4$ cup Triple Sec

2 cups heavy cream, scalded

SPECIAL TOOLS

4 shallow ovenproof plates

METHOD

Wash and dry the fruit and set aside.

In the top of a double boiler, beat the egg yolks until smooth and lemon colored.

Fold in the sugar.

Place the yolk mixture over simmering water and gradually whisk in the Triple Sec.

As the mixture begins to thicken, gradually add the hot cream.

When the mixture thickens enough to coat the whisk, remove from the heat and set aside.

Arrange the fruits on the plates and divide the sauce among them.

Place each plate on a pan under the broiler for 15 seconds, or long enough to glaze the cream.

Serves 4

Breakfast

JAMES BEARD'S SOURDOUGH RYE BREAD ○ BUTTER AND APRICOT JAM ○ FRESH BLACK FIGS ○ COFFEE

Sourdough bread is a popular favorite synonymous with San Francisco. The recipe given here, with the gracious permission of James Beard, is the best one I know. Nothing is more pleasing than running home with a loaf of bread warm from the oven of a local baker. Fresh local figs, sweet butter, and jam make an uncomplicated, satisfying breakfast.

JAMES BEARD'S SOURDOUGH RYE BREAD

INGREDIENTS

Three Days in Advance:

1 package active dry yeast

2 cups lukewarm water

2 cups all-purpose flour

One Day Advance:

2 cups rye flour

1 cup lukewarm water

Bread:

1 package active dry yeast

2 1/4 cups lukewarm water

2 teaspoons salt

1 tablespoon caraway seeds

1 1/2 teaspoons poppy seeds

2 tablespoons melted butter

3 tablespoons granulated sugar

6 cups all-purpose flour

Butter and cornmeal, for the baking sheets

1 egg lightly beaten with 1 tablespoon water, for egg wash

METHOD

Three days in advance:

In a bowl, combine the yeast with the lukewarm water.

Add the 2 cups flour and blend.

Pour the starter into a container and seal tightly.

Allow starter to sit at room temperature for 2 days; then place in the refrigerator for 1 day.

One day in advance:

Place 1 cup of the "starter" in a bowl.

Measure in the rye flour and lukewarm water.

Mix together and cover with plastic wrap.

Let stand overnight at room temperature.

Prepare the bread:

Dissolve the yeast with 1/4 cup of the lukewarm water. Stir down the dough that has been standing overnight.

Add the dissolved yeast, salt, caraway seeds, poppy seeds, melted butter, and sugar.

One cup at a time, add 4 cups of the flour, stirring to make a stiff dough.

Turn the dough out onto a clean surface and knead for 10 to 12 minutes.

Shape the dough into a ball and place in a buttered bowl.

Turn the dough over to coat it with butter.

Cover and place in a warm draft-free place to rise until doubled in bulk, approximately 2 hours.

Meanwhile, butter 2 baking sheets and generously sprinkle with cornmeal.

Punch down the dough and divide it in half.

Shape each piece of dough into a free-form loaf and place it on the prepared baking sheets.

Cover and let it rise for 1 hour.

Preheat the oven to 375° F.

Brush the loaves with the egg wash and bake for 30 minutes, or until the bread is golden and sounds hollow when the bottom is tapped.

Cover the sourdough loaves with kitchen towels to prevent the crust from hardening.

Makes 2 loaves

Fennel-Grilled Lunch

FENNEL-GRILLED SHRIMP ○ QUAIL ON POLENTA ○ CARAMELIZED ONIONS ○ MELTED BERRIES ○ ANGEL FOOD CAKE WITH STRAWBERRIES, RASPBERRIES, AND LEMON CREAM ○ Sterling Vineyards Pinot Gris, CA or Morgan Pinot Noir, CA

Throughout the Bay area, wild fennel is like the dandelion. Growing in fields, abandoned lots, and along roadsides, it's there for the taking. Bundles are tied and set to dry, and the fennel is used as cooking fuel to infuse fish with a marvelous flavor. If fennel isn't handy, you can always splash the fish with Pernod. Polenta is an Italian version of grits, favored by San Francisco Italians. The little quail are set on the polenta, soaking it with their juices while they are picked apart and eaten with the fingers. Berries with angel food cake are a must. The addition of this tart lemon sauce enhances the sweet, cottony cake.

FENNEL-GRILLED SHRIMP

INGREDIENTS
2 pounds medium shrimp in their shells
   (6 to 7 per person)
3/4 cup olive oil
1/2 cup fresh fennel sprigs, chopped

SPECIAL TOOLS
Dried fennel stalks

METHOD
Prepare a hardwood charcoal fire.
Place the shrimp in a bowl.
Add the olive oil and fennel and toss.

Off the heat, cover the rack with foil, and make slits in the foil with a paring knife.
Set the grill in place to heat up.
When the coals are dusty red, add the dried fennel stalks to the coals; they will ignite almost immediately.
Quickly arrange the shrimp on the grill to infuse with the fennel stalk flavor.
Grill the shrimp on each side for 1 to 2 minutes, until they turn pink.

Serves 4

QUAIL

INGREDIENTS
Salt and freshly milled pepper
8 quail, washed and patted dry
16 juniper berries, crushed
1/3 cup olive oil

METHOD
Prepare a hardwood charcoal fire.
Salt and pepper the cavities of the birds, and
place 2 juniper berries in each cavity.
Truss the birds, brush with olive oil, and set aside.
Preheat the oven to 400° F.
When the coals turn dusty red, lightly oil the grill.
Brown the birds on the grill, turning often.
Place on a heatproof pan and baste with a little
more oil.
Bake in the oven for 5 to 10 minutes, until rare
and juicy.
Serve the quail on the fried polenta cakes so the
polenta will absorb the juices.

Serves 4

POLENTA

INGREDIENTS
2 cups milk
1 teaspoon salt
1/2 cup yellow cornmeal
2 egg yolks, beaten
1/4 cup plus 1 tablespoon olive oil

METHOD
Lightly oil a baking sheet.
In a heavy saucepan, bring the milk to a low boil
over moderate heat and add the salt.
Slowly pour in the cornmeal, stirring constantly with
a wooden spoon.
Continue to cook, stirring constantly, for 30
minutes, or until the polenta pulls away from
the sides of the pan.
Remove from the heat and briskly mix in the eggs,
beating until incorporated.
Pour the polenta onto the prepared baking sheet
and spread out a little less than 1/2 inch thick.
Cool thoroughly and cut the polenta into
rectangular or diamond shapes large enough to
hold the birds.

In a cast-iron skillet, heat the olive oil over
moderate heat.

When the oil is hot, fry the polenta on each side
until golden.

Place the polenta in a serving dish and set a hot,
roasted bird on each slice of polenta.

Serve immediately.

Note: The consistency of cornmeal varies and the
addition of more liquid may be necessary. Have
ready a small pan of boiling water and, if the
mixture becomes too tough, add boiling water, a
little at a time, stirring vigorously to avoid any lumps.

Serves 4 to 8

CARAMELIZED ONIONS

INGREDIENTS
2 pints pearl onions
4 tablespoons unsalted butter
2 tablespoons sugar

METHOD
Cut an "X" into the root end of each onion.

In a pot of lightly salted boiling water, blanch the
onions for approximately 1 minute.

Drain, cool, and peel.

Return the onions to boiling water, reduce the
heat, and simmer until tender.

Drain.

In a skillet, melt the butter over moderate heat.

Add the onions, shaking the pan to coat the
onions with butter.

Sprinkle with the sugar and cook until the sugar
beings to caramelize.

When the onions take on a caramel color, serve.

Serves 8

MELTED BERRIES

INGREDIENTS
1 pint blueberries or huckleberries
2 tablespoons sugar
3 thin lemon slices
1 tablespoon fresh lemon juice

METHOD
In a saucepan, combine the berries with the sugar,
lemon slices, and lemon juice.

Warm the berries over moderate heat, gently
tossing to coat with the sugar.

Cover tightly and cook until the sugar has melted
and the berries begin to give off their juice.

Remove from the heat and serve immediately with
the birds.

Serves 4 to 8

ANGEL FOOD CAKE

INGREDIENTS
1 1/3 cups sugar
1 cup all-purpose flour
11 egg whites, at room temperature
1 1/2 teaspoons cream of tartar
1 teaspoon salt
1 teaspoon vanilla extract

SPECIAL TOOLS
10-inch tube pan, with a removable bottom,
   ungreased

METHOD
Preheat the oven to 350° F.
Sift the sugar 3 times into a mixing bowl.
In a separate mixing bowl, sift the flour 5 times.
Mix 1/3 cup of the sugar with the flour.
Beat the egg whites with an electric mixer
   until foamy.

Add the cream of tartar and salt and
   continue beating.
As the whites begin to stiffen, gradually add the
   remaining sugar and continue whipping until the
   whites form stiff glossy peaks.
Add the vanilla and beat for 1 to 2 seconds.
With a rubber spatula, gently fold in the flour,
   1/4 cup at a time.
Pour the cake batter into the pan and bake for
   40 minutes.
Invert the pan on a rack to cool, leaving at least
   1 inch of air space between the rack and
   the table. (You might want to "hang" the pan
   over the neck of a tall bottle to accomplish this.)
When completely cooled, pull the sides away from
   the pan with a fork and unmold the cake.
Serve with Lemon Cream and berries.

Serves 8 to 10

LEMON CREAM

INGREDIENTS
3/4 teaspoon arrowroot
1/2 cup fresh lemon juice
3 egg yolks
1/2 cup sugar

METHOD
In the top of a double boiler set over simmering
   water, whisk the arrowroot into the lemon juice
   until thick and shiny.
Cook until warmed through.
In a small bowl, whisk the egg yolks with the sugar
   until smooth and lemon colored.
Add the lemon juice mixture to the sugar and yolks
   and stir.
Return the mixture to the double boiler and
   whisk over simmering water for 10 minutes,
   or until thick.
Set aside and keep warm.
Serve the lemon cream with the angel food cake,
   accompanied with strawberries and raspberries.

Makes approximately 1 cup

Cioppino Dinner

SPAGHETTI CIOPPINO ○ DAY-OLD CAKE WITH FRESH STEWED FRUITS AND ZABAGLIONE
○ Foppiano Petite Sirah, CA or Concannon Sauvignon Blanc, CA

The availability of fresh pasta in countless forms has caused some of us to forget plain old spaghetti. The wonderful confusion of ingredients in this recipe calls for a sturdy pasta. The confusion continues in a fantasy dessert that offers a delicious way to rid yourself of day-old cake.

SPAGHETTI CIOPPINO

INGREDIENTS

1/2 lemon

8 tablespoons olive oil

12 baby artichokes, trimmed

1 clove garlic, crushed

1 medium yellow bell pepper, cored, seeded, deveined, and cut into julienne

1 medium sweet red bell pepper, cored, seeded, deveined, and cut into julienne

A pinch of hot red pepper flakes

2 large ripe tomatoes, peeled, seeded, and chopped with juice reserved

1 dozen small clams

1 dozen mussels, scrubbed and debearded

1/2 to 3/4 pounds spaghetti

1/2 pint bay scallops

1/2 pound small bay shrimp, cooked

METHOD

Squeeze the lemon into a large pot of salted boiling water, then add the rind and 1 tablespoon olive oil.

Add the artichokes and boil for 5 minutes.

Cool under cold running water and set aside.

Fill a large kettle with salted water and bring to
a boil.

Meanwhile, prepare the sauce:

In a large skillet, slowly heat the remaining
7 tablespoons olive oil with the garlic.

Add the peppers and sauté until they wilt.

Remove the garlic clove when it turns golden
and discard.

Add the hot red pepper flakes, tomatoes, and the
tomato juice and bring it to a simmer.

Add the clams, mussels, and artichokes and cover.

Add the spaghetti to the boiling water.

When the clams and mussels begin to open,
add the scallops and cook uncovered for
2 to 3 minutes.

Add the shrimp and cook just long enough to
warm through.

When the spaghetti is cooked but slightly firm,
drain in a colander and return to the pot.

Add a cup or two of the sauce to the spaghetti so
that it does not stick.

Divide the spaghetti onto heated plates and
divide the sauce and shellfish amongst them.

Note: Because of the quantity of the ingredients in
cioppino, 1/2 pound of spaghetti is really sufficient
for 4. However, there is enough cioppino for 3/4
pound of spaghetti.

Serves 4

DAY-OLD CAKE WITH FRESH STEWED FRUITS AND ZABAGLIONE

INGREDIENTS
1 cup raspberries
1 cup blueberries
1 cup strawberries
6 tablespoons sugar
Zabaglione Cream:
6 egg yolks
2/3 cup sugar
2/3 cup Marsala wine
2 cups heavy cream, whipped

Unsweetened cocoa powder
3 to 4 sliced day-old yellow cake or sponge-type
cake, cut into 1-inch cubes
Ground cinnamon

METHOD
Prepare the fruit:
Lightly stew the berries with the sugar, just until they
begin to give off their juices.

Set aside to cool.

Prepare the zabaglione cream:
Bring water to a simmer in the bottom of a
double boiler.

Off the heat, in a heatproof bowl, whisk the egg
yolks until they are smooth and lemon colored.

Set the bowl over the simmering water and,
whisking constantly, slowly add the sugar.

As the eggs begin to thicken, gradually add the
Marsala and continue to whisk for approximately
20 minutes, until the zabaglione coats the back
of a spoon. (If the mixture begins to curdle,
remove the bowl from the heat and whisk in a
little cold heavy cream).

Beat vigorously.

Place the mixture over a bowl of ice water to cool,
whisking from time to time.

Cover with a sheet of plastic placed directly on the
surface of the cream and refrigerate.

To assemble:
Fold the whipped cream into the zabaglione
mixture, but do not overblend.

Place the cubed cake onto a deep platter and
smother with the berries.

Spoon the zabaglione cream over the berries.

Allow to rest for 15 to 20 minutes before serving.

Liberally dust with cinnamon and cocoa
and serve.

Serves 6

Wine Tasting Picnic

HERBED GOAT CHEESE WITH CALIFORNIA OLIVE OIL ○ CRANBERRY AND FAVA BEANS WITH HERBS AND OLIVE OIL ○ SUN-DRIED TOMATOES ○ CALIFORNIA OLIVES ○ SOURDOUGH BREAD ○ FOCACCIA WITH GOAT CHEESE, OLIVES, AND ROSEMARY ○ SWISS CHARD AND ARUGULA SALAD ○ DRIED FRUITS, NUTS, AND GRAPES ○ Nickel & Nickel Chardonnay, "Truchard Vineyard", CA or Beaulieu Vineyard Chardonnay, CA

In addition to the great wineries spread across the valleys of California, there are numerous cottage industries producing all manner of cheeses, olive oils, breads, and preserved olives. This little feast is a tribute to those who toil for an eager and appreciative public. The menu, built around the wines served, is decidedly Mediterranean.

HERBED GOAT CHEESE WITH CALIFORNIA OLIVE OIL

INGREDIENTS
1 pound fresh soft goat cheese
1 tablespoon fresh thyme leaves
1/4 cup extra virgin California olive oil
Sea salt and freshly milled pepper

METHOD
Remove the cheese one hour before serving and
   bring to room temperature.
Mix the cheese with the thyme, olive oil,
   and seasonings.
Place in a serving bowl and drizzle with a little
   more oil and serve with crusty bread and
   additional olive oil.

Serves 6 or more

CRANBERRY AND FAVA BEANS WITH HERBS AND OLIVE OIL

INGREDIENTS
1 1/2 cups shelled fresh cranberry beans
1 1/2 cups shelled fresh fava beans
1 teaspoon fresh rosemary leaves, chopped

1 teaspoon fresh thyme leaves, chopped
Sea salt and freshly milled pepper
Extra virgin California olive oil

METHOD
In a pot of lightly salted boiling water, cook the
   cranberry beans for approximately 2 to 3 minutes
   and blanch under cold water.
Drain and set aside.
In another pot of lightly salted boiling water, cook
   the fava beans for 2 to 3 minutes and blanch
   under cold water. Drain.
Remove the outer casing.
In a serving bowl, combine the cooked beans,
   herbs, and seasonings.
Sprinkle with olive oil and serve.

Note: It is the Italian custom to serve the fava beans raw. Removing the outer skin from the fava bean is laborious. A quick blanch in boiling water makes it much easier.

Serves 4 to 6

Sun-dry for 8 to 10 days.

Remove the tomatoes from the rack and pack in sterilized canning jars with 1 clove of garlic and 1 sprig of rosemary per jar.

Fill each jar with olive oil.

Note: The tomatoes must be dried in a very dry climate. An alternative method is to roast the tomatoes in a hot oven, sprinkled with olive oil, baked at 400° F for 45 minutes or until they have collapsed and shrunken.

SUN-DRIED TOMATOES

INGREDIENTS
Kosher salt
Plum tomatoes
Garlic cloves
Rosemary sprigs
Olive oil

METHOD
Salt the tomatoes and set on a wire rack raised 12- to 18-inches off the ground, directly in hot sunlight.

FOCCACIA

INGREDIENTS
2 packages active dry yeast
1 cup lukewarm water
3 teaspoons salt
3 1/2 cups all-purpose flour
1/3 cup mashed potatoes
7 tablespoons olive oil
1/4 pound oil-cured black and green olives, pitted
1/4 medium-soft goat cheese, crumbled
1 tablespoon rosemary, lightly chopped

METHOD

In a bowl, dissolve the yeast in the lukewarm water.

Add the salt and set aside until it begins to foam and bubble.

Gradually add the flour and mashed potatoes, mixing until the dough forms a sticky ball.

Add 1 1/2 tablespoons of the olive oil.

Coat a bowl with 2 tablespoons of the olive oil.

Place the dough in the bowl and turn to coat with olive oil.

Cover with a damp cloth and let rise in a draft-free place for 25 minutes. Punch down the dough and place on a baking sheet coated with 1/2 tablespoon olive oil.

Shape it into a 1/2-inch-thick round or oval.

Randomly press the olives into the dough.

Sprinkle with the remaining 3 tablespoons olive oil, the goat cheese, and rosemary.

Allow to rest for 20 minutes.

Preheat the oven to 400° F.

Bake the focaccia for 30 minutes, or until golden and serve warm.

Serves 6

SWISS CHARD AND ARUGULA SALAD

INGREDIENTS

2 tablespoons butter

1/4 pound slivered almonds

Salt

2 bunches (approximately 1/2 pound) young, tender Swiss chard leaves without stems, washed and thoroughly dried

1 to 2 bunches arugula, washed and thoroughly dried

1/2 to 3/4 cup vinaigrette (see Basics, page 334)

Hard goat cheese, for grating

METHOD

In a small skillet, melt butter and sauté the almonds until they begin to turn golden.

Remove from the pan with a slotted spoon and salt lightly.

Toss the greens with the vinaigrette and divide among 6 plates.

Sprinkle with the warm almonds and grate a little goat cheese over each salad.

Serves 6

Street Food

Swan's Oyster Depot

Swan's Oyster Depot supplies San Francisco with some of the best and freshest fish. They make their own chowders and will poach a salmon to order. Their counter is open at eight o'clock in the morning, and I never fail to breakfast there on little oysters, Pacific coast clams, Dungeness crabmeat with homemade Louis dressing, good sourdough bread, coffee, and beer before catching a morning flight back home.

LOUIS DRESSING

INGREDIENTS

1 cup homemade mayonnaise
   (see Basics, page 334) or Hellmann's
1/4 cup ketchup
1 teaspoon fresh lemon juice
3 scallions, including some of the green,
   finely chopped
1/4 cup sweet or dill pickle, finely chopped
2 tablespoons fresh parsley, finely chopped
1 teaspoon Worcestershire sauce
3 to 4 drops Tabasco sauce

METHOD

Combine all the ingredients and refrigerate until
   ready to serve.

Note: Serve with cold crab, lobster, or shrimp.

Makes 1 1/2 cups

Hamburgers

I had my first drive-in meal in Los Angeles when I was 17. From the car window all I could see was a pair of legs in fishnet stockings. A tray was slapped on the side of the door with my lunch, and I thought I'd just been to the end of the plastic rainbow.

Dim Sum

The Golden Dragon rooms of Chinatown still offer platters of dim sum and tea. For the past couple of years, little holes in the wall have also been steaming up these savory pleasures as snack food.

Irish Coffee

Rumor has it that Irish coffee was first served in the bars on San Francisco's wharves. Whether this is true or not, the practice of a little nip in the coffee has become a warming habit, no matter what time of day. Unlike the flood of liqueurs with their johnny-come-lately coffee tricks, Irish coffee is the most straightforward of all coffee concoctions and is a perfect way to end a meal.

INGREDIENTS
1 teaspoon superfine sugar
1 $^1/_2$ ounces Irish whiskey

5 ounces hot espresso coffee
1 heaping tablespoon unsweetened
   whipped cream

METHOD
Warm a mug with boiling water and shake dry.
Place the sugar and whiskey in the glass.
Add the espresso and stir to dissolve the sugar.
Float the whipped cream on top.

Serves 1

NORTHWEST

NORTHWEST

The Pacific Northwest is still young and still wild. It is a revelation to sail its crystal waters through archipelagos of islands, to walk its rain forests of cascading ferns and silken moss, to climb its alpine heights carpeted with wildflowers, and to watch deer dance over the sponge of leaves and needles. This land is lush in spite of us. George Vancouver was 34 years old in 1792 when he set anchor in the sound with his Lieutenant, Peter Puget. The American Indians they met showed little interest in their arrival, leaving the navigators to explore on their own. By 1818, Britain and the United States shared the Northwest, and the Hudson's Bay Company soon followed, opening the wilds to fur traders. By 1843, settlers began to trickle in by land and water—scores of them—mostly pioneers from New England who came with their chowders and curries, bringing the settlement of America full circle.

The Natives Americans showed the newcomers where to fish for the great King salmon and where to harvest clams, mussels, and crabs. They themselves dined on clams and berries; clams, smoked and dried, were even strung and worn around the neck to be nibbled whenever hunger struck. They also roasted chunks of salmon or whole fish on spears, leaving gills and bladders standing like flags to mark that the fishing had been good. With nets, spears, and traps, they harvested salmon like a crop, just as land farmers pulled their crops from the earth. They taught the settlers how to make a flour from the inner stalks of cattails, and shared their meadows lush with wild chickweed, dandelion, burdock, nettles, and lambs' quarters. They also revealed the secrets of edible fungi. Spring morels, summer cepes, autumn's boletus, chanterelles, "cauliflower," and coral mushrooms were abundant, and some were dried for storage. The Olympic Mountains and Peninsula are among the greatest sources of wild mushrooms today.

The first settlers did not fish, but farmed instead, and their plantings flourished in these valleys of fertile volcanic soil protected from the cold salt air of the Pacific by the Cascade range. The apple seed was not indigenous to the Pacific Northwest, but by the mid-nineteenth century, Conestoga wagons filled with seedlings trundled over the plains. Today, of course, the reputation of these apples is unsurpassed, and Wasington apples and pears from the Yakima Valley are flown to the food halls of Europe and the Orient. The Northwest supplies the United States with nearly all of its lentils, not to mention most of its hops (for the beer industry) and soft wheat. Idaho potatoes are fried up on the boulevards of Paris and in the streets of Tokyo. Near Seattle, Dutch farmers cultivate acres of tulips, and Scottish descendants tend their flocks of clover-fattened sheep and cattle. Down in Kent, the Carnation milk factory continues to put up tins of condensed milk that have nourished countless American babies and become a family staple.

The Northwest of the 1890s was in a state of financial panic, just like the rest of the country. The Klondike gold strike was kept nearly secret for a year, until word leaked out in the July 17, 1897 *Seattle Post-Intelligencer* that the steamship Portland had arrived with more than a ton of gold from the Klondike on board. Desperate fortune-seekers—farmers, bank clerks, doctors, teachers, lawyers, policemen, prostitutes, missionaries, and firemen—abruptly packed their belongings and headed for Alaska, many with only the vaguest notion as to where that territory actually was. Not every prospector had luck, and few were prepared for the hardships of survival, but the rush to the Klondike was a boon to Seattle. Canada was decidedly hesitant, however, and the Mounted Police refused entry to anyone who wasn't carrying a year's food supply. Merchants got rich selling golddiggers the usual list of staples: bacon, 100 to 200 pounds; flour, 400 pounds; dried fruits, 75 pounds; cornmeal, 50 pounds; coffee, 25 pounds; sugar, 25 to 100 pounds; beans, 100 pounds; cases of condensed milk, and pounds and pounds of dried meat and fish—all weighing down a dogsled along with enough clothing and equipment to daunt even the most loyal team of huskies.

The French from Brittany, followed closely by the Scandinavians, were the first to show real interest in fishing. They homesteaded prime locations, at the mouths of estuaries and rivers on American Indian land holdings. Determined to claim this land for themselves, they often built too close to the banks, and their cabins and barns swept away time and again by rivers swollen with glacial run-off. These settlers challenged the fishing rights of the American Indians, whose belief that the right to fish these waters was God-given caused them to take great offense. They could scarcely fathom the notion of owning or selling land, sea, or air—their cherished collective holdings had always passed from generation to generation.

The Great Council of Walla Walla, signed in 1855, relieved five major American Indian tribes of all rights to fishing territories from the Columbia River through its tributaries to the Strait of San Juan de Fuca—a total of some 60,000 square miles in eastern Oregon and east-central Washington—prime land compensated at the equivalent of three cents an acre. The settlers lusted not so much after the fish that ran these waters as for the virgin timber that lined them. By 1888, the Northern Pacific Railroad had reached the terminus of Tacoma and logging went full tilt. Forests closest to the rivers fell first, the waterway itself providing the means of transporting the timber to the railways.

Logging gravely disrupted spawning and fish runs; this early manifestation of pollution seriously hindered species of fish that were accustomed to the clearest waters in the hemisphere. Powerboats appeared in the 1920s and exacerbated the downhill slide, as did the seal, the salmon's natural predator. Originally, the seal was overhunted by the Russian traders and the Hudson's Bay Company, causing the enactment of stricter regulations to protect them. But when it was later realized that a seal can effortlessly consume 200 to 300 pounds of salmon daily, it became clear that new laws were needed in order to protect both species.

Salmon have long sustained the American Indians of the Northwest. Before the Westerners arrived, traditional societies in the Pacific Northwest had communal institutions of property to protect marine resources. The Pacific Northwest Indians often had complex agreements between tribes to allow salmon to move up and down stream in order to maintain the spawning runs and ensure future fish supplies. Conflicts about the use and management of these resources have existed since 1853 when Washington first became a U.S. territory.

In 1854, Isaac Ingalls Stevens, the first territorial governor and superintendent of American Indian affairs concluded six treaties with the Washington Indians. These treaties recognized that they retained certain rights, including "the right of taking fish at all usual and accustomed grounds and stations in common with all citizens of the territory." One hundred and thirty years later, in 1974, the federal laws ruled that local American Indians were entitled to 50 percent of the harvestable salmon and steelheads. But the meaning of this has always been contested as non-native settlers as well as the state of Washington fought to control access to the region's rich fisheries. Commercial and sports fishermen argue that the tribes should not receive special rights and that native fisherman should be subject to the same laws and regulations as they are. The differing interpretations often lead to conflict and violence between these groups.

Along the coast all the way up to Alaskan waters, the Northwest is extraordinarily rich in shellfish—Dungeness, Alaskan King and snow crabs, shrimps, oysters, and clams of many varieties. The Pacific razor clam, which at maturity resembles a pen knife, is perhaps the most prized of the clams. Digging this clam requires a keen eye and vigorous work with a shovel, but that hasn't kept the razor clam population safe from extinction; a limit has been set on the number of clams that can be harvested per person, but the creature is perilously close to disappearing altogether.

The Northwest has always been a region of easy bounty, burgeoning with riches for the taking. The trees of valley orchards are heavy with fruit, the waters wait to be reaped of their harvest, and the air is full of life-giving moisture. It will take all of our discipline to keep the Northwest a frontier for future generations.

Breakfast

QUILCENE OYSTERS ○ LAMB SAUSAGE PATTIES ○ OOMA'S DILL BREAD ○ Iced Aquavit
○ Hogue Vineyards Chenin Blanc, WA or Rogue Shakespeare Stout, OR

The Pacific Northwest oyster is the only variety native to this region, and its little spoonful of flesh is a distillation of all the flavors of the best bivalves found in this country. There are some who absolutely love oysters, and there are those who are utterly horrified by the mucilaginous quality of them, and still others will eat ones the size of a catcher's mitt. What may seem an odd coupling, sausages and oysters, was a popular turn-of-the-century combination. Yeasty warm dill bread is a definite Scandinavian influence, and Aquavit is an eye-opener for this fisherman's breakfast.

LAMB SAUSAGE PATTIES

INGREDIENTS

1 pound lean lamb, ground twice
1/3 pound pork fat, ground twice
1 clove garlic, minced
2 teaspoons sage, rubbed and crumbled
1/2 teaspoon fresh rosemary, chopped
3/4 teaspoon salt
2 tablespoons unsalted butter

METHOD

In a mixing bowl, combine the lamb and pork fat.
Stir in the seasonings.
Shape the mixture into 12 small round patties,
    cover, and refrigerate until ready to cook.
Melt the butter in a skillet over moderately
    high heat.
Reduce the heat slightly and brown the patties
    evenly on both sides, turning once. Serve
    with freshly opened oysters.

Makes 12 patties

OOMA'S DILL BREAD

INGREDIENTS

1 package active dry yeast
1/4 cup lukewarm water
1 cup small curd cottage cheese, at room
    temperature
2 tablespoons sugar
1/2 small onion, minced
1 teaspoon salt
1 teaspoon baking soda
1 tablespoon unsalted butter, melted
4 teaspoons dill seed
3 fresh dill flower sprigs, chopped
1 egg
2 1/2 cups all-purpose flour, sifted
Vegetable oil, for the bowl
Sea or kosher salt

METHOD

In a small bowl, dissolve the yeast in the lukewarm
water and set aside until foamy.
In another bowl, combine the cottage cheese
    with the sugar, onion, salt, baking soda, butter,
    dill seed, dill flowers, and egg.
Stir in the yeast.
Stir in the flour and knead to make a stiff dough.
Place the dough in a lightly oiled bowl, cover with
    a damp cloth, and set in a warm, draft-free
    place until doubled, approximately 50 minutes.
Punch down the dough and place in a well-oiled
    1 1/2-quart baking mold or loaf pan.
Cover and let rise until doubled in volume,
    approximately 30 minutes.
Meanwhile, preheat the oven to 350° F.
Brush the top of the dough with water and sprinkle
    liberally with sea or kosher salt.
Bake for 50 minutes, or until golden brown.

Makes 1 loaf

Veal and Parsley Pie Dinner

CRUSTACEANS, HERRINGS, AND SMELTS ○
VEAL AND PARSLEY PIE ○ PLUM KETCHUP
○ BLACK PEPPER CAKE WITH STEWED
QUINCE ○ Ponzi Vineyards Pinot Noir, OR
or Eyrie Vineyards Pinot Gris, OR

*Complete meals are made from the abundance
of salted, cured, and pickled herring, smelts,
and the versatile Dungeness and Alaskan King
crab. The fishes are put up in true
Scandinavian fashion. It is arguable whether
the bigger-than-life crabs are comparable to the
blue crab of the East—they are a different
beast. Sweet and firm, they can be served hot
or cold, unadorned or enveloped in sauces.
They take to embellishment as gracefully as
lobsters. For this meal any selection of herrings,
smelts, or crustaceans, served simply, make for
a nice opening. Cold crab or shrimp with
Louis dressing, local oysters on the half shell
with a squeeze of lemon and a grinding of
pepper, mussels in a mustard-seasoned
mayonnaise, or any variety of pickled herring
or smelt would be ideal. Parsley pies, such as
shepherds' pie, were served from leftovers; the
dish included ground or chunked meats and
parsley was incorporated as a filler. These
Victorian meal extenders were covered with
pastry or mashed potatoes, but this Veal and
Parsley Pie starts fresh and is elevated by pieces
of white veal, chanterelles, and a piping of
mashed potatoes. The Oriental quince replaces
the spoonful of applesauce that so frequently
accompanied spice cakes.*

VEAL AND PARSLEY PIE

INGREDIENTS
Filling:
1/2 cup clarified butter
Salt and freshly milled black pepper
2 1/2 pounds lean veal, trimmed and cut into
    1 1/2-inch cubes
All-purpose flour for dredging
1 cup veal or beef stock (see Basics, page 332)
    or canned low-sodium beef broth
1/2 cup dry white wine
1 cup heavy cream
6 tablespoons unsalted butter
1 pound fresh chanterelles

Mashed Potato:
4 medium potatoes, peeled and quartered
1/2 cup milk, scalded
4 tablespoons unsalted butter
Salt and freshly milled black pepper
1 cup fresh parsley, minced

SPECIAL TOOLS
Pastry bag fitted with star tip

METHOD
Heat 1/4 cup of the butter in a large skillet over
    medium heat.
Salt and pepper the veal and lightly dredge
    with flour.
Working in batches, brown the meat, adding more
    butter as necessary.
If the pan becomes overly browned, deglaze with
    some of the stock, scraping up the bits with a
    wooden spoon and reserve.
Add more butter and continue to brown the veal.
When all the veal has been browned, drain off any
    excess fat from the pan.
Add the wine and deglaze the pan, scraping up
    the brown bits that cling to the bottom of the pan.
Add the reserved bits and juices and cook until
    reduced to a glaze.
Add the stock and simmer for 5 minutes.
Strain the liquid and return it to the pan.
Add the cream and bring it to a low boil.
Reduce the heat and simmer for 15 minutes.

Reserve.
Melt the butter in a medium skillet and lightly sauté
    the chanterelles over moderate heat just until
    they give off their juices.
Set aside the mushrooms and add the mushroom
    juices to the cream.
In a pot of lightly salted boiling water cook the
    potatoes for 20 minutes or until easily pierced
    with a paring knife.
In a warm bowl mash the potatoes with 1/3 cup
    of the scalded milk.
Stir in the butter, the remaining milk and season to
    taste with salt and pepper.

To assemble:
Preheat the oven to 350° F.
In the casserole, mix the veal and chanterelles.
Add the parsley to the cream sauce and pour
    over the meat mixture.
Fill a pastry bag with the potatoes and
    decoratively pipe the mixture over the meat.
Bake for 50 to 60 minutes, until the meat is tender
    and the piped potatoes are golden brown.

Note: If the potatoes brown before the meat is tender,
cover the casserole loosely with foil until done.

Serves 6

PLUM KETCHUP

INGREDIENTS
1 quart small, black Italian-type plums, pitted and
    cut into eighths (approximately 4 cups)
1/4 cup red or white wine vinegar
1 small cinnamon stick
1/4 teaspoon black peppercorns, crushed
2 strips lemon zest

METHOD
In a large pot, combine all of the ingredients.
Place over moderately low heat and simmer for 30
    minutes, or until most of the juice evaporates.
Cool and refrigerate in a sterilized jar.
The ketchup will keep 3 weeks.

Makes approximately 4 cups

BLACK PEPPER CAKE

INGREDIENTS
Butter and flour for the mold
$1/4$ pound plus 4 tablespoons unsalted butter
$3/4$ cup packed dark brown sugar
1 cup granulated sugar
3 eggs
1 teaspoon vanilla extract
$2 1/4$ cups all-purpose flour
1 teaspoon baking powder
$1/2$ teaspoon salt
$1/2$ teaspoon ground cloves
$1/4$ teaspoon ground ginger
$3/4$ teaspoon cinnamon
2 teaspoons freshly milled black pepper
1 cup buttermilk

SPECIAL TOOLS
1-quart Kugelhopf mold

METHOD
Preheat the oven to 350° F.
Butter and flour the mold and tap out the
    excess flour.
Set aside.
In a mixing bowl, cream together the butter
    and sugars.
One at a time, add the eggs and mix well.
Stir in the vanilla.
Sift the dry ingredients and spices together.

Alternately add the dry ingredients and the
    buttermilk to the batter.
Pour the batter into the mold and bake for 1 hour
    or until the cake pulls away from the sides of
    the pan.
Cool in the pan for 10 minutes.
Invert the cake onto a serving plate and unmold.

Serves 8 to 10

STEWED QUINCE

INGREDIENTS
4 large quince
Juice of 1 lemon
$3/4$ cup sugar
$1/4$ cup water
1 small cinnamon stick

METHOD
Peel, core, and roughly chop the quince.
Place the fruit in a small saucepan and toss with
    the lemon juice, sugar, and water.
Add the cinnamon, place over low heat,
    and cover.
Simmer, stirring occasionally, until the fruit begins to
    give off juice and soften.
Serve warm with the pepper cake.

Makes approximately 3 cups

Gravlax Lunch

GRAVLAX ○ MUSTARD DILL SAUCE (see Basics, page 334) ○ Snoqualmie Winery "Naked" Gewurztraminer, WA or Hair of the Dog Brewing Co. American Ale, "Ruth," OR

American Indians stood on catwalks that stretched across the river to spear salmon as the fish leapt to clear the barrier dams. Many salmon that escaped their spears tumbled into nets erected behind these dams. The first settlers were quick to adopt and apply these methods for catching salmon, and it became an early basis of their commerce. The endless supply was brought to the fishing stations, salt-cured, pickled, and barreled into 42-gallon casks. Curing preserved the fish for at least three years, and this salmon was considered emergency food throughout the interior. The age-old Northwest Indian method of smoking or kippering salmon has led to a separate industry. The Scandinavians were equally at home with this fish, using a quick salt-and-dill method of curing that is as popular here as in their homeland. Served with thinly sliced buttered black bread, gravlax is a perfect hors d'oeuvre or a nice little lunch.

GRAVLAX

INGREDIENTS
2 fresh salmon fillets with skin intact
   (approximately 3 pounds)
1/4 cup sea or kosher salt
1/3 cup sugar
2 tablespoons black peppercorns, crushed
2 large bunches dill
Mustard Dill sauce for serving
   (see Basics, page 334)

METHOD
Wash and pat the salmon dry with paper towels.
In a bowl, combine the salt, sugar, and pepper.
Arrange a few sprigs of dill in the center of a sheet
   of parchment large enough to envelop the fish.

Place 1 fillet, skin-side up, on top of the seasonings.
Sprinkle with the remaining seasonings and dill.
Tightly wrap the fish, set the fish on a baking dish,
   and weigh down with a weighted sheet pan
   or board.
Refrigerate for at least 2 days, turning once every
   12 hours and basting with its natural juices.
When the gravlax is ready, wipe off the dill and
   seasoning with a clean kitchen towel.
Thinly slice on the diagonal, removing the rosy flesh
   from the skin as you would a smoked salmon.
Serve with Mustard Dill sauce, freshly milled pepper,
   and buttered dark bread.

Serves at least 12

Baked Potato Supper

BAKED POTATO WITH INDIAN CURED SALMON ○ CHANTERELLE AND CORAL MUSHROOMS ○ PEAR-AND-BLACK-HEART-CHERRY STRUEDEL ○ Aquavit or Panther Creek Winemaker's Cuvee Pinot Noir, OR

The woodlands of the Pacific Northwest are a mycologist's dream come true—in fact the mushrooms grow practically everywhere. Platoons of hunters forage from spring to fall, and the markets are filled with heaps of morels, hedgehogs, boletus, the matsutake, and the most prolific of all, the yellow chanterelle. They are delectable and versatile fungi; morels are dried and used with game; the boletus, which is our porcini or cêpe, enliven pasta and risotto as well as soups. But the chanterelle remains the most available and popular of all. Although easily put up in brine, they are best served fresh as soon after picking as possible; some say the flavor is lost in 24 hours. I tend to agree. Like many regional foods, they are reasonable here, and the price doesn't soar until they wing their way East. This Pacific mushroom gives off an enormous quantity of liquid and should be drained before the sautéing process is complete. A rare coral mushroom was a present to me from a local purveyor, who had set it out to adorn his basket of chanterelles.

BAKED POTATO WITH INDIAN CURED SALMON

INGREDIENTS
4 baking potatoes
3 tablespoons butter
3 tablespoons all-purpose flour
1 teaspoon dry mustard
1/4 teaspoon cayenne pepper
1 cup milk, scalded
1 cup heavy cream, scalded
1 1/4 pounds Indian cured salmon or other
   smoked flaky fish, skinned and flaked
1/4 cup fresh dill, chopped

METHOD
Preheat the oven to 400° F.
Wash and dry the potatoes.
Bake the potatoes for 40 to 45 minutes or until
easily pierced with a sharp paring knife.
Melt the butter in a saucepan over
   moderate heat.
When the foam subsides, remove the pan from the
   heat and whisk in the flour.
Whisk in the mustard and cayenne.
Return to the heat and add the milk and cream.
Bring to a boil, whisking constantly.
Add the flaked salmon and dill, reduce the heat,
   and simmer for 4 minutes, or until the salmon is
   heated through.
Slit the top of the potatoes and scoop out a little
   of the flesh.
Place on warm serving plates and ladle the
   salmon mixture into each potato.
Serve immediately with the mushrooms.

Serves 4

CHANTERELLE AND CORAL MUSHROOMS

INGREDIENTS

1/2 pound fresh coral or boletus mushrooms
8 tablespoons unsalted butter
1/2 pound fresh chanterelles
Salt and freshly milled black pepper

METHOD

In a pot of salted boiling water, blanch the coral
    mushrooms for 2 minutes.
Drain and set aside.
In a large skillet, melt 4 tablespoons of the butter
    over moderate heat.
Sauté the chanterelles until tender, approximately
    8 minutes. Remove and set aside.
In the same skillet, melt the remaining 4
    tablespoons of the butter over moderate heat.
Sauté the coral mushrooms for 5 minutes,
    until tender and season.
Combine the mushrooms and serve.

Serves 4

PEAR-AND-BLACK-HEART-CHERRY STRUDEL

INGREDIENTS

6 pears, such as Bosc, Comice, or Anjou, peeled,
    cored, seeded, and chopped (approximately
    6 cups)
1 1/2 cups Black Heart or Bing cherries, pitted
1/2 teaspoon ground ginger
1/3 cup sugar
Grated zest and juice of 1/2 lemon
4 leaves strudel or phyllo dough
1/4 pound unsalted butter, melted
1/2 cup ground blanched almonds

SPECIAL TOOLS
Parchment paper

METHOD

Preheat the oven to 450° F.
In a bowl, combine the pears, cherries, ginger,
    sugar, lemon zest, and lemon juice.
Spread 1 leaf of strudel dough on a flat surface,
    with the long side facing you.
Brush with butter and sprinkle with 2 tablespoons
    of ground almonds.
Repeat this layering process, stacking the
    remaining 3 leaves.
Spoon the pear filling in a 3-inch strip along the
    edge nearest you, leaving 3 inches at each end.
Fold the ends over the filling and roll the dough
    around the filling, jelly roll fashion.
Brush the strudel with melted butter and place in
    the center of the baking sheet.
Bake for 10 minutes, reduce the heat to 400° F, and
    bake for 20 minutes more.
Cool for 1 hour before serving.
Serve warm with whipped cream.

Note: The strudel can be reheated.

Serves 6 to 8

Alderwood Grilled King Salmon

PACIFIC COAST CLAM CHOWDER (THE INDIAN WAY and THE WHITE MAN'S WAY)   ○
GRILLED SALMON   ○   LENTIL SALAD WITH YELLOW AND RED PEPPERS   ○   Chateau Ste. Michelle Sauvignon Blanc, WA or Deschutes Cinder Core Red Ale, OR

The American Indians have always revered salmon. From the moment the fish were caught, I felt as though we were witness to something ritual, sacrificial, and almost mythic. Each family member performs a single task, handed down from generation to generation. They work together like a primitive, living machine: one man catches the salmon, one man guts the fish and then builds the fire, and a woman braids the salmon on ironwood stakes that have been carved by yet another person. The stakes are set about the alderwood fire that perfumes the fish, and if a breeze comes up, logs fence the fire like totems to stay the wind. They used to cook clams and mussels gathered from the beach and rocks over hot coals, and cover them with kelp and seaweed to steam them. They still do.

CLAM CHOWDER THE INDIAN WAY

Skagit Clams and Broth:
Take a 1/2 bushel of Pacific coast clams and cover with seawater. Bring the clams to a boil over an open fire, and serve immediately after they open. Pick them from the pot and eat with bread dipped into the broth.

CURRIED CLAM CHOWDER THE WHITE MAN'S WAY

INGREDIENTS
3 tablespoons unsalted butter
3 tablespoons all-purpose flour
1 tablespoon curry powder
1 1/2 cups fish stock (see Basics, page 333)
3 cups heavy cream
4 dozen Pacific or East coast littleneck clams, scrubbed
Freshly milled black pepper

METHOD
In a heavy saucepan, melt the butter over moderate heat.

When the foam subsides, remove from the heat.
Whisk in the flour until smooth.
Return to heat and whisk in the curry powder.
Add the stock and cook until the mixture thickens.
Add the cream, reduce the heat, and simmer for
    15 minutes, stirring occasionally.
Add the clams and cover until the clams open.
Discard any that do not open.
Season with pepper and serve in heated bowls.

Serves 6

LENTIL SALAD WITH
YELLOW AND RED PEPPERS

INGREDIENTS
2 cups brown or French green lentils
1 small onion, peeled and studded with
    3 whole cloves
3 cloves garlic
2 teaspoons salt
1 sweet yellow bell peppers, cored, seeded,
    deveined, and diced
1 sweet red bell peppers, cored, seeded,
    deveined, and diced
1 tablespoon olive oil
1 cup vinaigrette (see Basics, page 334)
Salt and freshly milled black pepper

METHOD
Wash the lentils thoroughly and drain.
In a large pot, bring 2 quarts of water to a boil.
Add the lentils, onion, garlic, and salt.
Simmer for approximately 30 minutes, or until
    the lentils are tender but still hold their shape.
    Do not overcook.
Drain and set aside the lentils, discarding the
    onion and garlic.
In a skillet sauté the peppers in a light film of oil
    until tender.
Just before serving, toss the lentils with the peppers
    and vinaigrette; check for seasonings.
Serve at room temperature.

Serves 8 to 10

Street Food

Fish Soup at the Market

I know of no market in the entire country that glitters and sparkles with the region's produce as the Pike Place Market does in Seattle. The joy of this market is that you can find everything you need for a meal there, including meat and fish. Though it has been touted as a tourist trap, it serves Seattle residents as honestly today as 100 years ago. Tucked away in an alley behind the market is a restaurant-in-miniature, where one can sample local Quilcene oysters, chowders, smoked salmon, trout, crab, and a spicy fish soups.

Dungeness Crabmeat

One of the special delights of The Market is its offering of Dungeness Crab. This giant king crab and its cumbersome legs are sold separately and usually cooked and shipped frozen to all parts of the East and inland.

With little exception, the Dungeness crab is always sold in its shell and a good fishmonger might remove the meat for you. If doing it yourself, remove the back and spongy parts under the shell. Then remove the apron and split the body in two so you can remove the meat. Crack the claws and remove that meat as well.

Like all good crabmeat, the Dungeness is expensive. If serving it cold, accompany the dish with a homemade mayonnaise. If making a soup or salad, buy as much as the pocketbook can afford.

DUNGENESS CRAB SOUP

INGREDIENTS

Cream sauce:

3 tablespoon butter

3 tablespoons flour

1/2 cup light fish stock or chicken stock (see Basics, page 332) or canned low-sodium chicken broth

1 cup milk

Salt and freshly milled black pepper

Nutmeg

Dash of cayenne

Crab:

1 pound picked over crabmeat

1/2 cup milk

2 tablespoons butter

1 medium ripe tomato, peeled, seeded, and chopped

1 to 1 1/4 cups heavy cream

1/4 cup Scotch whiskey

2 tablespoons parsley, chopped

METHOD

Prepare the cream sauce:

Melt the butter in a medium saucepan over medium-high heat.

When the foam subsides, remove from the heat and whisk in the flour.

Return to the heat and cook the roux for approximately one minute.

Slowly pour in the stock while whisking vigorously over medium-high heat.

Bring to a simmer, add the milk, and continue to whisk until the mixture bubbles.

Add the seasonings, stir, and keep warm over low heat.

Stir occasionally while you prepare the crab.

In a medium soup kettle, add the crabmeat, milk, butter, and tomato and heat over medium heat.

When the mixture is hot, pour in the roux mixture and 1 cup of heavy cream.

Return to a boil.

Check for seasoning and add more cream if the soup is too thick.

Add the Scotch and stir.

Serve in heated bowls and sprinkle with parsley.

Makes 4 to 6 servings

BASICS

Basics

PIQUANT RELISH

INGREDIENTS

2 cups fresh parsley, chopped

8 fresh sage leaves, chopped

1 cup smoked eel, flaked

1 Cortland apple, peeled, cored, and grated

Salt and freshly milled pepper

1/4 cup olive oil

2 tablespoons white wine vinegar

METHOD

In a bowl, combine all of the ingredients.

Taste for seasonings and cover with plastic wrap.

Refrigerate for 3 hours and remove 30 minutes
 before serving.

Note: Serve with boiled meats, chicken, or with
crackers.

Makes approximately 2 cups

CHICKEN, BEEF, OR VEAL STOCK

INGREDIENTS

5 pounds chicken, beef, or veal bones

2 medium onions, peeled and coarsely chopped

3 celery ribs, coarsely chopped

2 leeks, green part only, washed and chopped

1 teaspoon thyme

1 teaspoon rosemary

2 bay leaves

15 peppercorns

6 parsley sprigs

1 large clove garlic

METHOD

Rinse the bones under cold running water.

Place the vegetables and remaining ingredients in
 the stockpot. Add the bones and enough cold
 water to cover.

Bring the stock to a boil, reduce the heat to low,
 and simmer for 2 hours, skimming the foam from
 the surface.

Line a strainer with a double thickness of
 dampened cheesecloth and set the strainer
 over a clean pot.

Ladle the stock into the strainer, pressing lightly on
 the bones and vegetables to release their liquid.

Discard the solids and allow the stock to
 cool completely.

Cover and refrigerate.

When the stock has chilled, remove the
 surface fat.

Note: The stock will keep refrigerated for 3 days. If
storing longer, freeze or boil the stock daily for 5
minutes and cool accordingly. The stock can be
kept frozen for 6 months or longer.

Makes approximately 4 quarts

COURT BOUILLON

INGREDIENTS

1 large carrot, peeled and chopped

3 shallots, peeled and chopped

1 leek, green part only, washed and chopped

1/2 cup celery leaves

1 bottle dry white wine

6 peppercorns, crushed

1/4 teaspoon thyme

1 bay leaf

Salt

3 clove garlic, crushed

METHOD

Combine all the ingredients in the stockpot.

Add 2 quarts of water and bring the bouillon
 to a boil.

Reduce the heat to low and simmer for 30 minutes.

Strain the court bouillon into a large, clean
 saucepan and discard the solids.

Refrigerate until ready to use or freeze in
 1-quart containers.

Makes approximately 2 1/2 quarts

FISH STOCK

INGREDIENTS

5 pounds white fish bones, tails and heads (do not use oily fish such as bluefish, mackerel, or salmon)
2 medium onions, coarsely chopped
3 celery ribs, coarsely chopped
1 teaspoon thyme
2 bay leaves
20 black peppercorns
6 parsley sprigs
2 cups white wine

METHOD

Rinse the fish bones under cold running water, making sure the gills and blood pockets have been removed.
Place the vegetables and remaining ingredients in a stockpot.
Add the fish bones and enough cold water to cover.
Bring the stock to a boil and reduce the heat to low.
Simmer for 30 minutes, skimming the foam that forms on the surface.
Line a strainer with a double thickness of dampened cheesecloth and place the strainer over a clean pot.
Ladle the stock into the strainer and discard the solids.
Allow the stock to cool completely.
Cover and refrigerate for up to 2 days or freeze indefinitely.

Makes approximately 3 quarts

BROWN SAUCE

INGREDIENTS

5 pounds veal knuckle and marrow bones or 4 pounds veal bones and 1 pound chicken bones
2 cups onion, coarsely chopped
2 cups carrot, coarsely chopped
2 cups celery, coarsely chopped
1 tablespoon peppercorns, crushed
2 bay leaves
2 cloves garlic, crushed
1 teaspoon thyme
1 cup parsley leaves and stems
2 ripe tomatoes, chopped
2 cups dry red wine

METHOD

Preheat the oven to 400° F.
Wash the bones under cold running water and drain.
In a roasting pan large enough to hold them, brown the bones in the oven, turning them every 30 minutes, for a total of $2^1/2$ hours. Scatter the vegetables over the bones for the last 20 minutes of roasting. The bones should be deep brown in color.
Transfer the bones and vegetables from the roasting pan to a stockpot.
Pour 1 quart of water into the roasting pan and deglaze, scraping the brown bits that stick to the bottom of the pan.
Pour the liquid into the stockpot. Add the remaining ingredients and enough water to cover by several inches.
Bring the stock to a boil and reduce the heat to low. Simmer, occasionally skimming the foam from the surface, for 8 to 10 hours.
Line a strainer with a double thickness of dampened cheesecloth or a clean cotton towel.
Place the strainer into a clean pot and ladle the stock into the strainer. Discard the solids and allow the stock to cool completely.
Cover and refrigerate for up to 3 days, or freeze indefinitely in small containers.

Makes approximately 2 quarts

CLARIFIED BUTTER

INGREDIENTS

1 pound unsalted butter

METHOD

In a saucepan, melt the butter over moderate heat.

When the butter has melted, skim off the foam from the top of the melted butter.

Set aside for 20 minutes to allow the milk solids to settle to the bottom.

Slowly pour the clear liquid into a clean container, carefully stopping before the milky white sediment pours out.

Discard the milky solids.

Note: Clarified butter will keep for weeks since the milk solids (the part that can spoil) have been removed.

Makes approximately 1 3/4 cups clarified butter

VINAIGRETTE

INGREDIENTS

1/3 cup red wine vinegar

1 teaspoon Dijon-style mustard

Salt and freshly milled black pepper to taste

2/3 cup olive oil

METHOD

In a small bowl, whisk together the vinegar, mustard, and seasonings.

In a steady stream, gradually whisk in the oil until the mixture thickens and emulsifies.

Makes 1 cup

MAYONNAISE

INGREDIENTS

4 egg yolks, at room temperature

1 teaspoon Dijon-style mustard

Salt and freshly milled white pepper

Dash of cayenne pepper

1 1/2 cups olive oil, or 3/4 cup olive oil and 3/4 cup canola oil

2 tablespoons fresh lemon juice

1 tablespoon boiling water

METHOD

Place the egg yolks, mustard, salt, pepper, and cayenne pepper in the bowl of a mixer or food processor and beat at high speed for 2 minutes, or until the mixture is creamy.

In a slow, thin stream, gradually add all of the oil.

Add the lemon juice and taste for seasoning.

Add the boiling water and mix for 2 or 3 seconds, just until incorporated.

Refrigerate the mayonnaise in a covered container.

Makes approximately 2 cups

TARTAR SAUCE

INGREDIENTS

1 cup homemade mayonnaise or Hellmann's

1/8 teaspoon cayenne pepper

1/2 teaspoon dry mustard

1 sweet dill pickle, thinly sliced and diced

4 scallions, including some of the green, finely chopped.

1 teaspoon fresh lemon juice

Grated zest of 1/2 lemon

METHOD

In a small bowl, combine the mayonnaise with the remaining ingredients.

Mix well, cover, and chill.

Makes approximately 1 cup

MUSTARD DILL SAUCE

INGREDIENTS

1/4 cup Dijon-style mustard

1/2 teaspoon dry mustard

2 tablespoons sugar

2 tablespoons white wine vinegar

2 tablespoons dry white wine

1/4 cup olive oil

1/4 cup fresh dill, chopped

METHOD

In a mixing bowl, combine the prepared and dry mustards.

Whisk in the sugar, vinegar, and wine.

Slowly whisk in the oil to make a sauce that is the consistency of mayonnaise.

Fold in the dill and chill.

Makes ³/4 cup

KETCHUP

INGREDIENTS

6 pounds very ripe tomatoes, peeled and seeded with juices reserved

1 onion

6 whole cloves

4 whole allspice berries

6 peppercorns

¹/4 teaspoon hot pepper flakes

1 sprig fresh rosemary

1 celery heart, with leaves

2 tablespoons brown sugar

¹/4 cup cider vinegar

Salt

METHOD

Coarsely chop the tomatoes and place them in the kettle with the reserved juice.

Stud the onion with the cloves and tie it in a double layer of dampened cheesecloth along with the allspice, peppercorns, hot pepper flakes, and rosemary.

Add the cheesecloth bag, celery heart, brown sugar, vinegar, and a little salt to the tomatoes and bring to a boil over high heat, stirring occasionally

Reduce the heat to low and simmer, stirring frequently, for 1 ¹/2 to 2 hours, or until reduced by half.

Remove the onion and herb packet.

Pass the mixture through a food mill or puree in a food processor and pass through a sieve, and taste for seasoning.

Return the mixture to the kettle and bring to a boil.

Reduce the heat and simmer for 15 minutes, or until the mixture is the consistency of store-bought ketchup.

Immediately pour the ketchup into sterilized jars and seal according to the manufacturer's directions.

Note: Tomatoes can be very watery. If not reduced enough, a layer of water will form in the bottom of the jars. If this should develop, unseal the jars and gently plunge a bulb baster to the bottom of the jar to extract the water. This ketchup will keep refrigerated for 2 weeks.

Makes approximately 2 ¹/2 pints

PIE DOUGH

INGREDIENTS

2 cups all-purpose flour

¹/8 teaspoon salt

12 tablespoons (³/4 cup) unsalted butter or lard, chilled and cut into bits

4 to 5 tablespoons ice water

METHOD

Place the flour, salt, and butter or lard in a mixing bowl.

Using a pastry blender, fork, or your fingers, cut the butter into the flour until the mixture resembles coarse meal.

One tablespoon at a time, toss the flour mixture with the ice water until the flour is damp and the pastry can be shaped into a ball.

Form the dough into a flat, fat round shape, wrap the dough in waxed paper or plastic, and refrigerate for at least 20 minutes before using.

To prebake the pie crust:

Preheat the oven to 350° F.

On a lightly floured surface, roll out the dough to ¹/4-inch thick.

Place the dough in a pie pan, fitting it evenly over the bottom of the pan and pressing gently against the inside edges.

Crimp the edges or trim away excess pie dough with a sharp paring knife.

Cover the dough with a sheet of foil and weigh

down with aluminum baking weights or dried beans.

Bake for 10 minutes.

Remove the weights and foil and bake for 15 minutes, or until golden brown.

Remove to a rack to cool.

Note: To make tartlets, roll out the dough to $1/8$-inch thick and fit rounds of the dough into the molds. Bake thoroughly to ensure that the shell will hold its shape.

Makes one 9-inch two-crust pie or 48 2-inch tartlets

COOKIE CRUST PIE DOUGH

INGREDIENTS

$1/4$ pound unsalted butter, at room temperature

$1/4$ cup sugar

2 eggs

$2 1/2$ cups all-purpose flour, sifted

2 to 3 tablespoons ice water

METHOD

Using an electric mixer, cream together the butter and sugar in a medium bowl.

Add the eggs and blend thoroughly.

Add the flour and blend, gradually adding the water, until the dough forms walnut-sized balls.

Shape the dough into a ball, wrap in waxed paper or plastic, and refrigerate for at least 20 minutes before using.

To prebake the pie crust:

Preheat the oven to 350° F.

On a lightly floured surface, roll out the dough to $1/4$-inch thick.

Place the dough in a pie pan, fitting it evenly over the bottom of the pan and pressing gently against the inside edges.

Crimp the edges or trim away excess pie dough with a sharp paring knife.

Cover the dough with a sheet of foil and weight down with aluminum baking weights or dried beans.

Bake for 10 minutes.

Remove the weights and foil and continue to bake for 15 minutes, or until golden.

Remove to a rack to cool.

Makes one 9- to 11-inch pie crust

PARKER HOUSE ROLLS

INGREDIENTS

1 package active dry yeast

1 teaspoon sugar

$1 1/4$ cups milk, warmed

$2 3/4$ cups all-purpose flour

3 tablespoons butter, melted

1 teaspoon salt

Vegetable oil, for the bowl and the baking sheet

1 egg, lightly beaten with 1 tablespoon cold water, for the egg wash

METHOD

In a large bowl, dissolve the yeast and sugar in the warm milk.

Set aside until the mixture becomes frothy.

Add the flour, melted butter, and salt.

Stir until the mixture becomes a firm dough.

On a lightly floured surface, knead the dough until it becomes elastic and smooth.

Form into a ball and place in an oiled bowl.

Turn the dough in the bowl to coat it with oil.

Cover with a clean kitchen towel and set aside in a warm, draft-free place to rise until doubled, approximately 2 hours.

Lightly oil a baking sheet.

Turn out the dough on a lightly floured surface and roll out to $3/4$-inch thick.

Using a 3-inch round cutter or an upturned wineglass dipped in flour, cut out rounds of dough, using all of the dough.

Crease the center of each round with the back of a floured table knife.

Fold the dough along the crease and press down on the fold; the edges will fan out.

Arrange the rolls 2 inches apart on the baking sheet and set aside in a warm, draft-free place to rise for 30 minutes.

Meanwhile, preheat the oven to 400° F.
Brush the tops of the rolls with the egg wash.
Bake the rolls for 20 minutes, or until the bottoms
 sound hollow when tapped.
Serve hot with sweet butter.

Makes approximately 15 rolls

SIMPLE SYRUP

INGREDIENTS
2 cups sugar
4 cups cold water

METHOD
Place the sugar and 4 cups of cold water in
 a saucepan.
Bring to a boil over high heat, stirring with a
 wooden spoon, until the sugar has dissolved.
Continue to boil for 5 minutes and remove from
 the heat.
When the syrup is cool, refrigerate in a
 covered container.
The syrup will keep for two weeks under
 refrigeration and can be frozen indefinitely.

Makes 1 quart

RUM HARD SAUCE

INGREDIENTS
1/2 pound unsalted butter at room temperature
3/4 cup confectioners' sugar
2 tablespoons rum or brandy

METHOD
With an electric mixer, cream the butter until fluffy.
Gradually add the sugar and cream together with
 the butter. Gradually add the rum or brandy.
Scrape the butter onto a sheet of plastic wrap.
Roll the plastic wrap around the butter and
 shape into a log that is approximately
 1 1/2-inches in diameter.
Chill until hardened.

Remove the hard sauce log about 20 minutes
 before serving.
Cut into 1/4-inch medallions and serve on top of
 hot mincemeat or with steamed puddings.

Makes approximately 1 cup

ENGLISH CREAM

INGREDIENTS
1 quart milk
2 vanilla beans, split lengthwise
12 egg yolks
1 cup sugar

METHOD
In a heavy saucepan, scald the milk with the
 vanilla beans.
Set aside.
In the top of a double boiler, whisk the egg yolks
 with the sugar until frothy and lemon colored.
Place over simmering water and cook gently,
 stirring constantly, until the yolks are
 warmed through.
Slowly pour in the scalded milk and cook while
 stirring, until the cream coats the back of a
 metal spoon, approximately 20 minutes.
Strain the English Cream into a clean bowl and set
 in a larger bowl of ice and water.
Stir until completely cooled.
Cover and refrigerate.
The sauce will keep up to 3 days.

Makes approximately 1 1/2 quarts.

TOASTED NUTS

For all types of raw nuts— pignolis, walnuts,
almonds, etc.

METHOD
Preheat the oven to 400° F.
Spread raw nuts evenly over a dry baking sheet.
Place the baking sheet in the oven and toast for

4 minutes, tossing the nuts to ensure even browning.

Watch the nuts closely and remove from the oven when they turn golden brown.

Allow the nuts to cool slightly before removing from the baking sheet.

Rub the nuts between the folds of a kitchen towel to remove the outer skins.

Store in a tightly covered container.

ROASTED PEPPERS

For all types of peppers—bell peppers, jalapeños, or green chiles.

METHOD

Char the peppers directly on an open flame, preferably on an outdoor charcoal grill or a gas stovetop range.

Using long kitchen tongs, turn the peppers until blackened on all sides.

Remove, place the peppers in a paper bag, and close tightly.

Allow them to steam in the bag for 3 to 5 minutes.

Remove the peppers and peel off the outside skins.

Remove the core, ribs, and seeds and discard.

Proceed with the appropriate recipe.

Old Standbys

MACARONI AND CHEESE

INGREDIENTS

$1/2$ pound elbow macaroni

8 tablespoons butter

$1/4$ cup all-purpose flour

1 teaspoon dry mustard

3 cups milk

$1/2$ teaspoon salt

$1/8$ teaspoon cayenne pepper

$3/4$ pound sharp cheddar cheese, shredded

$1/2$ cup fresh bread crumbs

METHOD

In a pot of lightly salted boiling water, cook the macaroni until almost tender. Do not overcook.

Cool under cold running water, drain, and reserve.

Butter an 8-inch square ovenproof baking dish.

In a heavy saucepan, melt 4 tablespoons of the butter over moderate heat.

Off the heat, whisk in the flour.

Return the saucepan to moderate heat and whisk for 3 to 4 minutes, until the flour is cooked.

Blend in the dry mustard and add the milk, whisking constantly.

When the mixture bubbles and begins to thicken, remove from the heat and add the salt and cayenne pepper.

Fold in the cheese and blend.

Fold in the macaroni, pour the mixture into the baking dish, and set aside.

Preheat the oven to 350° F.

In a small sauté pan, heat the remaining 4 tablespoons butter over moderate heat.

Add the bread crumbs and toss for 1 or 2 minutes, until lightly toasted.

Sprinkle the crumb mixture over the macaroni.

Bake for 25 minutes and serve hot.

Serves 6

HAM SALAD

INGREDIENTS

1 pound sugar-cured baked ham, trimmed of all fat, cut into small bite-size pieces (approximately $3 1/2$ cups)

$1/2$ red bell pepper, cut in strips and diced

$1 1/2$ celery ribs, peeled, cut in strips, and diced

2 dill pickles, cut in strips and diced (approximately 1 cup)

$1/2$ to $3/4$ cup homemade mayonnaise (see Basics, page 334) or Hellmann's

3 tablespoons fresh chives, snipped

METHOD

In a bowl, combine the ham and diced vegetables.

Toss with mayonnaise and sprinkle with chives.
Chill completely and remove from the refrigerator
  20 minutes before serving.

Serves 3 to 4

CHICKEN SANDWICHES

INGREDIENTS
1 large roasted chicken breast, skin removed.
Thinly sliced white bread or white toast
Homemade mayonnaise (see Basics, page 334)
  or Hellmann's
Salt and freshly milled pepper
Leafy lettuce such as Boston, oak leaf,
  or butter crunch

METHOD
Thinly slice the chicken breasts.
Lightly coat the bread slices with the mayonnaise.
Place one or two layers of chicken on half of the
  slices of the bread.
Lightly season the chicken slices with salt
  and pepper.
Cover with one piece of lettuce and top with a
  slice of bread.
Trim the crusts and cut the sandwiches in half.

Note: The breast of a 3 1/2-pound roasted chicken
will yield 4 to 5 sandwiches. The combination of
sweet chicken, sweet white bread, and sweet
mayonnaise was a specialty available at most
soda fountains and good hotels until the 1960s.
It has since fallen on hard times.

Serves 4 to 5

MEATLOAF

INGREDIENTS
1 pound ground lean beef
1/2 pound ground lean veal
1/2 pound ground lean pork
1 medium onion, finely chopped

1 clove garlic, minced
1 teaspoon fresh tarragon, chopped
1/4 cup fresh parsley, chopped
1 cup fresh whole wheat bread crumbs
  (from 4 very thin slices of bread)
1 egg
1/2 cup store-bought chili sauce
1 tablespoon heavy cream
Salt and freshly milled black pepper
4 thick slices slab bacon cut 1/4-inch thick
3/4 cup sour cream, at room temperature

METHOD
Preheat the oven to 325° F.
In a large mixing bowl, combine all of the
  ingredients except the bacon and sour cream
  and mix well.
Shape the mixture and place it in a loaf pan.
Cover the top with the bacon slices, tucking the
  bacon between the meatloaf and the sides of
  the pan.
Cover the meatloaf with foil and bake for 1 hour.
Remove the foil and bake for an additional
  15 minutes.
Remove the bacon and suction off the cooking
  liquid with a bulb baster, or carefully pour it out
  of the pan into a bowl.
Measure 1/4 cup of the cooking liquid and stir it
  into the reserved sour cream.
Blend thoroughly and serve with the meatloaf.
To serve cold, thinly slice the meatloaf and
  accompany with hot pepper relish or corn relish.

Serves 6

EPILOGUE

The pond broke last night, as it must have done numberless times over the centuries. When the brackish waters creep too high, the ponds on the south fork of Long Island overrun their banks and rush in a flood to the ocean a few hundred feet away. Carving out a channel, the waters snake their way to the ocean—the seasonal infusion of salty water with the fresh water run-off rests in shallow pools. These shallows are the breeding ground for the blue crabs, eels, silver minnows, and oysters that fed the Indians from Shinnecock to Montauk. These Indians have all but disappeared but they left legacy to the Bonacers, descendants of the British who settled here in the 17th century, many of whom still support themselves with local fishing.

Before the pond breaks, long before dawn, the light of an occasional battery lamp can be seen shining on its surface. The shallow pond dances with light when everyone comes out to net the season's last crabs and eels as the waters rush out. Crabs not already burrowed or safe in the grasses will wash into the sea. Nature flushes these ponds annually, and if she should forget, the local townships will bulldoze a path to the sea, to prevent the ponds from flooding the nearby fields and farms that stretch to the dunes, the same fields tilled by American Indians so long ago.

The fishing season has ended. The men who haul seine have stored their dories in the barn. A lonely trawler can be seen a few miles out to sea. Hunters tread back and forth stealthily. With the occasional shot, a duck falls from the sky, and a flurry of ducks and honking geese speed away, flying out beyond the breakers and sandbars, stretching their number out in one long, dark thread on the horizon where they bob on the ocean like decoys, waiting for the shooting to stop. The potato fields are carpeted with new green rye, a winter's rest before spring's planting.

Winter
Sagaponack, New York

WEB AND MAIL ORDER SOURCES

American wineries by state
www.allamericanwineries.com
www.weekendwinery.com
www.wineweb.com

Beer
www.beeradvocate.com

Buffalo meat and sausage
www.buffalogal.com
507-896-2345

Cajun and Creole ingredients
(file powder, hot sauces, shrimp boil, etc.)
www.cajungrocer.com
888-272-9347
www.zatarain.com
888-264-5460

Cake flour
www.whitelily.com
800-264-5459

Cheese, California olive oil, honey, and other ingredients
www.zingermans.com
888-636-8162

Chesapeake Bay crabs
Harbour House Crabs
www.ilovecrabs.com
888-458-8272

Demi-glace and stocks
www.morethangourmet.com
800-860-9385

Dried heirloom beans
www.beanbag.net
800-845-2326

Duck specialties, meat, and game
www.dartagnan.com
800-327-8246

Elk meat
www.jamisonfarms.com
800-ELK-MEAT

Farmers' markets by state
www.ams.usda.gov/farmersmarkets
www.foodroutes.org

Flour
www.bobsredmill.com
800-349-2173

Freshly ground grits and cornmeal
www.hoppinjohns.com
800-828-4412

Fresh seafood and alderwood smoked salmon
www.freshseafood.com
800-392-3474

Fresh wild morels and chanterelles
www.wild-harvest.com
800-367-4709

Fresh wild Northwest mushrooms
www.mushroomsbymillard.net
541-563-7371

Gooseberry and currant bushes
www.noursefarms.com
413-665-2658

Heirloom turkey, lamb, pork, and goose
www.heritagefoodsusa.com
212-980-6603

Hominy
www.redcorn.com
800-280-9745

Kitchen equipment
www.kitchenemporium.com
888-858-7920
www.chefscatalog.com
800-884-8433
www.cooking.com
800-663-8810

Linguiça sausage
www.portuguesefood.com
508-676-0167

Pecans
www.rosaliepecans.com
877-772-3139

Smithfield ham
www.smithfieldhams.com
800-926-8448

Smoked trout
www.ducktrap.com
800-828-3825

Southwestern ingredients
(dried peppers, corn husks, blue corn meal, etc.)
www.hotchilepepper.com
505-471-6967

Sustainable fishing, farming, and food issues
www.passionfish.org
www.baumforum.org
www.slowfoodusa.org

Sustainably raised beef, pork, and lamb
www.nimanranch.com
866-808-0340

Wild rice, hominy, and maple syrup
www.nativeharvest.com
888-274-8318

SELECTED BIBLIOGRAPHY

Adams, Ramon F. *Come An Get It: The Story of the Old Cowboy Cook*. Norman, Okla.: University of Oklahoma Press, 1952.

Anderson, Ken. *Eagle Claw Fish Cookbook*. Cambridge, Mass.: Dorison House, 1977.

Baker, Charles H., Jr. *The Gentleman's Companion: An Exotic Drinking Book*. New York: Crown, 1946.

Bandera Library Association. *Cooking Recipes of the Pioneers*. Bander, Texas: Frontier Times, 1936.

Beard, James. *Beard on Bread*. New York: Knopf, 1977.
   James Beard's New Fish Cookery. Boston: Little, Brown, 1976.
   James Beard's New American Cookery. Boston: Little, Brown. 1972.

Beecher, Catherine Esther. *Domestic Receipt Book*. New York: Harper and Brothers, 1846.

Beeton, Mrs. Isabella. *The Book of Household Management*. London: Warwick House, Salisbury Square, E.C.: Ward and Lock Company, 1880.

Berglund, Berndt, and Clair E. Bolsby. *The Edible Wild*. Toronto: Pagurian Press, 1971.

Bivins, S. Thomas. *The Southern Cookbook*. Hampton, Va.: Press of the Hampton Institute, 1912.

Boorstin, Daniel J. *The Americans: The Democratic Experience*. New York: Random House, 1973.

Borthwick, J.D. *Three Years in California*. Edinburgh and London: Wm. Blackwood and Sons, 1857.

Brown, Dale. *American Cooking: The Northwest*. Alexandria, Va.: Time-Life Books, 1970.

Bujzek, Beatrice Ross. *The Cranberry Connection*. Brattleboro, Vt.: The Stephen Green Press, 1978.

Carson, Jane. *Colonial Virginia Cooking*. Williamsburg, Va.: University Press of Virginia in Charlottesville, 1968.

Challenger, Jean. *How to Cook Your Catch*. Sidney, B.C.: Sallire Publishing Co., 1973.

Chase, Joan. *During the Reign of the Queen of Persia*. New York: Ballantine Books, 1983.

Christ Church. *Christ Church Cook Book*. Savannah, Ga.: Kennickell Printing Co., 1978.

Colquit, Harriet Ross. *The Savannah Cookbook*. New York: Farrar and Rinehart, 1933.

Commercial Fisherman Wives, Port of Coos Bay. *Cookbook Presented by the Wives of Charleston*. Or.: Wegford Publications, 1972.

Cone, Joan. *Easy Game Cooking*. Mclean, Va.: EPM Publications, 1974.

The Democratic Women of Maine. *The State of Maine Cookbook*. 1924.

Dillow, Louise B., and Deenie B. Carver. *Mrs. Blackwell's Heart of Texas Cookbook*. San Antonio: Corona Publishing Co., 1980.

Doar, David. *Rice and Rice Planting in the South Carolina Low Country*. Charleston: The Charleston Museum, 1936.

Field, S.S. *The American Drink Book*. New York: Farrar, Straus, Young, 1953.

Fisher, M.F.K. *As They Were*. New York: Knopf, 1982.

Fox, Minnie C. *The Blue Grass Cook Book*. New York: Fox, Dunnfield and Co., 1904.

Frederick, J. George. *The Pennsylvania Dutch and Their Cookery*. New York: The Business Bourse, 1935.

The Friday Club. *The Friday Club Menus: A Capecod Cookbook*. Yarmouthport, Ma.: The Register Press, 1912.

Glasse, Hannah. *The Art of Cookery. made Plain and Easy; Which far exceeds any Thing of the Kind yet published*. London: Wm. Strahan, 1770.

Gleig, George Robert. *A Narrative of the Campaigns of the British Army of Washington and New Orleans, under Generals Ross, Pakenhanm, and Lambert, in the years 1814 and 1815*. 2d ed. London: John Murray, Albermarle Street, 1826.

Hack, Virginia, and Ann Andersen, eds. *100 Years of Good Cooking*. St. Paul: Minnesota Statehood Centennial Commission, 1958.

Hawkins, Nancy and Arthur, and Mary Allen Havermeyer. *Nantucket and Other New England Cooking*. New York: Hastings House, 1976.

Hayes, W.T. *Kentucky Cookbook*. St. Louis. J.H. Tomkins Printing Co., 1912.

Hearn, Lafcadio. *La Cuisine Creole*. New Orleans: Pelican Publishing House, 1967.

Hess, John L. and Karen Hess. *The Taste of America*. New York: Grossman Publishers, 1977.

Hewitt, Jean. *The New York Times Southern Heritage Cookbook*. New York: G.P. Putnam's Sons, 1976.

Horne, Viola, comp. *Milton Cookbook*. Boston: Boston Press of George H. Ellis, 1918.

Hosmer, Susan Harris Coleman. *Nantucket Recipes*. Nantucket, Ma.: The Inquirer and Mirror Press, 1915.

Howard, Mrs. B. *Fifty Years in a Maryland Kitchen*. Baltimore: Norman Remington Co., 1913.

Jones, Cranston. *Home of the American Presidents*. New York: Bonanza Publishers, 1962.

Jones, Evans. *American Food: The Gastronomic Story*. New York: E.P. Dutton, 1975.

Junior League of Baton Rouge. *River Road Recipes*. Baton Rouge, La.: 1972.

Junior League of Charleston. *Charleston Recipes*. Charleston: Walker, Evans, Cogswell Co., 1966.

Junior League of Shreveport. *A Cook's Tour of Shreveport*. 1964.

Junior League of Tampa. *The Gasparilla Cookbook*. 1961.

Kahn, E.J., Jr. "The Staffs of Life." *The New Yorker*, June 18, November 12, December 17, 1985.

Kimball, Marie. *Thomas Jefferson's Cook Book*. Charlottesville: University Press of Virginia, 1976.

King, Caroline B. *Victorian Cakes*. Idaho: Caxton Printers, 1941.

Kramer, Mark. *Three Farms*. Boston: Little, Brown, 1977.

Lang Varley. *Follow the Water*. Winston-Salem: John F. Blair, 1961.

Lewis, Meriwether, and William Clark. *The Journals of Lewis and Clark*. Edited by Bernard DeVoto. Boston: Houghton Miflin Company, 1953.

Lunchetti, Cathy. *Women of the West*. St. George, Utah: Antelope Island Press, 1982.

MacFayden, J. Tevere. *Gaining Ground: The Renewal of America's Small Farms*. New York: Holt, Rinehart and Winston, 1984.

Marrow, Kay. *The New England Cookbook*. Reading, Pa.: Culinary Arts Press, 1936.

McClare, A.K. *The Encyclopedia of Fish Cookery*. New York: Holt, Rhinehart and Winston, 1977.

McCulloch-Williams, Martha. *Dishes and Beverages of the Old South*. New York: McBride, Nast and Co., 1913.

Michaux, Francois Andre. *Travel to the West of the Allegheny Mountains*. 2d ed. London, D.N. Shury for B. Crosby and Co., 1805.

Michener, James A. *Chesapeake*. New York: Random House, 1978.

Mitcham, Howard. *Creole Gumbo and All That Jazz: A New Orleans Seafood Cookbook*. Reading, Pa.: Addison-Wesley Publishing Co., 1978.

Morgan, Edmund S.*Virginians at Home*. Williamsburg: The Colonial Williamsburg Foundation, 1983.

Morgan, Murray. *Puget's Sound*. Seattle: University of Washington Press, 1980.

Morison, Samuel Eliot. *The Maritime History of Massachusetts. 1783–1860*. Boston: Houghton Miflin Company, 1922.

Mosser, Marjorie. *Good Maine Food*. New York: Doubleday, 1947.

Ortiz, Elisabeth Lambert. *The Book of Latin American Cooking*. New York: Random House, 1979.

Ott, Eleanore. *Plantation Cooking of Old Louisiana*. New Orleans: Harmanson Publisher, 1938.

Parkman, Francis. *The Oregon Trail*. Boston: Little, Brown, 1902.

Perl, Lila. *Hunter's Stew and Hangtown Fry: What Pioneer America Ate and Why*. New York: a Clarion Book, Seabury Press, 1977.
   Slumps, Grunts, and Snickerdoodles: What Colonial America Ate and Why. New York: Houghton Miffling, 1975.

Pixley, Aristene. *The Green Mountain Cook Book*. New York: Stephen Day Press, 1934.

Randolph, Mary. *Virginia Housewife*. Baltimore: J. Plaskett, 1836.

Reidpath, Stewart. *The Angler's Cookbook*. London: A.H. and A.W. Reed, 1973.

Rombauer, Irma S., and Marion Rombauer Becker. *Joy of Cooking*. Indianapolis and New York: Bobbs-Merrill Company, 1979.

Ronald, Mary. *Mary Ronald's Century Cook Book*. New York: Century Company, 1897.

Root, Waverly. *Food*. New York: Simon and Schuster, 1980.

Russel, Howard S. *A Long Deep Furrow: Three Centuries of Farming in New England*. Hanover. N.H.: University Press of New England, 1976.

The Silver Thimble Society. *How We Cook in Tennessee*. Jackson, Tenn.: The Silver Thimble Society of the First Baptist Church, 1906.

Scott, Natalie Vivian. *Two Hundred Years of New Orleans Cooking*. New York: J. Cape and H. Smith, 1931.

Stieff, Frederick Phillip. *Eat, Drink and Be Merry in Maryland*. New York: G.P. Putnam's Sons, 1932.

Stratton, Dorothy. *Pioneer Women*. New York: Simon and Schuster, 1981.

Talmadge, Betty. *How to Cook a Pig: And Other Back-to-the-Farm Recipes*. New York: Simon and Schuster, 1977.

Thoreu, Henry David. *The Annotated Walden, or Life in the Woods*. New York: Clarkson Potter, 1970.
   Cap Cod. Cambridge, Mass., Hougton Miflin, Riverside Press, 1914.
   A Week on the Concord and Merrimack Rivers. Princeton: Princeton University Press, 1980.

Tocqueville, Alexis de. *Journey to America*. Translated by George Lawrence. New Haven: Yale University Press, 1960.

Turner, Harry Baker. *Nantucket Cookbook*. Nantucket, Mass.: Inquirer and Mirror Press, 1927.

Twain, Mark. *A Tramp Abroad*. New York: Harper and Brothers, 1907.

Tyree, Marion Cabell, ed. *Housekeeping in Old Virginia*. Louisville, Ky.: J.P. Morton and Co., 1890.

Voltz, Jeanne A. *The Flavor of the South*. New York: Doubleday, 1977.

Warner, William. *Beautiful Swimmers*. Boston: Atlantic, Little, Brown 1976.

Weatherwax, Paul. *Indian Corn in Old America*. New York: Macmillan, 1954.

Weygandt, Cornelius. *A Passing America: Considerations of Things Yesterday Fast Fading from Our World*. New York: Henry Holt and Co., 1932.

White, Mrs. Peter A. *Kentucky Cookery Book*. Chicago: Belford Clarke Co., 1891.

INDEX

ACKNOWLEDGMENTS

For this revised edition, I wish to thank Lena Tabori for bringing me back to Welcome Enterprises. From the very beginning she has believed in this book and worked so hard to keep it in the public eye. I also want to thank the people at Welcome who reinvigorated this edition, particularly Katrina Fried—my devoted editor and Gregory Wakabayashi for his splendid art direction that has brought new life into these pages. I am indebted to Diana Van Buren who so enthusiastically embraced this work and lent her cooking, wine, beer, and editing skills and did it with humor and intelligence. For Mary Anne Page—my beacon of truth and beauty—for her art of critiquing me with a velvet covered hammer. Also to my Dad, and brother Philip and his wife Mayda who over time have made many of these recipes— and made them well. To Jon Gilman for accurately refreshing my memories of the foods of the Northwest, Robert and Bobbie Meyzen for their generosity and encouragement, and Lee Brian Schrager—a wine authority in his own right. Also Rick Bishop—the Union Square Greenmarket's potato king, environmentalist, and raconteur of all things agricultural. And my dearest friend and critic, Geraldine Stutz.

For the people who opened their kitchen doors, their family cooking secrets and their hearts, I want to thank all of them once again. Some have passed away, some have passed away from my life and I from theirs—but I remember them all:

NEW ENGLAND
Felecity Pratt Morgan
Ralph Gray
Nicholas Love
Mrs. Ruth P. James
Thomas, Susie and Seth Wilbur
Norman Miller
Randy Durkee
K. Eric Weiss
Vernon B. Miller
Diana Conklin
Clifford Klenk
Polly and Joseph Kraft
Peaches and Raymond Halsey and their family
Ceil and Stanley Knight
East Hampton Town Baymen's Association and the haulsteiners;
    Bill Lester, Calvin Lester, Donald Eams, Ernie Green, Jr.,
    Walter Burnett
William Serter
John Hassler—The Seafood Shop
Andrea Terry—The Lobster Roll
Bruce and Maryann Bozzi—The Palm restaurants
Peter Schub
Robert Bear
Eric Villency
Mark Sudack
Robert Dash
Marjorie Benchley
Joachim Esteve
Elizabeth Esteve Vardinoyannis
Kiminho Esteve

MID-ATLANTIC
Judith Van Amringe
Jean de Castella Delley
Beati and Hart Berry
Everett Nak
Leo Steiner—Carnegie Deli
Big Apple Circus: Eileen Condon, Ruth Schuman, Jane Lahr
Bill Blass
Mrs. Kenyon Boocock

Frolic Weymouth
Joanne Dupont
Manuel Nunez
Jessica Meyers
Lisa Babinksi
Mrs. John M. Gates
Zoe Lewis
Felipe Rojas—Lombardi
Helen Fraser
Gail Levenstein

SOUTH
Nancy and Neil Smith
Bart Murphy and The Ruby Ford
Billy Wood Bradshaw and The Maggie Lee
Ralph Ruark and the Wilma Lee
Corporal Nick Nazare, Jr., and Sgt. Joseph H. Jones—Maryland
    Natural Resources Police
Didi and Neil Rheiland
William R. "Bill" Jones—The Crab Claw
Caleb Cliff
Richard Jenerette
Bob Bray
Nell Dillow Thomas
Beth Spary
Owen Lee
Mrs. Marti Atkins
Mrs. Perry Lewis
Mrs. Sidney Le Gendre
Sam Washington
Fleeta Fox—Charleston Foundation
The Stockpot—Charleston
Mrs. A.L. Jennings

DEEP SOUTH
Mr. and Mrs. Jimmy Boulet
Henri Boulet
Sheila Duplessis
Douglas Hayward—Belle Helene Plantation
J. Lawrence Hill

Joe Mizelle
Michael Myers
Russell Albright
Mrs. Donald J. Nalty
Adam Steg
Soniat House—Rodney Smith
Shirley Ratterree
Flo Treadway, Scott Ratterree—Longuev>eue House and Gardens
Edith Morgan
Ella Brennan
Edmund McIlhenny—Avery Island
Acme Oyster House
Mr. and Mrs. Lloyd English Jr.—Mandiche1s
Dr. and Mrs. Anthony Petro
Mr. and Mrs. John Peet, Jr.
Mrs. and Mrs. Thomas E. Goodman
Mr. and Mrs. William Wallace
Carol Puckett Daily—The Everyday Gourmet
Ernie Knight

MIDWEST
Mary Reisinger
Deborah Buell
Nancy and George Buell
Marcia Goldberg
Gladys Delight Hilgert

NORTHERN REGIONS
Snake River Ranch: Nancy and Chuck Resor, Jane and Stan Resor,
    Story and Bill Resor, Susan Hauge
Ted Kimmel
Bernie Shrable—Wyoming Department of Fish and Game
The Hardeman Ranch: Earl Hardeman, Jerry Jacobson
Dick Best
Ad Lib
Ann Stewart
Coty Bliss

SOUTHWEST
Janie and Hank Coleman
The Bar K Ranch: Ann and Hamp Stead, John and Leah Darby,
    Jeff and Catherine Steinmeyer, Ab Crawford, David Smelley,
    Derwood Semlley, Mary and Sylvester Perry, Gaspar Herrera,
    Dale Savell, Grady Crawford, C.W. Bardwell, Cotton McLeroy
Rose and Kenneth Kirkpatrick
Billy Sue Turner Antiques
Sunny Bryant's
Joan Baker
Sarah Moody
Michelle Tsosie Naranjo—Santa Clara Pueblo
Mr. and Mrs. Keith Wofford
Mr. and Mrs. Arturo Jaramillo
Forrest Moses
Ramona Scholder
Anna Ferrier
Rosalea Murphy
Alan Smith—The Stockpot
Nedra Mateucci

WEST COAST
The Rio Bravo Ranch: Mr. and Mrs. George Nickel, Kathi and
    Miller Nickel, Andre Honeste
Steve Couture

John J. Kovacevich
Jacinto Sarabia
Sue Campoy
Mr. and Mrs. Arthur C. Withrow II
Suzannah Love
Tom and Patty Skouras
Ames Cushing
Gijsbert Paul Bozuwa
Maggie Waldron
Mrs. Richard K. Miller
David Miller
Jim Mays
Ira Kirlander
Mrs. Ivy Rosequit
Carmella Scaggs
Sal Sancimino and Sons— Swan's Oyster Depot
Wendra Liang
Haywood Winery: Peter Haywood and Dennis Bowker
Rutherford Hill Winery: Mr. and Mrs. William Jaeger, Robert Hardy
Belle Rhodes
Laurie Chenel—Laurie Chenel California Chevre
Ignazio A. Vella—Vella Cheese Company

NORTHWEST
Astrida R. Blukis Onat
Don Foster
Rosalynn G. Powell
Benjamin Woo—The Morel Society
Michael Erikson
Peter Hasson—Hasson Brothers Fruit and Produce
Mike Osborn—Pure Food Fish Market
Emmett Watson's Oyster Bar
Larry Hansen
Members of the Swinomish tribe: Maxine Williams,
    Gus "Stoney" Stone, Bernadette Stone, Ken Edwards

The New York Public Library
The New York Society Library
The New York Academy of Medicine Library
The American Cookbooks and Wine Books 1797–1950 exhibition
    from the collection of Janice Bluestein Longone and
    Daniel T. Longone, courtesy of the William L. Clements Library
    of American History and the Food Library, Ann Arbor, Michigan

For the original Random House Publication, I wish to thank:

Jason Epstein
Rena and Gary Coyle
Penni Wisner
Laura Schultz
Bob Scudellari
Mardee Haidin Regan
Todd Weinstein
Tom Eckerle
Jimmy Eckerle
Chechi Gallini

and the late James Beard

Published in 2005 by Welcome Books®
An imprint of Welcome Enterprises, Inc.
6 West 18th Street, New York, NY, 10011
(212) 989-3200; Fax (212) 989-3205
www.welcomebooks.com

Publisher: Lena Tabori
Editor: Katrina Fried

Designed by Gregory Wakabayashi

ISBN-13: 978-1-932183-74-0
ISBN-10: 1-932183-74-4

Library of Congress Cataloging-in-Publication Data on file

Printed in Hong Kong

First Edition

10 9 8 7 6 5 4 3 2